Content-Area Reader

TEACHER'S GUIDE

The United States
Change and Challenge

Senior Consultant
Dr. Judith Irvin
Florida State University

HOLT, RINEHART AND WINSTON
A Harcourt Classroom Education Company
Austin · New York · Orlando · Atlanta · San Francisco · Boston · Dallas · Toronto · London

Staff Credits

EDITORIAL

Manager of Editorial Operations
Bill Wahlgren
Executive Editor
Patricia McCambridge
Senior Editor and Project Editor
Eileen Joyce
Component Editors: Jane Archer Feinstein, Carolyn Logan, Pamela Thompson
Assistant Editor: Tracy DeMont
Copyediting: Michael Neibergall, *Copyediting Manager;* Mary Malone, *Copyediting Supervisor;* Christine Altgelt, Joel Bourgeois, Elizabeth Dickson, Emily Force, Julie A. Hill, Julia Thomas Hu, Jennifer Kirkland, Millicent Ondras, Dennis Scharnberg, *Copyeditors*
Project Administration: Marie Price, *Managing Editor;* Lori De La Garza, *Editorial Operations Coordinator;* Heather Cheyne, Mark Holland, Marcus Johnson, Jennifer Renteria, Janet Riley, Kelly Tankersley, *Project Administration;* Ruth Hooker, Casey Kelly, Joie Pickett, Margaret Sanchez, *Word Processing*
Editorial Permissions: Susan Lowrance, *Permissions Editor*
Writers: Judith Austin Mills, Matthew Pangborn, Trudy Williams

ART, DESIGN, AND PHOTO

Book Design
Richard Metzger, *Design Director*
Graphic Services
Kristen Darby, *Manager*
Design Implementation
The Format Group, LLC
Image Acquisitions
Joe London, *Director;* Jeannie Taylor, *Photo Research Supervisor;* Sarah Hudgens, Robert McClellan, *Photo Researcher;* Michelle Rumpf, *Art Buyer Supervisor;* Gillian Brody, *Art Buyer*
Cover Design
Curtis Riker, *Director,* Sunday Patterson, *Designer*

PRODUCTION

Belinda Barbosa Lopez, *Senior Production Coordinator*
Beth Prevelige, *Prepress Manager*
Carol Trammel, *Production Supervisor*

MANUFACTURING/INVENTORY

Shirley Cantrell, *Supervisor of Inventory and Manufacturing*
Wilonda Ieans, *Manufacturing Coordinator*
Mark McDonald, *Inventory Planner*

Cover Photo Credits: (Guadalupe Mountains National Park, *El Capitan Peak with Boulders*), © Laurence Parent; (steam train), © Kim Todd/Picture Quest; (train track), Digital Imagery © 2001 Photodisc, Inc.; (launch of the space shuttle *Discovery*), NASA/Roger Ressmeyer/CORBIS; (stars in the night sky), © Digital Art/CORBIS.

For permission to reprint copyrighted material, grateful acknowledgment is made to the following source:

Stanley Lucero: From synopsis of "Cielito Lindo" lyrics written by Stanley A. Lucero from *Dos Voces–Un Espiritu,* at *http://www.lucerito.net/dosvoces.htm,* accessed June 4, 2001. Copyright © 1999 by Lucerito's Music (Madera, California).

6 7 8 9   018   10 09 08 07

Contents

CHAPTER 6

American Issues: The United States from 1914 to the Present

Content-Area Reading Strategies

Blackline Masters for Graphic Organizers

Using This Teacher's Guide

This Teacher's Guide is intended to

- *provide maximum versatility and flexibility*
- *serve as a ready resource for background information on each selection*
- *act as a catalyst for discussion, analysis, interpretation, activities, and further research*
- *provide reproducible blackline masters that can be used for either individual or collaborative work, including discussions and projects*
- *provide multiple options for evaluating students' progress*

The Selection Notes, Selection Tests, reading strategies essay, and blackline masters in this Teacher's Guide have been created to provide support for teaching the selections and features in the *Content-Area Reader* Pupil's Edition. In this Teacher's Guide, you will find instructional background and other resources that will help you to teach content-area reading skills effectively to all of your students.

Selection Notes

Selection Notes, arranged by chapter and selection, are included for every selection in the Pupil's Edition, providing teachers with the tools they need to help students get the most out of their content-area reading.

- **Before Reading** activities introduce students to important issues in the selection, provide further background for the teacher, offer instruction in both high-utility and content-area vocabulary, and present basic reading skills and reading strategies to implement those skills.
- **During Reading** activities provide extra information about selection features, such as the side-margin features and the art that accompanies the selection. In addition, teaching suggestions for Learners Having

Difficulty, English-Language Learners, and Advanced Learners are offered to help teachers meet the needs of all students.

- **After Reading** activities provide answers to the **Reading Check** questions in the Pupil's Edition so that you can assess students' content comprehension. A **Reteaching** feature for students who had difficulty with the reading skill and strategy helps ensure that all students learn content-area reading skills. **Connecting to Language Arts** activities offer students in the language arts classroom a chance to create a personalized response to the selection, using such approaches as journal entry writing, ad or brochure copy writing, video presentations, and interviews involving role-playing. **Connecting Across the Curriculum** provides activities to extend students' interest by researching materials related to the selection topic and completing a project based on their investigations. **Rubrics for Cross-Curricular Activities** in the Pupil's Edition are provided at the end of each chapter.

Selection Tests

- A **Selection Test** for each title offers multiple-choice questions about the content and multiple-choice or matching questions to assess vocabulary comprehension. The vocabulary that is tested appears underscored in the selections in the Pupil's Edition.

Content-Area Reading Strategies for the Language Arts Classroom

In this section of the Teacher's Guide, Senior Consultant Dr. Judith Irvin provides an informative essay on content-area reading skills and offers eleven strategies for approaching content-area reading in the classroom. In order to successfully read expository text, students need to be aware of the basic text structures used in nonfiction literature. Students also need to have access to a variety of tools—strategies—for understanding expository text. Dr. Irvin's reading strategies are cross-referenced throughout the Selection Notes in the first section of the Teacher's Guide, and graphic organizers to support various reading strategies are provided in reproducible blackline masters in the final section of the Teacher's Guide.

Graphic Organizers

A selection of various graphic organizers in reproducible blackline masters form appears at the back of the Teacher's Guide. These graphic organizers can be used with the various reading strategies presented in the selection Teaching Notes.

CHAPTER 1

A City Upon a Hill
The Colonial Period 1608–1775

Droughts Played Major Role in Jamestown, "Lost Colony" Tragedies	**CONTENT-AREA CONNECTIONS** SCIENCE • HISTORY •

from *William and Mary News*
by PEGGY SHAW
(student text page 3)

Reading Level: Above average

Text Summary

This newspaper article explains how a team of historians, archaeologists, and climatologists uncovered a possible cause for the "starving time" of the early Jamestown settlement and of the disappearance of the Roanoke Colony. By examining tree rings from centuries-old bald cypresses along the border of present-day Virginia and North Carolina, scientists discovered that the area faced the worst drought in an eight-hundred-year span during the colonies' first years. The article points out that scientists from different disciplines working together can solve mysteries that alone they could not unravel.

BEFORE READING

Make the Connection

Ask students what issues they would consider if they were moving to a remote wilderness area without cell phones, shopping, electricity, or access to the Internet. [sources of food and water; support in cases of medical, military, or natural emergency; organization of society and laws] What conditions would be necessary for survival? [a livable climate, food sources, water and fuel supply, resources for building shelters]

BUILD BACKGROUND
■ More About the Topic
Jamestown was named for King James I of England. The first successful colony in North America, Jamestown was destroyed later in the seventeenth century when its inhabitants rebelled against the Virginia governor.

Vocabulary Development

The following words are underscored and defined in the student text.
implicated: to be involved in or connected with.
enigmatic: puzzling; mysterious.
archaeology: a branch of science that studies past human cultures by looking at the clues they left behind.
subsistence: existence; life.
decimated: destroyed; killed.

Before assigning the reading, you may want to introduce students to any words that could cause pronunciation or definition problems.

┌─ *Vocabulary Tip* ─
Using Suffixes Tell students that the suffix *–logy* means "a branch of learning" and that it is preceded by an *o* when combined with Greek roots. When combined with the root *archaeo* (which means "ancient"), the word *archaeology* is formed ("the study of ancient things"). Ask students how many other words they can think of that end in *–ology*. [*geology, psychology, ontology, cosmetology, meteorology*]

Although the following words are important to understanding the text selection, some of them may be unfamiliar to students. You will want to introduce the words to students before they begin reading. Ask students what they predict they will read about in a selection using these words and the vocabulary words in the student text.

conducted*: performed in an orderly manner.
correlated: compared to show how they are related.
anomaly: a specific case that may differ from a general rule or trend.
climatic: relating to the climate.
determinist: someone who believes events can be traced back to a single cause or set of circumstances.

*Although students may be familiar with other meanings of this word, the word as used in the selection has a specific meaning that pertains to the content area.

Reading Informational Material

Reading Skill
Identifying Structure and Main Idea
Tell students that a selection's main idea is the central point that the author is trying to make. Analyzing the organizational structure of a text selection can often help students to identify its main idea.

▶ **Teaching Tip**
Investigative Reporting Point out to students that the article is an investigative piece of newspaper reporting. There are many facts and statistics given to support the article's main idea. Students should be prepared to take note of these facts and statistics and use them when expressing in their own words the main idea of the article.

Reading Strategy
Constructing Concept Maps (Strategy 4)
To help students identify the main idea and structure of the article, use Strategy 4 described in Content-Area Reading Strategies. Have students create a Concept Map or provide them with a Cause-and-Effect Chart (Graphic Organizer 2) to help them organize their thoughts as they read.

DURING READING

Differentiating Instruction
■ Learners Having Difficulty
If students are having difficulty organizing the details of the selection, have them work in pairs to take notes on the text as they read. Students should use the Key Points and Details Chart (Graphic Organizer 5). Have students read through the selection together, pausing after each paragraph to note its main idea and record any supporting statistics, facts, or examples in the corresponding column.

AFTER READING

 **Reading Check**

The following are sample answers to questions on student text page 7.

1. The most extreme drought in eight hundred years occurred between the years 1587 and 1589.

2. The climatologists looked for information about rainfall and temperatures during the Tidewater region's growing season.

3. The drought destroyed the corn crops on which the colonists depended for food. The Indians' inability to provide the settlers with corn may have caused a conflict between the two groups. The drought affected the quality of the colony's water supply, which may have led to illness among the colonists. [Accept any two.]

4. Researchers from the areas of history, archaeology, and climatology worked together on the project.

5. When experts from different disciplines work together, they can achieve exciting, important results.

Reteaching
If students are still having difficulty identifying and arranging supporting ideas under the article's main idea, have students meet in small groups to identify the main idea in each paragraph. Once the groups have done so, solicit student answers and

input as you arrange the ideas hierarchically on the chalkboard or on an overhead transparency of a Cluster Diagram (Graphic Organizer 3). First, begin with the quotation at the end of the first paragraph, which serves as the article's thesis statement. Then, arrange the supporting ideas around the statement, showing which are reasons for the scientists' conclusion and which are effects of the drought.

Connecting to Language Arts

▪ Writing

Editorial Cartoon The article describes many harsh effects of the drought on the fledgling Jamestown colony. Ask students to imagine how they would feel about the situation if they were Jamestown colonists. Then, have students create editorial cartoons for the colony's newspaper. You may want to bring to class examples of editorial cartoons from local and national newspapers that students can use as models.

▪ Speaking and Listening

Historical Scene Have students study the effects of the drought on the settlers and write a speech proposing ways of coping with these problems. Students can address their ideas to either the colony's leaders or the English businessmen who launched the colony. Students' speeches should last no longer than three minutes and should include at least two items of support for their solutions.

Connecting Across the Curriculum: Science

Bad Weather Assign students to find out more about weather-related catastrophes, including droughts, floods, tornadoes, hurricanes, and lightning and hail storms. What circumstances produce these phenomena? What are their effects and worst recorded instances of damage? Have each student choose a weather phenomenon as the subject for an informative poster. Display students' posters in the classroom.

Further Resources

▪ Books

Temperate Deciduous Forest (Exploring Earth's Biomes) by April Pulley Sayre.
The Paradox of Jamestown: 1585–1700 by Christopher Collier and James Lincoln Collier.

▪ Video

Lost Colony of Roanoke. A&E Entertainment, 1998. Not rated.

Assessment

Turn to page 117 for a multiple-choice test on the selection.

Test Answers

1. c 2. a 3. b 4. a 5. d
6. d 7. a 8. d 9. c 10. a

from "The Time of Most Distress"

from *William Bradford: Rock of Plymouth*
by KIERAN DOHERTY
(*student text page 8*)

Reading Level: Average

Text Summary

This selection describes the settlement of the Mayflower Pilgrims at Plymouth Rock and the settlers' preparations for surviving their first winter in New England. The account describes the hardships the Pilgrims faced as well as their surprising adventures.

BEFORE READING

Make the Connection

Discuss with students how they might go about establishing a small town or settlement. How would they divide the work among the people who lived there? [according to skill, physical ability, age] What would the most important tasks be? [providing food, shelter, and a supply of drinking water] Write students' suggestions on the chalkboard, and introduce the Pilgrims' story by asking students how the setting up of such a settlement would be made more dangerous and difficult by a harsh winter, disease, and the possible threat of conflict.

BUILD BACKGROUND

▪ More About the Topic

Many of the early Pilgrims were Separatists, Puritans who had decided they could not reform the Church of England from within and who thus formed their own churches. Separatist groups were illegal in England, however, and many Separatists were arrested and jailed. In 1607, a number of Separatists fled to Holland, but after a few years they worried about bringing up their children as foreigners to their native land. What they needed was a *new* native land: America. Along with the English citizens on board the *Mayflower* were forty-one members of the Separatist congregation from Holland, weary outcasts who hungered for freedom—and a new home.

Vocabulary Development

The following words are underscored and defined in the student text.

enduring: lasting.
allocated: given out in portions according to a plan.
scourged: punished; made to suffer.
vehemently: forcefully; with intensity.
install: to secure in the correct position to be used. Before assigning the reading, you may want to introduce students to any words that could cause pronunciation or definition problems.

┌─ *Vocabulary Tip* ─────────────────

Using Prefixes Point out to students that the prefix *in–* may have one of two incompatible meanings. In one, the prefix means "not," as in *inconclusive*. In the other, the prefix means "into," as in *infuse*. Ask students which meaning they think the prefix in *install* has, and have students check their answers by looking up the word in the dictionary.

└──────────────────────────────────

(**CONTENT-AREA VOCABULARY**)

Although the following words are important to understanding the text selection, they may be unfamiliar to students. Point out to students that all the words are nouns. Have students visualize or draw a picture of each word.

anchorage: a ship's anchored position in a bay or harbor.
mud flats: muddy ground at the sea's edge.
wharf: a structure much like a bridge or pier, used to provide a link between ship and land.
rushes*: reedy plants.
shellfish: edible sea creatures with shells, such as crabs, mussels, and oysters.

*Although students may be familiar with other meanings of this word, the word as used in the selection has a specific meaning that pertains to the content area.

Reading Informational Material

Reading Skill

Analyzing Text Structure: Chronological Order

Tell students that keeping the events in the selection in chronological order—the order in which they happen—will help them understand the development of the Plymouth Colony.

Reading Strategy

Understanding Text (Strategy 2)

To help students follow the chronology of the events in the selection, use Strategy 2 described in Content-Area Reading Strategies. You may wish to provide students with a list of signal words to use with the Sequence and Chronological Order Chart (Graphic Organizer 10).

▶ **Teaching Tip**

Pilgrim Life Tell students that the description in the selection of the Pilgrims' life covers two kinds of information: the daily life of the settlement and the long-term projects of the settlers. Encourage students to take notes on their reading using a Key Points and Details Chart (Graphic Organizer 5).

DURING READING

Using the Side-Margin Feature

▪ **Meeting the Neighbors**

You can use the brief feature on the Pilgrims' first meeting with Samoset to start a discussion with students about what they know of the first interactions of settlers and Native Americans in the region. What were some problems the two groups overcame together? What were causes of conflict?

Differentiating Instruction

▪ **Learners Having Difficulty**

Students may skip over the facts and statistics in the selection, or they may become confused trying to make use of the numbers in their reading. Encourage students to rewrite each statistic and make a judgment about it in their reading notes. Students can write, for example, "Twenty men to build the houses—that doesn't sound like very many. I wonder how many houses they had to build?" Taking such notes will help students remember and understand the statistics.

AFTER READING

✔ Reading Check

The following are sample answers to questions on student text page 15.

1. The Pilgrims used the rock as a kind of pier, stepping onto it from a boat and then crossing from it over a walkway to the shore.

2. Their first houses were one-room structures made of twigs covered with mud. They had fireplaces and chimneys made of logs and covered with clay. The roofs were thatched with rushes.

3. The structure was first used to store supplies. Later, it became a hospital.

4. The Pilgrims buried their dead in secret because they believed they were being watched by Indians and did not want to reveal that the settlement was being weakened by disease.

5. The Pilgrim boys gathered rushes, fished, and hunted. Girls prepared meals, helped with the sewing, and did other household chores.

Reteaching

If students still have difficulty arranging the events in the selection in chronological order, have them make a calendar of the Pilgrims' landing and settling at Plymouth. Students' calendars should begin on December 16, 1620, and end in the summer of 1621. Students can mark specific dates for events as they are given in the article and shade areas on their calendars for approximate dates of events. Ask volunteers to share their calendars with the class.

Connecting to Language Arts

▪ **Writing**

Diary Have students imagine they are a member of the Plymouth Colony. Ask them to write a diary entry detailing an unusual or significant event that occurred while they were performing a daily chore. Students can base their accounts on the description of the Pilgrims' lives given in the selection. Ask volunteers to share their entries with the class.

- **Speaking and Listening**

Interview Pair students and have them choose either the role of Samoset or of an interviewer asking Samoset for his views and opinions on the Pilgrim settlers. Direct the interviewers to prepare three questions and to ask three follow-up questions. Students taking the role of Samoset should base their answers on the facts in the selection. The pairs can take turns performing their interviews for one another in groups of four to eight.

Connecting Across the Curriculum: Health

Have students choose one of the diseases suffered by the Pilgrims—scurvy, pneumonia, or typhus—and research its causes and treatments. How well-equipped were the Pilgrims to fight such illnesses? What about the Pilgrims' experiences or conditions might promote the outbreak of these diseases? Have students who have chosen the same disease present their findings to the class in a round-table discussion. Students should suggest remedies the Pilgrims could have used.

Further Resources

- **Books**

    A Journey to the New World: The Diary of Remember Patience Whipple by Kathryn Lasky.
    Landing of the Pilgrims by James Daugherty.
    Squanto, Friend of the Pilgrims by Clyde Robert Bulla.

- **Video**

    The Mayflower Pilgrims, directed by Alan Mumby, 43 minutes, 1996.

- **Museum**

For more information on Plymouth and the Pilgrims, you can visit the Pilgrim Hall Museum in Plymouth, Massachusetts, or the museum's Web site.

Assessment

Turn to page 118 for a multiple-choice test on the selection.

Test Answers

1. a   2. c   3. d   4. d   5. d
6. b   7. c   8. d   9. a   10. a

from Smallpox

from *Invisible Enemies: Stories of Infectious Disease*
by JEANETTE FARRELL
(student text page 16)

Reading Level: Average

Special Considerations

The selection treats in passing many of the horrifying details of the practice of slavery. Students may find it difficult to pass over such details quickly and without discussion. You may want to set aside some time to be able to discuss the subject more fully.

Text Summary

The selection recounts the efforts of some colonists, including Cotton Mather and Benjamin Franklin, to promote the practice of inoculating against smallpox, an idea brought to the colonies by an African slave, Onesimus. The practice inspired fear and met with fierce objections from the people of eighteenth-century Boston. Acceptance of inoculation came as the result of the brave stands of many men and women.

BEFORE READING

Make the Connection

Have students write a brief journal entry describing a time when they had to do something that scared them but that was for their own good. [Students may write about visiting a doctor or dentist, taking a test, or taking an unpopular position in which they believed strongly.] Then, introduce the tough decision described in the selection: Would students take their chances on a relatively new medical practice, or choose to test their luck by risking infection by a deadly disease?

Build Background

■ Motivate

Students will probably be unfamiliar with the health conditions of the time period and may find them hard to imagine. Have students brainstorm health products or practices they feel they could not do without. [Students might suggest toothpaste, hot running water, aspirin, basic antiseptics, or modern dentistry.] Discuss with students what challenges and health concerns they would face without these products and practices.

Vocabulary Development

The following words are underscored and defined in the student text.

immune: unable to contract a disease.

epidemic: an outbreak of a disease that spreads quickly among many people in a given area.

distraction: a state of mental agitation and disturbance.

intervening: coming between.

virus: a disease caused by a tiny living particle that reproduces inside cells.

Before assigning the reading, you may want to introduce students to any words that could cause pronunciation or definition problems.

Vocabulary Tip

Analyzing Analogies Students may be more familiar with the word *virus* as it relates to computers. Have students compare and contrast a natural virus and a computer virus. [Both invade their hosts and reproduce themselves, causing damage; a natural virus is a living thing that can cause death, while a computer virus is a program by which data may be lost.]

CONTENT-AREA VOCABULARY

Although the following words are important to understanding the text selection, they may be unfamiliar to students. From this list of words have students predict what the selection is about.

pidgin: a simplified hybrid of a language.
contagion: infection; disease.
seethed*: raged.
distemper: a disease.

*Although students may be familiar with other meanings of this word, the word as used in the selection has a specific meaning that pertains to the content area.

Reading Skill

Analyzing Text Structures: Cause and Effect

Tell students that the selection will discuss many causes and effects, and comprehending the material will depend largely on understanding these relationships.

Reading Strategy

Using Graphic Organizers (Strategy 3)

To help students track causes and effects in the selection, use Strategy 3 described in Content-Area Reading Strategies. You may wish to provide students with a Cause-and-Effect Chart (Graphic Organizer 2), to help them analyze the relationships in the selection.

▶ **Teaching Tip**

Excerpt Point out to students that since the selection is part of a larger work, a book on infectious disease, the selection's main focus will be on the smallpox disease and the efforts made to combat it. Historical figures of the time and important events in the life of the Colonies will be mentioned only as they relate to this main idea.

DURING READING

Differentiating Instruction

▪ Advanced Learners

This selection touches upon many historical figures and events without going into detail. Encourage students to investigate further any topic that interests them, and allow students time to share their findings with the class. Possible topics include the slave trade, the history of various infectious diseases, and the lives of Cotton Mather and Benjamin Franklin.

AFTER READING

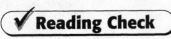
✔ Reading Check

The following are sample answers to questions on student text page 22.

1. Cotton Mather's African slave, Onesimus, told Mather about the practice, which was common in his homeland.

2. When a person was inoculated, a scratch was made on his or her arm. A small amount of the virus was then put into the scratch. In the days that followed, the person suffered a mild case of smallpox but was afterwards immune.

3. The outbreak was severe because the last epidemic had occurred nineteen years earlier, so that many people had not been exposed to the disease and were not immune. Also, the virus could be spread through the air and a single particle could cause disease.

4. Franklin had promoted inoculation, so many people assumed that Franklin's son had been given the smallpox virus through inoculation. In fact, Franklin had not yet inoculated his son.

5. Inoculation required days of preparation in addition to time for isolation and recovery.

Reteaching

If students still have difficulty identifying the cause-and-effect relationships in the text, have them review the selection and make a list, in chronological order, of the events described. Then, ask students to think of ways each event was influenced by the ones preceding it. You may also want students to consider if the events could have happened in a different order. For example: Would Cotton Mather have written so much about inoculation if Onesimus had not told him about the scar on his own arm? Why or why not?

Connecting to Language Arts

▪ Writing

Invitation Ask students to imagine they are planning an inoculation party of their own. Have students write invitations for their party outlining the health benefits of inoculation and detailing the entertainment and refreshment they will provide. Students might want to experiment with a word-processing program to find the right fonts, type size, and graphics for their invitations.

- **Speaking and Listening**

Debate Arrange students into three-person teams and assign each team a position on the question of inoculation as it was viewed in the time period covered in the selection. Then, stage debates among the teams. Each team member should contribute one of the following: opening statement, rebuttal, closing statement. You may want to videotape the debates.

Connecting Across the Curriculum: Social Studies

Colonial Government Have students research the local governments in the colonies in the early and mid-eighteenth century. What background did the leaders come from and how were they chosen? How did they use their power? Students can work in small groups to carry out their research and then choose a spokesperson from the group to present their findings to the class.

Further Resources
- **Books**

Smallpox Strikes! Cotton Mather's Bold Experiment (the American Adventure) by Jean Lutz recounts the 1721 smallpox epidemic and inoculation debate in Boston through the eyes of eleven-year-old Rob Allerton.

The subject of plagues is discussed across time and cultures in *When Plague Strikes: The Black Death, Smallpox, AIDS* by James Cross Giblin, woodcut illustrations by James Frampton.

Assessment

Turn to page 119 for a multiple-choice test on the selection.

Test Answers

1. b **2.** a **3.** c **4.** a **5.** d
6. d **7.** a **8.** b **9.** c **10.** d

The Young Witch Hunters

from *Muse*
by RHODA BLUMBERG
(student text page 23)

Reading Level: Below average

Special Considerations

The selection discusses the Salem witch trials of 1692 and may spark student discussion of their own religious beliefs. Remind students to be respectful of the beliefs of others, and assure them that they need not share any information that they would be uncomfortable discussing.

Text Summary

This magazine article details the events that led to the hanging of nineteen innocent people for witch-craft in the town of Salem, Massachusetts, in 1692. The article describes how the harmless game of two young girls culminated in tragedy and discusses possible explanations for the behavior of those involved.

BEFORE READING

Make the Connection

Ask students to draw a two-column chart on a sheet of paper. In the first column have students write their impressions of witches from stories, cartoons, and other sources. List the impressions on the chalkboard or on an overhead transparency. Have students discuss why they think these impressions might or might not be historically accurate. Tell students they will be reading about a witchcraft trial that actually took place in Puritan New England. Ask them to use the second column of their charts to record any material that verifies or disputes their original impressions.

Build Background
■ More About the Topic

The Salem witch trials made such an impression on the American consciousness that "witch hunt" has become a common term for any campaign during which people are accused of subversive activities on flimsy or nonexistent evidence. One such campaign was Senator Joseph McCarthy's investigations of alleged U.S. Communists in the early 1950s. He was officially censured by the Senate in 1954.

Vocabulary Development

The following words are underscored and defined in the student text.

supernatural: relating to the world beyond time and space; spiritual.

contagious: able to spread from one person to another.

bizarre: very surprising and incredible.

accusation: formal statement finding a person guilty of wrongdoing.

torment: to cause physical or emotional pain; torture.

Before assigning the reading, you may want to introduce students to any words that could cause pronunciation or definition problems.

Vocabulary Tip

Distinguishing Between Commonly Confused Words Students may confuse the words *bizarre* and *bazaar*, since both words have an unusual spelling. Point out to students that the word that means "incredible" has an *i*, just like *witch* has. The other word, *bazaar*, means "a market" and thus has an a (market). Ask students for their own strategies in remembering the number of *r*'s in each word.

CONTENT-AREA VOCABULARY

Although the following words are important to an understanding of the text selection, some of them may be unfamiliar to students. You may wish to present this list of words and definitions to students. Write the words on the chalkboard or on an overhead transparency. Pronounce each word, and ask students for their definitions of the words.

dabbling: playing with.

hags: ugly, evil women.

fasting: purposefully going without food for a certain period of time.

dungeon: underground jail cell.

Reading Informational Material

Reading Skill
Making Generalizations

Tell students that comprehending the selection will require them to make decisions and judgments about the information presented. Students should base their generalizations on facts given in the text.

Reading Strategy
Anticipating Information (Strategy 9)

To help students make generalizations about the themes in the selection, use Strategy 9 described in Content-Area Reading Strategies. Provide students with an Anticipation Guide (Graphic Organizer 1) to help them record their thoughts and findings.

DURING READING

Using the Side-Margin Feature
- Witch or Snitch

Students may benefit from discussing games and pranks that in their own realm of experience and knowledge may lead to larger problems. You may want to use the discussion as a springboard to investigate some of the real issues students face, such as how teasing, bullying, and alienation may lead to violent retribution.

Differentiating Instruction
- Learners Having Difficulty

Direct students to work with partners to organize the events in the selection into causes and effects. Students can do this by paying attention to cause-and-effect signal words such as *because, since,* and *therefore.* By investigating the causes and effects of events, students will be better able to get to the roots of the problem presented.

AFTER READING

✔ Reading Check

The following are sample answers to questions on student text page 28.

1. Witches were thought to create storms, sink ships, ruin crops, cause disease, sour milk, put fleas in food, cause nightmares, and cause quarrels. [Accept any two.]

2. After they conducted their egg-white experiment, Betty Parris and Abigail Williams felt terribly guilty because they believed they had committed a sin.

3. The villagers had suffered through a recent drought; they had had a brutally cold winter; many had died during a smallpox epidemic; nearby Indians threatened to attack. [Accept any two.]

4. Tituba made up stories about being possessed because she had been tortured and wanted to be left in peace.

5. The witch hunt was stopped when one of the girls accused the president of Harvard College and the wife of the Massachusetts governor of witchcraft. The judges believed that such important citizens could not truly be witches. As a result of the witch hunt, 150 people were arrested, and 22 people died. Some of the accused remained in prison for months.

Reteaching

If students still have difficulty making generalizations about the selection, they may be having trouble connecting the situation described to their own lives. Have students freewrite for five minutes on the kind of problems that can result from fear and suspicion. Then, have students review the text, paying close attention to the emotions of the people involved. Why might the inhabitants of Salem be afraid of witches? What kind of people would be suspected? Students can discuss their ideas in small groups and work together to make generalizations.

Reading Informational Material

Connecting to Language Arts

▪ Writing

Legal Brief Ask students to imagine they are lawyers taking up the defense of the Parrises' slave Tituba, who was one of the first to be accused by the girls. Students should write a brief description of the charges and the situation, giving reasons for maintaining their client's innocence and telling what they think is the true crime occuring in Salem in 1692. Remind students to support their persuasive arguments with facts, statistics, and anecdotes.

Connecting Across the Curriculum: Social Studies

Court Case Have students research another real-life "witch hunt." Students should choose a famous controversial trial in U.S. history and investigate the factors that led to the jury's judgment. Have students present their cases in short speeches in which they describe the case and suggest ways to avoid such mistakes in the future.

Further Resources

▪ Books

The Witchcraft of Salem Village by Shirley Jackson examines the story of the witch trials. *Tituba of Salem Village* by Ann Petry tells the story of the Salem witch trials from the point of view of one of the accused.

Advanced students may enjoy reading the play *The Crucible* by Arthur Miller.

▪ Video

Salem Witch Trials, A&E Home Video, 2000. Not rated.

▪ Online resources

For more information about the Salem witch trials, visit the National Geographic Web site.

Assessment

Turn to page 120 for a multiple-choice test on the selection.

Test Answers

1. c   **2.** a   **3.** b   **4.** b   **5.** a
6. d   **7.** a   **8.** d   **9.** b   **10.** a

The Slave Ship

from *The Kidnapped Prince: The Life of Olaudah Equiano*

by OLAUDAH EQUIANO, ADAPTED BY ANN CAMERON
(student text page 29)

Reading Level: Average

Special Considerations

The selection describes in terrifying detail the experiences of kidnapped Africans aboard slave ships. Students may find some of the material upsetting. You may want to discuss with students how keeping alive the memory of such historical events can help to prevent similar events from happening again.

Text Summary

In this selection, an excerpt from an adapted biography, an African youth sold into slavery in the mid-1700s tells about his experiences on a slave ship. The firsthand account offers a unique perspective on one of history's most disturbing chapters.

BEFORE READING

Make the Connection

Ask students what they know about the slave trade that brought Africans to the United States. [Students may mention crowded, filthy conditions, a high death rate, cruel treatment.] Write students' comments on the chalkboard, and then tell students they are about to read an account of life aboard a slave ship from the point of view of an African sold into slavery.

Build Background
■ More about the Topic

The slave trade operated from the seventeenth to the nineteenth century, bringing Africans to both North and South America. In 1808, Congress passed a law banning the importation of any more slaves into the U.S. In 1863, during the height of the Civil War, President Lincoln delivered his Emancipation Proclamation, declaring that all slaves were now free. The Fourteenth Amendment to the Constitution, passed by Congress in 1868, officially defined the rights of freed slaves.

Vocabulary Development

The following words are underscored and defined in the student text.

complexion: the appearance of the skin, especially the face.
lot: a person's situation in life.
consternation: alarm; dismay; bewilderment.
flogged: beaten with a stick or whip.
fetid: having a foul or rotten smell.

Before assigning the reading, you may want to introduce students to any words that could cause pronunciation or definition problems.

Vocabulary Tip

Finding Synonyms Seeking out synonyms and learning to use them is a good way for students to expand their vocabularies. Some words have more synonyms than others, however, and *fetid* is one such word. Challenge students to use a thesaurus or dictionary to find as many synonyms as they can for the word. [Students may list *malodorous, musty, putrid, rank, smelly,* or *stinking.*]

CONTENT-AREA VOCABULARY

Although the following words are important to an understanding of the text selection, some of them may be unfamiliar to students. You may wish to present this list of words and definitions to your students. Ask students what they predict they will read about in a selection using these words and the glossary words in the student text.

vast: great; huge.
vessel*: ship.
exceedingly: very much.
astonishment: surprise.
unmercifully: without pity.

*Although students may be familiar with other meanings of this word, the word as used in the selection has a specific meaning that pertains to the content area.

Reading Skill

Analyzing Multiple Text Structures

Tell students that the selection has a twofold structure: The author recounts in chronological order his experiences in his first days on a slave ship, and he also compares and contrasts the whites' ways with his own. Students should pay attention to both structures to ensure comprehension.

Reading Strategy

Understanding Text (Strategy 2)

To help students follow the structures of the text in the selection, use Strategy 2 described in Content-Area Reading Strategies. You may wish to provide students with lists of signal words to use with a Cluster Diagram (Graphic Organizer 3) to help them identify the structures used in the selection.

Teaching Tip

▶ *Adaptation* Students may be curious about the method of adaptation of Equiano's story. If possible, provide an excerpt from the original so that students can compare and contrast the styles. You might also provide students with an excerpt of any document from the same time period and have students comment on the language. Discuss with students the benefits and pitfalls of adapting someone else's story. After reading the selection, students may want to share their opinions on how faithful Cameron is to Equiano's experiences.

DURING READING

Using the Side-Margin Feature

■ Early Artisans Break the Mold

Students may want to investigate further examples of African and African American art. Set aside a class period in which students present the poetry, fiction, speeches, music, and artwork they discover.

Differentiating Instruction

■ Learners Having Difficulty

Students may be confused by the division between the sophisticated language used by the author and some of his seemingly naïve comments and questions. Point out to students that the author wrote this account many years after the experience but wanted to share the shock and bewilderment

he felt at the time. Students may be more understanding if they try their hand at describing something that at one time seemed strange but is now familiar—school, for example, or a sport they play.

AFTER READING

✓ Reading Check

The following are sample answers to questions on student text page 34.

1. When he first boards the ship, Equiano is terrified. He sees a furnace on the deck, Africans in chains, and white people who look strange to him.

2. Nets were stretched along the sides of the ships, and the sailors watched over the captives at all times.

3. Equiano believes the white people are spirits from another world.

4. It was very cramped below deck where the captives were kept. Tubs were used for toilets. It was hot and the air was foul. The screams of the sick and dying could be heard at all hours.

5. The sailors threw the fish back into the water.

Reteaching

If students still have difficulty understanding the structures in the text, point out that Equiano's account can be divided into descriptions of action, descriptions of setting and people, and general observations. Have students find examples of each. Then, point out that the descriptions of action are generally arranged chronologically and tell Equiano's story. The other descriptions and general observations for the most part consist of Equiano making meaning of his experiences and feelings—often by using comparisons.

Connecting to Language Arts

■ Writing

Diary Entry Point out to students that surviving conditions such as those on the slave ship required considerable mental strength and fortitude. Ask students to imagine that they have been taken against their will to live in a strange place under inhuman conditions. What hopes, dreams, and plans would keep them going? [Possible answers: hope of returning home and seeing their families again, hope of escape, hope that the new land will offer opportunities] Have students write their ideas in the form of a series of diary entries.

▪ Speaking and Listening

Eulogy   Remind students that Equiano believed an event to be important only if a person learns from it to be better and wiser. Ask students: *If the horrors of the slave trade are an important historical fact, what have we learned from that fact?* [Possible answers: to abolish slavery, to fight against mistreatment of minorities around the world] Have students frame their ideas as a eulogy for those who suffered and died.

Connecting Across the Curriculum: Social Studies

Lessons from History The slave trade between Africa and the Americas from the 1600s to the 1800s is, unfortunately, not the only great tragedy in world history. Have students research another such event and encourage them to concentrate, as Equiano would, on the lessons that can be learned from such horrors. Students may choose anything from the Roman persecution of Christians to the Jewish Holocaust during World War II and should share their findings orally with the class.

Further Resources
▪ **Online resources**

The *Henrietta Marie,* a slave ship that sank near Key West in 1701, was salvaged and exhibited at the Historical Museum of Southern Florida in 1997. For more information on the ship and its current location, visit the museum's Web site. More information may be available on the Museum of African Slavery Web site.

Assessment

Turn to page 121 for a multiple-choice test on the selection.

Test Answers

1. a   **2.** d   **3.** a   **4.** d   **5.** a

6. d   **7.** a   **8.** c   **9.** b   **10.** b

Lacrosse Yesterday and Today

from *Cobblestone*
by STANLEY A. FREED
(*student text page 35*)

Reading Level: Average

Text Summary

This selection is a magazine article that describes the origins and the current state of the field game called lacrosse. The author emphasizes the importance of the game in the cultures of the eastern North American Indian tribes and tells how American Indians today take pride in competing at the highest level.

BEFORE READING

Make the Connection

Ask students if any of them have played lacrosse, watched a game, or heard of the game. Have students describe lacrosse and write students' descriptions on the chalkboard. Encourage students to compare their comments to the description of the game in the article.

Build Background

▪ Building Prerequisite Skills

Students may or may not be well practiced in using graphic organizers to analyze the structure of text. For students unfamiliar with Venn Diagrams (Graphic Organizer 11), you may want to introduce the organizer by comparing an apple and an orange. [Both are fruits that grow on trees, information that may be written in the overlap of the two circles; apples are crisp and their cores are not usually eaten, while oranges are soft and their skins usually not eaten.] Write the similarities and differences between the fruits in a Venn diagram on the chalkboard or overhead transparency.

Vocabulary Development

The following words are underscored and defined in the student text.

modified: changed or altered.
agility: speed and gracefulness of movement.
stamina: staying power.

procession: a group of people moving forward together in an orderly way.
mayhem: purposeful injury of another person; deliberate violence.

Before assigning the reading, you may want to introduce students to any words that could cause pronunciation or definition problems.

Vocabulary Tip

Using Etymology The word *stamina* comes from the Latin *stamen* (the same as the English word for the seed-producing part of a plant), which means "warp," or "thread." The word was applied in classical mythology to the thread spun by the Fates. The Greeks believed that the Fates, a group of goddesses, spun a thread that represented the length of a person's life. Discuss with students the aptness of the metaphor, in that the course of one's life depends upon one's stamina, or staying power.

CONTENT-AREA VOCABULARY

Although the following words are important to an understanding of the text selection, some of them may be unfamiliar to students. You may wish to present this list of words and definitions to your students. Ask students what they predict they will read about in a selection using these words and the glossary words from the student text.

festival: celebration.
bounty*: abundance.
predating: coming before.
feasting: eating large meals for a special occasion.
assembled: gathered.

*Although students may be familiar with other meanings of this word, the word as used in the selection has a specific meaning that pertains to the content area.

Reading Skill

Analyzing Text Structure: Comparison and Contrast

Tell students that the selection compares and contrasts lacrosse as it was played by the American Indians centuries ago and as it is played today. Understanding the selection will require that students comprehend the comparisons being made.

Reading Strategy

Using Graphic Organizers (Strategy 3)

To help students analyze the comparison-and-contrast structure of the selection, use Strategy 3 described in Content-Area Reading Strategies. You may wish to provide students with a copy of a Venn Diagram (Graphic Organizer 11) to help them analyze the comparisons made in the selection.

▶ **Teaching Tip**

Comparison and Contrast Students will be familiar with writing comparison-contrast essays in either point-by-point or block style but may be confused by the selection's mixture of the two organizing patterns. You may want to make copies of the selection for students and have them color-code the details given, using one color for lacrosse "yesterday" and one for lacrosse "today."

DURING READING

Differentiating Instruction

■ Advanced Learners

Students may be interested in learning more about other American Indian cultures' games and celebrations. Encourage students to research another sport or game and its origins, rules, and significance, and have them display their findings on posters you hang in the classroom.

AFTER READING

✔ Reading Check

The following are sample answers to questions on student text page 38.

1. The game got its name from the French settlers' term for the racket used, which resembled a bishop's staff or "crosier."

2. Early lacrosse was more violent, had a varying number of players and size of field, was part of a religious festival, had no time limit, and required no protective equipment.

3. Both early and modern lacrosse are played with rackets and both are rough, fast games in which teams try to score by making the ball cross the other team's goal.

4. George Catlin attended a Choctaw lacrosse game in 1834, painted it, and wrote about it.

5. In 1990, an American Indian team competed in the World Cup Lacrosse Championship, which marked the American Indians' return to competing in lacrosse at its highest level.

Reteaching

If students still have difficulty understanding the comparison-and-contrast structure of the text, they may need to reread the article more than once, each time with a specific, focused goal. On one rereading, students can use one column of a two-column organizer to record details about the American Indian game of lacrosse. On the next rereading, students can note in the second column details about the modern game. Students can then compare their two columns, circling similarities and numbering differences.

Connecting to Language Arts

■ Writing

List of Rules Have students write a list of rules for the game of lacrosse as it was played in the past by the early American Indians tribes. Students can either research the game further or make up rules that are consistent with the descriptions of the game given in the article.

■ Speaking and Listening

Halftime Speech Tell students to imagine they are coaching a team playing in the final of the World Cup Lacrosse Championship games. Their team is behind by one goal, and their best player is lost to injury for the rest of the game. What can they say to motivate their team to win? Ask volunteers to deliver their speeches to the class.

Connecting Across the Curriculum: Physical Education

Skills Workshop Sports require that players perform very precise, graceful actions under incredible strain and pressure. Have students choose an action from their favorite sport (a jump shot in basketball, a bicycle kick in soccer, throwing a curveball in baseball, and so forth) and write a brief "how-to" article describing how best to perform the action. You may want to assemble students' articles in a class sports handbook.

Further Resources

▪ Books

Lacrosse: The National Game of the Iroquois, written by Diane Hoyt-Goldsmith and illustrated by Lawrence Migdale, features three generations of lacrosse players. Lacrosse—the game, the sport, and its importance to the Iroquois culture—is presented through the life of a contemporary thirteen-year-old American Indian.

The Man Who Painted Indians: George Catlin by Nancy Plain is illustrated by full-color reproductions of the artist's paintings.

George Catlin: Painter of the Indian West by Mark Sufrin expands on the material in Plain's biography.

Ten Bears by Miles Harrison Jr. and Chip Silverman tells the story of the first African American college lacrosse team to compete in the NCAA.

Assessment

Turn to page 122 for a multiple-choice test on the selection.

Test Answers

1. a **2.** a **3.** c **4.** b **5.** c
6. d **7.** d **8.** c **9.** a **10.** d

The following criteria can help you evaluate each student's success in completing the activities prompted by the Cross-Curricular Activities feature in the student textbook.

Science/Art
A Day in the Life

- The student conducts research to learn more about viruses.
- The student creates a chart or poster that reflects his or her research.
- The student's poster demonstrates imagination and creativity.

History/Drama
Meeting the Neighbors

- The student uses resources to find out more about the colonists' relationships with neighboring American Indian tribes.
- The student plans a short skit that reflects what he or she has learned about these relationships.
- As performed, the skit is plausible and effectively conveys the relationship between colonists and neighboring American Indians.
- The performance of the skit is relatively free of performance errors. If used, props, costumes, music, sound effects, and other enhancements contribute to the overall effectiveness of the skit.
- The skit shows imagination and creativity.

Language Arts/Health
What's for Dinner?

- The student conducts research to find out what typical colonial meals were like.
- The student plans a menu for a Colonial American meal that reflects his or her research and describes or gives the history of each dish.
- The menu is relatively free of errors in spelling, grammar, usage, and mechanics.

Social Studies/Art
Sailing to Slavery

- The student re-reads "The Slave Ship" (pages 29–34) and uses other resources to gather more information about slave ships.
- Based on this research, the student creates a diagram of a typical slave ship of the 1700s.
- The diagram is labeled accurately and includes brief captions that explain the function of each part of the ship.

Art/Speech
"Play Ball!"

- The student conducts research on the history of a modern sport.
- Based on this research, the student creates a chart that accurately compares the original rules of the game with today's rules, including illustrations of equipment and uniforms.
- The student presents his or her findings and chart to the class.
- The student's presentation is clear and well organized and effectively contrasts the original and modern versions of the game.
- The presentation is relatively free of performance errors.

CHAPTER 2

With Liberty and Justice for All
The New Nation 1776–1804

from Inventor and Scientist

from *Benjamin Franklin: The New American*

by MILTON MELTZER
(student text page 43)

Reading Level: Above average

Text Summary

This excerpt from *Benjamin Franklin: The New American* examines Franklin's post-retirement period during which he devoted himself to science. His desire to discover the why and how of his surroundings led to numerous useful inventions, and his unique method of experimentation paved the way for modern science.

BEFORE READING

Make the Connection

Ask students what happens if they are curious about their environment. Have students look around the classroom for objects that arouse their scientific curiosity. For example, they might ask, "How could we design a window blind that adjusts automatically to the angle and height of the sun?" List students' suggestions on the chalkboard. Tell students that they will follow up on their ideas later.

Build Background

■ More About the Topic

When Benjamin Franklin encountered a problem, his scientific curiosity enabled him to find a solution. For example, Franklin needed glasses to read but got tired of removing the glasses when he was not reading. As a result, he invented bifocals, eyeglasses that enabled him to see clearly both near and far objects. As he grew older, he had trouble reaching the books on the high shelves of his library. Therefore, he invented a tool called a long arm—a long wooden pole with a grasping claw at

the end—to help him reach the books. Franklin's list of useful inventions is long and varied.

Vocabulary Development

The following words are underscored and defined in the student text.

inventiveness: the quality of being able to make something that did not exist before.

genius*: the intellectual and creative powers of human beings.

amateur: a person who participates in an activity for enjoyment rather than money.

voracious: having an enormous appetite for something.

analytic: able to study carefully to determine what something is or how it works.

*Although students may be familiar with other meanings of this word, the word as used in the selection has a specific meaning that pertains to the content area. Before assigning the reading, you may want to introduce students to any words that could cause pronunciation or definition problems.

┌─ *Vocabulary Tip* ─────────────

Recognizing Homophones Tell students that a homophone is a word that sounds like another word or words but that has a different meaning. Homophones for *flue* are *flu*, the abbreviated form of *influenza*, and *flew*, the past tense of *fly*.

└─────────────────────────────

Although the following words are important to an understanding of the text selection, some of them may be unfamiliar to students.

trivial: not very important.

dissenters: persons who disagree or who strongly differ in beliefs.

ingenious: clever at devising things.

flue: a tube or pipe through which smoke, steam, hot air, and so forth may travel.

contemporaries: persons living during the same time period.

Reading Informational Material

Reading Skill

Determining the Main Idea

Explain to students that the main idea is an overall topic developed in a selection or in parts of a selection.

Reading Strategy

Previewing the Text (Strategy 1)

To help students organize their thinking and set goals before reading, use Strategy 1 described in Content-Area Reading Strategies. Have students look through the selection, noting text features. Then, ask students to complete the three-column PIC chart, labeling columns: "Purpose of Reading," "Important Ideas," and "Connecting to Prior Knowledge." Explain to students that the ideas they generate in the second column of the chart can help them establish the main idea.

▶ **Teaching Tip**

Previewing Text Features Explain to students that how they preview a text will depend on its text features. In previewing this selection, ask students to look at the headnote, title, pictures, and comprehension questions. Remind them that other selections may have headings, subheadings, charts, and design features such as bullets and boldface type.

DURING READING

Using the Side-Margin Feature

■ What Tombstones Tell

You may want to have students brainstorm about the meaning of Ben Franklin's epitaph. Explain

that his occupation at the time was printing. Ask students if they think his tone is serious or humorous, and elicit discussion about the identity of "the Author."

Differentiating Instruction

■ Learners Having Difficulty

You may wish to provide students with self-adhesive notes to use while reading. Tell students to use the notes to mark words, passages, or paragraphs that seem confusing. Encourage students to jot down on each note why that particular piece of information is confusing. Then, pair students and have them discuss their questions and find answers.

AFTER READING

✔ Reading Check

The following are sample answers to questions on student text page 49.

1. After retiring at age forty-two, Ben Franklin plunged into the life of a scientist.

2. There were no sources for research funds such as corporations or universities. Scientists did not work together in laboratories. There was no formal training for scientists. Most scientists worked alone, at home, and financed their own experiments.

3. Ben Franklin helped start the American Philosophical Society.

4. Ben Franklin refused to patent his inventions because he felt that people should be glad to serve others through their inventions.

5. According to the author, Ben Franklin's most important contribution to science was his experimental approach.

Reteaching

If students are still struggling with the concept of finding the main idea, write a question about the selection in the center of a Cluster Diagram (Graphic Organizer 3) and distribute copies to the class. [Example: What was scientific research?] Ask students to fill in the next level with supporting statements [people (amateurs) conducted research for their own enjoyment, no funds for support, no training, worked alone]. Then, tell them to answer the question in one sentence. [Other questions might be, What is the best example of Franklin's inventiveness? Why did Franklin bring scientists and thinkers together?]

Connecting to Language Arts

▪ Writing

Epitaph On page 48 is the epitaph that Ben Franklin wrote for himself when he was twenty-two years old. Have students note the style, form, and capitalization used. Explain that epitaphs generally focus on the qualities or achievements for which an individual wants to be remembered. Then, ask students to write epitaphs for themselves. Students can choose to use Ben Franklin's epitaph as a model, or they can create a style of their own. You may want to post the epitaphs on a bulletin board.

Connecting Across the Curriculum: Science

Young Inventors Review the students' suggestions for improvements to the classroom environment. Have books available that highlight students' inventions. Possibilities include *The Kids' Invention Book* by Arlene Erlbach or *Brainstorm!: The Stories of Twenty American Kid Inventors* by Tom Tucker. Then, working in small groups, have students select an idea from the chalkboard or come up with a new idea and propose an invention for the classroom. Ask students to prepare a description of the invention or a working model or drawing and present it to the class.

Further Resources

National Geographic World has an interesting Web site for inventive minds called *Inventions*.

Check out the Web site for the National Inventors Hall of Fame Index of Inventions—inventions range from ACTA Scanner to Zirconium.

The Franklin Institute Online includes a list of Franklin's inventions along with other resources and a museum visit.

The life of Franklin can be viewed on the video *Biography-Benjamin Franklin*, released by A & E Entertainment. Other figures prominent in Amercian History, such as George Washington, are represented in this series of biographies, all rated NR.

Assessment

Turn to page 123 for a multiple-choice test on the selection.

Test Answers
1. b   2. c   3. c   4. d   5. a
6. d   7. a   8. b   9. b   10. c

The Women of the American Revolution

from *Who Were the Founding Fathers? Two Hundred Years of Reinventing American History*

by STEVEN H. JAFFE
(student text page 50)

Reading Level: Average

Text Summary

This selection focuses on the many contributions that women made during the American Revolution. As his main source of information, the author uses a nineteenth-century book that was based on primary sources—old diaries, letters, and interviews. The description of women's roles and courageous feats showed women to be capable of much more than household duties.

BEFORE READING

Make the Connection

Ask students whether they have ever believed in something so strongly that they were willing to speak out publicly to demonstrate their support. Elicit discussion about the rewards and challenges of standing up for your beliefs when they go against current thinking.

Build Background

▪ Motivate

Have students think about how women's roles in America have changed throughout history. During the Revolutionary War, a woman's place was in the home, but even then some women courageously forged new roles. Ask students to give examples of girls or women who have proven that a particular accomplishment or vocation was not for men only.

Vocabulary Development

The following words are underscored and defined in the student text.

revive*: to remember; to bring to mind.

crucial: extremely important.

skirmish: a minor fight or conflict.

exploits: acts of bravery.

stereotypes: oversimplified ideas or beliefs about a group of people.

*Although students may be familiar with other meanings of this word, the word as used in the selection has a specific meaning that pertains to the content area.

Before assigning the reading, you may want to introduce students to any words that could cause pronunciation or definition problems.

Vocabulary Tip

Using Derivations The word *boycott* was derived from a person's name: Captain Charles Cunningham Boycott. In 1880, Captain Boycott was hired to manage an estate in Ireland. His strict rules and inflexibility caused his tenants to launch a campaign against him. Boycott's property was destroyed; his mail was not delivered; he was denied service in local stores; and his life was threatened. So effective was this campaign that *boycott* became synonymous with the refusal to buy, sell, or use goods or services.

CONTENT-AREA VOCABULARY

Although the following words are important to an understanding of the text selection, some of them may be unfamiliar to students. Put the words on the chalkboard or on an overhead transparency. Pronounce each word and ask students to define the words if they can. Write their definitions and add the ones given below if students have not covered those particular meanings.

boycotted: refused to buy.

anguish: great pain or suffering.

inferiority: the condition of a lower rank.

Reading Informational Material

Reading Skill
Identifying Supporting Details

Explain to students that the supporting details are the information included to explain the main idea, which is the focus or key idea in a piece of writing.

Reading Strategy
Taking Effective Notes (Strategy 10)

To help students identify the supporting details in this selection, use Strategy 10 described in Content-Area Reading Strategies. After students have labeled the text using INSERT symbols, they can organize their notes using a Concept Map or a Cluster Diagram (Graphic Organizer 3).

Teaching Tip

Identifying Supporting Details Explain to students that a selection such as this one has two kinds of supporting details. One kind of detail supports the main idea of the piece of writing—in this case, that women's efforts during the Revolutionary War helped prove that women deserved equal rights. Other details support the main idea of a paragraph.

DURING READING

Correcting Misconceptions

Because women's contributions to the Revolutionary War effort were not usually documented, much of what is known today is a compilation of primary source material. Researchers have sifted through such sources as court records, newspaper articles, diaries, and letters to piece together information. Depending on the source, the information might be unreliable. For example, Dr. Linda Grant DePauw, President of the Minerva Center (an educational and research corporation for the study of war and women in the military), proposes that Molly Pitcher is a legendary figure. Because of the pension she received, it is assumed that the real Mary McCauley did do something special, but no evidence supports that she assumed the name "Molly Pitcher" or was one of the two women who fought in the Battle of Monmouth.

Using the Side-Margin Feature
▪ **What Primary Sources Tell**

Explain to students that the excerpt from Abigail Adams's letter on student text page 53 is a primary source—firsthand, original information. After they have read the letter, ask students what conclusions they might draw about Mrs. Adams or the time period in which she lived.

Differentiating Instruction
▪ **Learners Having Difficulty**

If some students have difficulty identifying main ideas and supporting details using the INSERT symbols, you can create a Cloze Concept Map (see Strategy 4 in Content-Area Reading Strategies) on which you have filled in key words. Students can work in pairs to complete the map.

▪ **English-Language Learners**

You may want to ask students to share from their cultures stories of heroic women. Making such cross-cultural connections might inspire students to learn more about these women as well as the heroic women of the American Revolution.

AFTER READING

✔ Reading Check

The following are sample answers to questions on student text page 55.

1. Ellet read old diaries and letters and interviewed people who were alive during the American Revolution.

2. Accept any two: Women boycotted British imports such as tea and textiles; they raised money for the army; they served as spies and messengers; they took care of family businesses; they advised important politicians; they sometimes participated in battles.

3. Deborah Sampson disguised herself as a man and enlisted in the army.

4. In 1802, Sampson went on tour, giving an onstage address (written for her by Herman Mann) that described her experiences as a soldier.

5. As both a soldier and lecturer, Sampson showed that women could be successful at tasks that it was generally believed they were unable to do.

Reteaching

If students are still struggling with the concept of supporting details, write the following sentences on the chalkboard, but scramble the order and omit the outlining. Then, help students organize the information into outline form showing how certain details form a hierarchy to support a main idea. You may also want to illustrate how these same details can be transferred to a concept map.

I. Women contributed to the Revolutionary War cause in various ways.

  A. Women advised important politicians.

   1. Many of the Founding Fathers asked the opinion of Mercy Warren.

   2. Abigail Adams advised her husband, who later became President.

  B. Women acted as spies and messengers behind enemy lines.

  C. Wives and daughters took care of family businesses.

Connecting Language Arts

▪ Writing

Brochure Tell students to imagine that women were actually recruited for the Revolutionary War. Have students work in small groups to create brochures to promote the recruiting process. What tasks would Revolutionary-era women have been best equipped for? If possible, have several brochures available that students can look at for design ideas. You may want to review persuasive writing techniques before students begin.

Connecting Across the Curriculum: Art

Ask students to design a stamp commemorating the brave deeds of women during the Revolutionary War. Display the stamps in the classroom. To extend the activity, suggest that students research how the United States Postal Service determines which stamps should be issued and how the stamps are designed.

Further Resources

The Minerva Center is a nonprofit educational foundation that supports the study of women in war. Contact them on their Web site or at

> The Minerva Center
> 20 Granada Road
> Pasadena, MD 21122-2708
> Telephone (410) 437-5379

Liberty-American Revolution, a video on the American Revolution produced by PBS Home Video, is a six-hour documentary beginning with the Stamp Act in 1765 through to the U.S. Constitution and the Bill of Rights in 1789. This video may be a useful resource for this and other selections in this chapter.

Assessment

Turn to page 124 for a multiple-choice test on the selection.

Test Answers

1. d   2. a   3. c   4. d   5. b
6. c   7. a   8. c   9. c   10. b

from Ground Truth

from *Breaking Ground, Breaking Silence:*
The Story of New York's African Burial Ground

by JOYCE HANSEN and GARY McGOWAN
(student text page 56)

Reading Level: Above average

Text Summary

This excerpt examines how archaeological research sheds information on the past. In 1991, archaeologists discovered a burial site deep under the streets of New York City. From the painstaking investigation of the skeleton and artifacts within the site, archaeologists hypothesized that the buried individual may have been an African American man who served in the British navy during the American Revolution.

BEFORE READING

Make the Connection

Ask students if they have ever unearthed or found an object, such as an old coin, and wondered about its origin. What steps could they take to uncover the object's history? [look in reference books, do online research, ask an expert, look for identifying marks] What conclusions did they come to about the origin of the object based on their research?

Build Background

■ More About the Topic

African Americans in the Revolutionary War
African American soldiers served on both sides during the war. Initially, African Americans were not enlisted in the United States Army for fear of an armed uprising. Eventually, however, men were needed to fill depleted ranks. It is estimated that 5,000 to 8,000 African Americans—both slaves and free blacks—joined the patriot cause. A much greater number—tens of thousands—sided with the British army, for many believed that a British victory would bring freedom for the slaves.

Vocabulary Development

The following words are underscored and defined in the student text.

phase: stage.
critical*: important.
organic: of or related to a living thing.
particles: very small pieces.
extracted: taken out.
immersed: dipped completely into.
eroded: worn away.
verify: to show the truth of.
deceased: dead.
corroded: rusted; worn away.

*Although students may be familiar with other meanings of this word, the word as used in this selection has a specific meaning that pertains to the content area. Before assigning the reading, you may want to introduce students to any words that could cause pronunciation or definition problems. Ask students to notice what many of the words have in common. [Many are verbs ending in *-ed*, which indicates past tense.]

CONTENT-AREA VOCABULARY

Although the following words are important to an understanding of the text selection, some of them may be unfamiliar to students. Before you introduce the content-area vocabulary words, you may want to remind students that breaking down a word and examining its parts can offer clues to the word's meaning. For example, the prefix *in-* meaning "in" or "within" paired with *sign* can give students a clue to the meaning of *insignia*. The word *exhume* contains the prefix *ex-* meaning "out" and *hume* (*humus* meaning "earth").

distorted: falsely represented.
oppress: to keep down unfairly.
inadvertently: accidentally.
insignia: a distinguishing mark indicating membership or rank.

pewter: an alloy of tin with lead, copper, and other metals.

excavation: the process of digging out.

exhume: to dig up or remove from the earth.

Vocabulary Tip

Using Context Clues Not all of the selection's challenging vocabulary words are included in the previous lists because the author defines many within the text. Have students look for the following signals that indicate definition/restatement context clues:

- commas, dashes, or parentheses
- words and phrases such as *or, called, other, known as,* or *referred to as*

Among the words that students should find defined in the text are *thorax, flotation, osteologists, shroud, acrylic resin, reconstructed, analyzed, hypothesis, gilded,* and *raking.*

Reading Informational Material

Reading Skill
Identifying Chronological Order

Tell students that keeping the events described in the selection in chronological order—the order in which they happen—will make it easier to understand the excavation process.

Reading Strategy
Understanding the Text (Strategy 2)

To help students follow the chronology of the events in the selection, use Strategy 2 described in Content-Area Reading Strategies. Provide students with a list of signal words to use with the Sequence and Chronological Order chart (Graphic Organizer 10), to help keep the events in chronological order.

DURING READING

Reading Informational Material

▶ **Teaching Tip**

Identifying Chronological Order Point out to students that the chronology of the events in this particular selection is not limited to the lettered steps on student text pages 58–59. A number of events occur before the steps for processing arti-

facts are listed. These steps are further explained in the text that follows them.

Differentiating Instruction
■ **English-Language Learners**

Establish a Listening Center in your classroom. First, either you or one of your advanced readers can read aloud and record difficult reading selections, such as this one, on audiocassette tapes. Then, English-language learners can listen to the selections while they silently read along.

■ **Advanced Learners**

Not all authors present sequence in a linear manner (one event occurs, then a second, and so forth). Sometimes events may be presented in reversed order, or flashbacks and/or flash-forwards might be used. Have students rewrite portions of this selection as a newspaper article or television story to demonstrate reversed order, a flashback, and a flash-forward.

AFTER READING

✔ Reading Check

The following are sample answers to questions on student text page 60.

1. Thin metal pins and an iron pellet—probably a bullet—were also found in the grave.

2. To archaeologists, "ground truth" means the truth that can be told only through artifacts, especially when history gives an incomplete or unfair picture of a people or culture.

3. To process artifacts, archaeologists must clean the artifact, label it, stabilize it, reconstruct it, and analyze it.

4. On some of the buttons, the anchor and rope symbol of the British navy can be clearly seen.

5. The archaeologists hypothesized that the skeleton may have been that of an African American man who served in the British navy during the American Revolution.

Reteaching

You may want to provide students with the following list of events, but scramble the order. Then, ask students to list the events in chronological order. Allow students to refer to the selection. Remind them to look for transitional words and phrases in the text to help them locate the events.

- The archaeologists removed the dirt from the skeleton's surface.
- Artifacts were discovered on the skeleton's midsection.
- Osteologists analyzed the skeleton and drew conclusions.
- Thin metal pins and an iron pellet were found in the grave.
- The artifacts and skeleton were taken to laboratories for further study.
- The artifacts were cleaned.
- The artifacts were labeled.
- The artifacts were stabilized.
- The artifacts were reconstructed.
- The artifacts were analyzed.
- The archaeologists formed a hypothesis.

Connecting to Language Arts

- Writing

Biographical Sketch Have students work in small groups to write a biographical sketch of the individual in Burial #6. Suggest that they use print sources as well as the Internet to research background information. (See suggestions under **Further Resources** on this page.) If information about African Americans during the Revolutionary War period is hard to find, students may fill in details by using what they know about the time period and what they can imagine.

Connecting Across the Curriculum: Science

Studying Bones This selection focuses mainly on the processing of artifacts to provide information about the past. Skeletal remains also have a story to tell. Have students research the field of forensic anthropology—the examination of skeletal remains. The selection mentions osteology, which is one branch of forensic study, but the field is much broader. Have students share their findings with the rest of the class.

Further Resources

Information about African Americans in the American Revolution can be found on Washington State University's *World Civilizations* Web site.

The Web site of The American History Archive Project also contains information about African Americans in the American Revolution.

Assessment

Turn to page 125 for a test on the selection.

Test Answers

1. d   2. b   3. c   4. a   5. d
6. d   7. g   8. e   9. b   10. f
11. f   12. d   13. g   14. a   15. b

Your Rights and Mine

from *Give Me Liberty! The Story of the Declaration of Independence*

by RUSSELL FREEDMAN
(student text page 61)

Reading Level: Above average

Text Summary

This excerpt examines the lasting effect of the Declaration of Independence on society. Its principles, particularly the passage "all men are created equal," continued to motivate oppressed groups, such as women and slaves, to secure the equal rights they believed they deserved. The influence of the Declaration of Independence is still being felt today.

BEFORE READING

Make the Connection

Point out that Thomas Jefferson knew that people were not equal in all respects—some have greater athletic ability, others are musically gifted, some are particularly insightful and empathetic, others are extremely intelligent or physically beautiful. He also knew that some were born into wealth while others were born into families of more modest means. What, then, did Jefferson mean when he said that "all men are created equal"? [Perhaps he meant they should be equal before the law or that everyone should have equal opportunities to develop their abilities.] Have students brainstorm to answer this question, and write students' responses on the chalkboard or an overhead transparency.

Build Background

■ More About the Topic

At the end of the French and Indian War, Great Britain tightened its control in the Colonies, and the colonists resisted. The resistance led to a boycott of British goods and eventually to violence. To punish the unlawful colonists—particularly the Bostonians who during the Boston Tea Party had thrown overboard 342 chests of British tea—the British Parliament passed in 1774 what the colonists called the Intolerable Acts. These five acts seemed to colonists to severely limit

their political and geographical freedom. Mounting tension and the unwillingness to compromise are sometimes considered to have led to war and the colonists' Declaration of Independence.

Vocabulary Development

The following words are underscored and defined in the student text.

indictment: accusation.
affirmation: a statement or declaration that something is true or right.
abolish: to do away with.
denounced: condemned as wicked or wrong.
eliminated: gotten rid of.

Before assigning the reading, you may want to introduce each word by pronouncing it and asking students to give a definition. Then, have students check and refine these definitions as they read the selection.

CONTENT-AREA VOCABULARY

Although the following words are important to an understanding of the text selection, some of them may be unfamiliar to students.

violated: disregarded or broke (as an agreement or law).
values: principles or qualities considered worthwhile or desirable.
embedded: set in firmly.
prevailed: triumphed; lasted.

Vocabulary Tip

Investigating Multiple Meanings Point out to students that *value* has multiple meanings. You may want to have students use dictionaries to check out the word's meanings and to find the one that applies to this selection.

Reading Informational Material

Reading Skill
Finding the Main Idea
Explain to students that the main idea is the central statement that the writer wants to make about a topic in a piece of writing. Some writers directly state their main ideas, while others only suggest or imply them. To identify an implied main idea, the reader can use prior knowledge to infer the content of the idea.

Reading Strategy
Anticipating Information (Strategy 9)
To help students activate prior knowledge about the selection's topic and identify the main idea, use Strategy 9 described in Content-Area Reading Strategies. You may wish to provide students with an Anticipation Guide (Graphic Organizer 1) to help them record their thoughts and findings.

DURING READING

▶ **Teaching Tip**
Using Quotations Point out to students that this selection is sprinkled with quotations by Thomas Jefferson, Abraham Lincoln, and Dr. Martin Luther King, Jr. Discuss how the author weaves the quotations into his sentences, and brainstorm with students the reasons for including direct quotations in a piece of writing. [to give validity to the writing, to support or state a main idea, to create an emotional response]

Differentiating Instruction
■ Learners Having Difficulty
You may want to pull out from the selection some of the more challenging phrases and clauses, particularly some of the quoted material. Write a phrase or clause on the chalkboard and model for students how to break the groups of words down to foster understanding. For example, substitute synonyms for challenging words, pull out extraneous prepositional phrases, and talk through the meaning. Then, have students work in small groups to continue the procedure. Encourage students as they read to create their own lists of word groups that need clarification.

■ English-Language Learners
To help with reading comprehension, you may want to pair an English-language learner with a more advanced speaker of English. Ask the students to take turns reading aloud a small section to their partners and then to discuss what has been read. You may want to model the process before pairing the students.

AFTER READING

✔ Reading Check

The following are sample answers to questions on student text page 65.

1. According to Thomas Jefferson, the purpose of the Declaration of Independence was to explain why the colonies were separating from England.

2. He meant that if a government does not protect its citizens' rights, then those citizens have the right to create a new government.

3. In 1848, a group of women's rights advocates declared that "all men and women are created equal."

4. Abraham Lincoln believed that equality in America was an ideal to work toward even though it might never be perfectly achieved.

5. In 1963, Dr. Martin Luther King, Jr., echoed Jefferson's belief that "all men are created equal."

Reteaching
If some students have difficulty identifying the main ideas of the selection, create a Cloze Concept Map (see Strategy 4 in Content-Area Reading Strategies) on which you have filled in key words. Students can work in pairs to complete the map.

Connecting Language Arts
■ Writing
Bill of Responsibilities The first ten amendments to the Constitution, the Bill of Rights, contain provisions that protect an individual's fundamental rights. Congress believed that each citizen had certain responsibilities, although those responsibilities were not enumerated. Have students work in small

groups to review the Constitution's Bill of Rights. Then, ask each group to create a Bill of Responsibilities. What should society expect from good citizens? What duties do citizens owe their communities? [Students may say citizens should show respect for others when exercising their rights to free speech, not leave firearms in the reach of children, support the democratic process by voting and communicating concerns to government representatives, and so on.]

■ Speaking and Listening

Interview Have students work in pairs to plan and conduct an interview of Thomas Jefferson during the time he was writing the Declaration of Independence. One student will play the role of Jefferson, and the other student will be the interviewer. Encourage students to go beyond this selection to find more historical information for their interviews. If time permits, have students perform their interviews for the rest of the class.

Connecting Across the Curriculum: Science

Document Preservation The Declaration of Independence is on display at the National Archives in Washington, D.C. This original document, however, wasn't always preserved under the best of conditions. First, have students research the scientific procedures for preserving historical documents. Then, ask students to focus on the specific measures taken to preserve the Declaration of Independence. Have students report their findings to the rest of the class.

Further Resources

Access information about the Declaration of Independence on the National Archives and Library of Congress Web sites.

Assessment

Turn to page 126 for a multiple-choice test on the selection.

Test Answers

1. c **2.** d **3.** c **4.** a **5.** b
6. d **7.** a **8.** b **9.** a **10.** b

Benjamin Banneker

from *Pioneers of Discovery*
(Profiles of Great Black Americans)

edited by RICHARD RENNERT
(student text page 66)

Reading Level: Average

Special Considerations

During Benjamin Banneker's time, the supporters of slavery believed that people of European ancestry were more intelligent than African Americans. Discuss with students the causes of such cultural stereotyping—also called *racism.* [ignorance, a desire to control] Have students comment on why the people who supported slavery held this belief.

Text Summary

This excerpt examines the life of Benjamin Banneker (1731–1806), an African American astronomer, mathematician, surveyor, and author. Banneker's accomplishments won him respect and fame, and he used his reputation to promote an end to racism and slavery.

BEFORE READING

Make the Connection

Ask students whether they have ever taught themselves to do something just because it interested them. Have they ever taken anything apart just to see how it works? In this age of information—when computers, televisions, and print material offer endless possibilities for knowledge, ask students if they have ever been so fascinated by a topic that they couldn't seem to learn enough about it.

Build Background
■ More About the Topic

Benjamin Banneker was a black man born of free parents. Other ways that African Americans in the late 1700s could achieve freedom was to buy it, to be set free by their masters, or to be set free by law. Although not bound by slavery, these free blacks did not lead easy lives. Treated by most whites as inferior, they were barred from many public places, and their activities were often limited. For example, in parts of New England, special passes

were required if African Americans wished to visit a town, and they needed permission to socialize with slaves. Faced with such severe discrimination, many—such as Banneker—still emerged as leaders.

Vocabulary Development

The following words are underscored and defined in the student text.

servitude: labor or service.

contemplative: thoughtful.

statistics: facts or data collected as numbers and arranged so as to give information.

surveyor: a person who measures the size and shape of a piece of land.

censure: blame or disapproval.

Before assigning the reading, you may want to introduce students to any words that could cause pronunciation or definition problems.

┌─ *Vocabulary Tip* ─────────────────

Making Inferences Before you introduce the content-area vocabulary words, point out to students that associating parts of an unknown word with more familiar words can offer valuable clues to the word's meaning. For example, associating the word *deported* with the familiar words *imported* and *exported* can give clues to the meaning of *deported.*

└────────────────────────────────────

CONTENT-AREA VOCABULARY

Although the following words are important to an understanding of the text selection, some of them may be unfamiliar to students.

deported: sent out of the country.

heritage: something—such as a trait, tradition, or culture—that has been passed down from ancestors.

abolition: doing away with.

Reading Informational Material

Reading Skill
Identifying Cause-and-Effect Relationships

Explain to students that a cause-and-effect relationship shows how one thing leads to another. A cause makes something happen. An effect is the result of the cause.

Reading Strategy
Using Graphic Organizers (Strategy 3)

To help your students track causes and effects in the selection, use Strategy 2 described in Content-Area Reading Strategies. You may wish to provide students with a Cause and Effect Chart (Graphic Organizer 2), to help them analyze the relationships in the selection.

▶ **Teaching Tip**

Analyzing Text Structures Point out to students that writers often use more than one text structure in a piece of writing. For example, the overall structure of this selection is narrative nonfiction, with events arranged in chronological order. However, within the narrative are cause-and-effect text structures.

DURING READING

Reading Informational Material

▶ **Teaching Tip**

Analyzing Cause and Effect Cause-and-effect relationships are often signaled by clue words such as *because, since, consequently,* and *as a result of.* Explain to students that when no clue words appear in the text, the cause-and-effect relationship is an *implied* one. To recognize an implied relationship, students should ask these questions:

- What happened?
- How or why did it happen?
- What was the result?

Using the Side-Margin Feature
- Letter to Thomas Jefferson

Because of the language of the time period, students may be challenged when reading the letter's excerpt. You may want to discuss its main points: Banneker says that although Jefferson claims that all men are created equal and therefore are entitled

to certain God-given rights, Jefferson owns slaves and is therefore guilty of "fraud and violence." If students are interested, Banneker's complete letter as well as Jefferson's response can be found online by using the keywords "Thomas Jefferson and Benjamin Banneker."

Differentiating Instruction
- Learners Having Difficulty

Students can better understand cause-and-effect relationships by becoming more familiar with signal words. Pair students and provide each pair with a list of cause-and-effect signal words (see Strategy 2) and sentences summarizing causes and effects from the selection. Have students combine these sentences using signal words from the list. For example, "Because Molly Welsh was accused of stealing milk, she was deported to the Colonies."

AFTER READING

✔ Reading Check

The following are sample answers to questions on student text page 71.

1. Banneker's mother and his father, a freed slave, met when they lived on neighboring farms.

2. At the age of 21, Banneker built a clock.

3. Banneker helped survey the land on which the national capitol would be built.

4. In his letter to Jefferson, Banneker compared the enslavement of blacks to the oppression of the American Colonies by the British government before the Revolution.

5. Abolitionists used Banneker's almanac to show that the intellectual ability of African Americans' was equal to that of whites.

Reteaching

If students are still struggling with the concept of cause-and-effect relationships, you may want to create a Cloze Concept Map (see Strategy 4 in Content-Area Reading Strategies). For each cause-and-effect relationship in the selection, fill in either the cause(s) or effect(s), and have students complete the relationship. Here is a list of some of the cause-and-effect relationships: Because Banneker's father died, Banneker was responsible for the farm; because Banneker was a free black, he led a lonely life; because Banneker taught himself astronomy, he predicted eclipses and created ephemerides; Banneker became a celebrity because of his correspondence with Jefferson and through publication of his almanac.

Connecting Language Arts

■ Writing

News Story Have students write a news story about the fire that destroyed Benjamin Banneker's home. Students should create an eye-catching headline, describe the event, and give background information. Upon completion, have students share their stories.

■ Speaking and Listening

The Winner Is... Have students work in pairs to plan and perform the presentation of a "Distinguished Citizen" award to Benjamin Banneker. One of the students will play the role of the presenter, and the other will be Banneker. The presenter should tell about Banneker's many accomplishments and contributions, and the recipient should tell why winning such an award is an honor.

Connecting Across the Curriculum: Science

Stargazing Encourage students to become stargazers. To familiarize themselves with the night sky, students should locate star charts specific to their latitude and the time of year. (These are available in various bookstores and nature stores, in astronomy magazines, and on the Web.) You may want to begin this activity by determining your students' experience with astronomy; amateur astronomers in your class can be a valuable source of information.

Further Resources

Access the *Lemelson-MIT Awards Program* Web site for information on Banneker and his inventions.

The Banneker Center for Economic Justice has information on Banneker and can be contacted on its Web site or at

> The Benjamin Banneker Center
> 647 Plymouth Road
> Baltimore, Maryland 21229

Assessment

Turn to page 127 for a multiple-choice test on the selection.

Test Answers

1. b **2.** a **3.** d **4.** c **5.** b
6. c **7.** a **8.** d **9.** a **10.** b

from **Thomas Jefferson**

from *Science in Colonial America*

by BRENDAN JANUARY
(student text page 72)

Reading Level: Average

Text Summary

This excerpt examines Thomas Jefferson's interest in natural science. This interest, as well as a desire to prove North America's merit, motivated him to sponsor several scientific expeditions. The first was to find fossilized animal bones to support his belief that woolly mammoths had lived in North America. The second was to explore the nation's newly acquired Louisiana Purchase.

BEFORE READING

Make the Connection

Tell students they will be reading about an individual whose fame and fortune partly reflect a childhood passion. Then, ask students to think about their own hobbies or interests. Might students' current interests affect future goals and accomplishments? How? [Students interested in computer games and the Internet might seek a career in computers; those involved in the school music, art, or acting programs may be headed for careers in the arts.]

Build Background

▪ Motivate

Have students discuss with a partner a time when someone challenged them to "prove" something— for example, their athletic or academic ability, the truth of a belief, the value of a special interest, or the worth of a sports team or organization they belonged to. Then, ask students what positive benefits resulted from this challenge. [Students may say they were challenged to become more skilled or knowledgeable in their area of interest, that they became more convinced of the truth of a belief, or that they deepened their loyalty to a team or organization.]

Vocabulary Development

The following words are underscored and defined in the student text.

geology: study of the nature and history of the earth.

inferior: lower in rank or class.

impressive: producing a strong effect.

specimens: examples; representatives of a larger group.

sponsored: organized; supported.

Before assigning the reading, you may want to introduce students to any words that could cause pronunciation or definition problems.

┌─ *Vocabulary Tip* ─────────────

Making Inferences Before you introduce the vocabulary words, ask a volunteer to define *crippled*. [unable to use the limbs or body properly] Tell students that in Jefferson's time, many Europeans believed that North America was crippled. Have students brainstorm definitions for *crippled* used in this context. [swampy and covered with stunted bushes and trees, and simple people]

└────────────────────────────

⟨ **CONTENT-AREA VOCABULARY** ⟩

Although the following words are important to an understanding of the text selection, some of them may be unfamiliar to students. You may wish to present this list of words and definitions to your students. Encourage students to discuss other meanings they know for some of these words.

brilliance: the quality of showing great intelligence, talent, or skill.

philosophers: persons who study the general principles and laws of a field of knowledge.

practical: serving a useful purpose.

crippled: unable to use the limbs or body properly.

stunted: abnormally short or small.

Reading Skill

Summarizing

Explain to students that summarizing is restating and condensing a writer's main ideas. Summarizing helps a reader to understand the key points of a selection.

Reading Strategy

Activating and Using Prior Knowledge (Strategy 8)

To help your students summarize a writer's main ideas, use Strategy 8 described in Content-Area Reading Strategies. Students should use their completed KWL chart (Graphic Organizer 6) to help them construct a concept map, then write their summaries based on the map.

▶ **Teaching Tip**

Summarizing Explain to students that in summarizing they are trying to determine the most direct and accurate answer to the question, "What is this selection about?" Remind students that they should use their own words but include only the ideas contained in the selection. Students should not include personal judgments and comments.

DURING READING

Differentiating Instruction

▪ **Advanced Learners**

Challenge students to think of practical, daily uses for summarizing. For example, students might summarize the school day when a parent asks "What did you do in school today?" During a peer-editing session students might summarize if their partner asks "What did you like about my paper?" Encourage students to share their examples with the rest of the class.

AFTER READING

✔ Reading Check

The following are sample answers to questions on student text page 76.

1. In 1780, a French statesman asked Jefferson to answer some questions about Virginia's people, climate, plants and animals, and landscape.

2. Most Europeans believed that North America was a "crippled" land of stunted plants and animals and simple people.

3. From Paris, Jefferson asked his friends to send the skeletons of several large animals. He wanted to use the skeletons to show that North America was a land of mighty creatures.

4. The bones of the woolly mammoth and the *Megalonyx*, or giant ground sloth, were discovered in North America and examined by Jefferson.

5. According to the selection, both the Louisiana Purchase and Lewis and Clark's expedition were related to Jefferson's interest in natural science.

Reteaching

To successfully summarize, students must be able to separate the important from the unimportant. Therefore, you may want to provide guided practice in locating the main ideas of the paragraphs in the selection. Have students read the first paragraph, and then work together to identify the main idea and to provide a summarizing statement. Remind students that in summarizing, they condense and use their own words. Continue with the next paragraph, and so on. Listed below are summarizing statements for the first six paragraphs.

▪ Thomas Jefferson was an intelligent man with many talents and interests.
▪ Jefferson's love of science began at an early age.
▪ Jefferson wrote a book about Virginia's natural history.
▪ Jefferson wanted Europeans to have a positive impression of North America.
▪ Jefferson believed that large animal skeletons would impress the Europeans. (paragraphs 5 and 6)

Connecting Language Arts

▪ **Writing**

Tall Tale Based on fantastic pioneer and American Indian stories, Thomas Jefferson believed that woolly mammoths still existed in North America. Have students write a tall tale proclaiming the existence of an extinct or imaginary creature. Encourage students to illustrate their tall tales. You may want to post them in the classroom for all to enjoy.

■ Speaking and Listening

Visit This Beautiful Spot Jefferson was proud of his state and spoke highly of it. Have students work in small groups to produce a sixty-second radio spot praising the town, area, or state in which they live. Have students mention the people, plants, animals, climate, landscape, and enjoyable activities. Their purpose for creating the commercial is to persuade others to visit. Have each group write its script and practice performing before presenting the commercial to the rest of the class.

Connecting Across the Curriculum: History

Time Line Have students create a time line highlighting the events of Thomas Jefferson's life. Encourage students to include on the time line important events that shaped United States history, such as 1774—First Continental Congress meets. Upon completion, have students compare time lines and discuss why they included the events they did.

Further Resources

The University of Virginia maintains a Web site that contains information about Thomas Jefferson.

A film titled *Thomas Jefferson* produced by Ken Burns and released by PBS Home Video, is available on video. PBS Online has information about Jefferson, the making of Ken Burns's film, and archives of Jefferson's writings.

The Web site Monticello, named for the home of Thomas Jefferson, contains information about Jefferson, his house and its grounds, the plantation, as well as useful additional resources.

Assessment

Turn to page 128 for a multiple-choice test on the selection.

Test Answers

1. a **2.** c **3.** d **4.** a **5.** c
6. a **7.** c **8.** c **9.** b **10.** a

The following criteria can help you evaluate each student's success in completing the activities prompted by the Cross-Curricular Activities feature in the student textbook.

Science
How Does This Work?
- The student selects a common object and conducts research to determine how it works.
- The student makes a detailed drawing that reflects his or her research.
- The student presents his or her findings to the class.
- The student's presentation is clear and well organized.

Music/Language Arts
Keeping Time
- The student writes two verses to be sung to the tune of "Yankee Doodle" that tell the story of a recent conflict.
- The verses accurately convey the facts of the conflict and effectively communicate the student's view of the events.
- The student performs the verses for the class and then discusses the message he or she was trying to convey.
- The student's performance is well prepared.

Drama/History
"I Was There!"
- The student chooses a historical figure from Chapter 2, "With Liberty and Justice for All," and writes a first-person monologue that tells about one of the person's experiences.
- The student's monologue shows imagination and creativity.
- The student's monologue is memorized and well rehearsed.

Drama/Dance
Show, Not Tell
- The student chooses a selection from Chapter 2, "With Liberty and Justice for All," that would make an interesting performance piece.
- The student chooses an effective means of telling the story he or she has chosen, creating a pageant, pantomime, or dance.
- The student's performance effectively conveys the event, leaving the audience with a clear picture of what happened.
- The performance is relatively free of performance errors. If used, props, costumes, music, sound effects, and other enhancements contribute to the overall effectiveness of the performance piece.
- The student's performance piece shows imagination and creativity.

Language Arts/History
Who Said That?
- The student compiles a class almanac or playing-card game of sayings of famous Americans.
- The student accurately labels the origin of each saying.
- The almanac or playing cards are made neatly.

CHAPTER 3

Separate Roads
The United States from 1800–1850

Into the Unknown: The Incredible Adventures of Lewis and Clark

from *National Geographic World*
by MARGARET McKELWAY
(student text page 81)

CONTENT-AREA CONNECTIONS

HISTORY •
GEOGRAPHY •

Reading Level: Below average

Text Summary

This selection recounts the journey of Meriwether Lewis and William Clark, who, with the aid of American Indians, much determination, and a little luck, became the first U.S. citizens to cross the continent to the Pacific Coast. The selection tells how the expedition helped shape the course of the young country.

BEFORE READING

Make the Connection

Ask students to imagine they are going on a journey into an unexplored wilderness with very slow means of communicating and of getting supplies. How would they prepare? What possible emergencies would they need to anticipate? [illness or accident, loss of some food supplies to animals, possible extreme weather conditions, lack of good water sources, and so on] What supplies would they take along? [compact extra food sources such as jerky or dried fruit, medical kit, compass (more than one), water purification tablets, items to trade with any native people they meet] What knowledge or skills would they need to have before leaving? [navigation, how to build a fire, basic first aid, how to repair tents or rafts, tracking, weather signs, and so on]

Build Background
■ More About the Topic

President Thomas Jefferson was eager to buy France's territory in North America in part because of fears among Americans that Napoleon Bonaparte might want to build an empire there. Napoleon, who crowned himself emperor of France in 1804, would later go on to conquer much of Europe before losing a decisive battle to Britain at the Battle of Waterloo in Belgium in 1815.

Vocabulary Development

The following words are underscored and defined in the student text.

acquired: gained possession of something by one's own efforts.

commissioned: given an assignment or an order.

reunion: a meeting of people who have been separated from one another.

obstacle: something that stands in the way.

treacherous: dangerous.

Before assigning the reading, you may want to introduce students to any words that could cause pronunciation or definition problems.

Vocabulary Tip

Using Roots Tell students that the Latin root of the word *commission* (*commissio* or "to bring together") is found in a number of very useful words. There is the verb *commit*, which means "to put into action" or "to entrust or bind"; the noun *commitment*, which means a "trust or pledge"; and the noun *committee*, which designates a "group charged to take action on some subject." Discuss with students how the meanings of the words are related.

CONTENT-AREA VOCABULARY

Although the following words are important to an understanding of the text selection, some of them may be unfamiliar to students. You will want to introduce the words to students before they begin reading. Ask students what they predict they will read about in a selection using these words. [The words *bluff, fork,* and *pass* suggest that the selection will probably involve exploration or travel.]

quarters*: official lodging.
corps: organized group.
bluff*: cliff.
fork*: split in a river.
pass*: a gap between mountains that allows travel through them.

*Although students may be familiar with other meanings of these words, the words as used in the selection have a specific meaning that pertains to the content area.

Reading Informational Material

Reading Skill
Interpreting Graphic Information
Tell students that interpreting graphic information (such as maps, charts, or diagrams) means relating the information in the visual graphic to information in the text.

Reading Strategy
Visualizing Information (Strategy 5)
To help students understand the map of Lewis and Clark's journey, use Strategy 5 in Content-Area Reading Strategies. Show the class a map of the journey. After previewing the map, have students write questions based on the map in the left-hand column of a chart on their own paper. After reading the selection, have students write their answers in the right-hand column. Then, have students discuss with a partner how well the map represented the information in the text.

▶ **Teaching Tip**
Previewing Text Features Preview with students the text headings in the selection. Point out to students that the headings indicate the information in the selection will be given in chronological order, starting with Lewis and Clark's planning of the trip and concluding with the journey's end.

DURING READING

Using the Side-Margin Feature
- **She Moved in Mysterious Ways**

You can use the brief feature on Sacagawea to interest students in the other members of the expedition and their stories. Students may want to research Sacagawea, the Shoshone Indians, or the life of a French fur trapper in North America in the early nineteenth century. Encourage students to present their research to the class in the form of first-person monologues.

Differentiating Instruction
- **Learners Having Difficulty**

Students may have trouble making sense of the many facts and statistics in the selection. Encourage students to relate the information to standards from their own lives. For example, to help students visualize the limitations put on supplies transported by Lewis and Clark, you can show them a ten-pound stack of books. You can also provide students with distances to local landmarks to give them a standard for distances traveled by the Corps of Discovery.

AFTER READING

✓ Reading Check

The following are sample answers to questions on student text page 86.

1. President Thomas Jefferson sent Lewis and Clark on their expedition.

2. The expedition's mission was to find the source of the Missouri River, cross the Rocky Mountains, and follow a large river to the Pacific Ocean.

3. Lewis decided that travel by water would be impossible when the expedition approached the towering Rocky Mountains. To solve this problem, the group bought horses from the Shoshone Indians.

4. Accept any two: They had to climb steep hills and hack through thick undergrowth; the horses got hurt and sometimes died; they suffered hail and snow; they had little to eat; they became ill from food given to them by American Indians; they had to navigate fierce rapids.

5. Accept any one: They made maps; they gathered information; they discovered new species of plants and animals; they paved the way for the United States to claim the Oregon region.

Reteaching

If students still have difficulty visualizing the information in the selection, have students work in small groups to redraw the map of Lewis and Clark's journey. If possible, have group members determine how long it took the explorers to complete a certain section of their trek. Group members can then determine how far the expedition traveled in an average day and compare that distance to a distance familiar to them in the area. Have groups each choose a representative to present their maps and calculations to the class.

Connecting to Language Arts

- Writing

Annotated Map Have students each make a detailed map of one section of Lewis and Clark's journey, with captions that describe what happened on their route. Students may want to work with a partner to research the expedition and choose a section of the trip. You may wish to assign students sections and provide research materials in order to have the class cover the entire trip. Display students' maps in the classroom.

- Speaking and Listening

Interview Arrange students in groups of four. Have group members each choose one of the following roles: Lewis, Clark, Sacagawea, or interviewer. Have group members work together to prepare interview questions and responses. Then, ask the groups to present to the class their interviews as part of a talk show.

Connecting Across the Curriculum: Science

Finding Flora and Fauna Have students research a specific plant or animal discovered by Lewis and Clark on their journey. Students can draw their plants or animals and provide with their drawings a description of the species and where it may be found. Display students' drawings in the classroom.

Further Resources

Video

For more information on the subject, show the documentary "Lewis & Clark: The Journey of the Corps of Discovery" by award-winning director Ken Burns and author Dayton Duncan (1997).

Assessment

Turn to page 129 for a multiple-choice test on the selection.

Test Answers

1. a   2. b   3. d   4. a   5. a
6. c   7. a   8. d   9. b   10. a

from The Oregon Trail

by LEONARD EVERETT FISHER
(student text page 87)

Reading Level: Average

Text Summary

This selection explains the rise of "Oregon fever" and describes the wagons and the daily lives of settlers in wagon trains along the Oregon Trail. It includes quotations from primary sources (journals, newspaper articles, and so on).

BEFORE READING

Make the Connection

Tell students that even in the technological world of the twenty-first century, there are some people who have decided to return to a simpler, more independent way of life (using solar power, growing their own food, weaving, using water cisterns, and so on.) Ask students to imagine that their family decides to move to a very remote part of the country to "live off the land." The journey there is along back roads with no shopping, and the family is taking only what will fit in their pickup truck camper. What will students pack? [mementos such as family heirlooms, photos, awards, and scrapbooks; necessities such as basic kitchen equipment, first-aid kits, tools] What will they leave behind? [unnecessary clothing, CD collections, video games, magazine collections] How will they decide what to bring? What can they make or buy once the family gets to their new home? What items are just luxuries—not necessary to daily life? What items are unnecessary but of special personal value? List students' ideas on the chalkboard.

Build Background

■ More About the Topic

One of the earliest travelers along the Oregon Trail was Marcus Whitman, a young Presbyterian minister and doctor who, with his wife Narcissa, settled among the Cayuse Indians near Walla Walla, Washington, in 1836. Whitman gained respect for his ability to treat illnesses and surgically remove arrowheads. Tensions began to build among the Cayuse, however, as thousands of white settlers colonized their land. When a measles epidemic killed half their tribe in 1847, the Cayuse blamed the Whitmans and slaughtered them and others at the mission. Outraged, white settlers attacked the Cayuse in retaliation.

Vocabulary Development

The following words are underscored and defined in the student text.

emigrants: people who move out of one country or region into another.

multitude: a great many.

maneuver: a planned move.

durable: long lasting despite hard use.

brackish: having a disagreeable taste; sickening.

Before assigning the reading, you may want to introduce students to any words that could cause pronunciation or definition problems.

┌─ *Vocabulary Tip* ─────────────

Recognizing Commonly Confused Words The words *emigrant* and *immigrant* are often confused. Both come from the Latin *migrare*, meaning "to migrate or move." The *e*– prefix means "out of," and so *emigrate* means "to leave a place." The *im*– prefix means "in, into," and so *immigrate* means "to enter a place."

└──────────────────────────────

(**CONTENT-AREA VOCABULARY**)

Although the following words are important to an understanding of the text selection, some of them may be unfamiliar to students. You will want to introduce the words to students before they begin reading. Have students discuss the multiple meanings of the words *posts* and *admit*.

posts*: stations or forts.

tonics: liquid mixtures supposed to have medicinal value.

admit*: allow to enter.

*Although students may be familiar with other meanings of these words, the words as used in the selection have a specific meaning that pertains to the content area.

(Reading Informational Material)

Reading Skill
Making Predictions

Tell students that to make predictions about a text, they use prior knowledge to make an inference about the text's topic.

Reading Strategy
Building Background Information (Strategy 6)

To help students better understand the conditions discussed in the selection, use Strategy 6 in Content-Area Reading Strategies. After giving students background information and posing a general question about the topic, have students write their predictions about the text in the first column of the Predicting and Confirming Activity chart (Graphic Organizer 8). After providing students with additional background information, have them turn their predictions into questions and record these in the second column. (You may wish to model this for students.) After reading, encourage students to answer their questions in the third column of the chart.

▶ **Teaching Tip**
Finding the Main Idea Point out to students that the selection is an excerpt from a larger work rather than an article divided into sections with subheadings. Consequently, students checking their predictions will have to pay close attention to the shifts from one main idea to the next. Tell students that often the first sentence of a paragraph will reveal the main idea of that paragraph. You may want to lead students in discussing the main ideas of the first three paragraphs, as revealed in the first sentence of each.

DURING READING

Using the Side-Margin Feature
▪ Too Much, Too Little, Too Late

Connect the feature on the high prices of some food items on the Oregon Trail with students' own experiences of the often exorbitant prices charged for snacks at a movie theater. Point out to students

that a settler, like a theater patron, couldn't just shop for the better bargain but had to take what he or she could get.

Differentiating Instruction
▪ Learners Having Difficulty

Because of the primary source quotations and absence of subheadings, some students may have trouble following the progression of ideas in the selection. Provide students with category headings for the ideas in the selection (for example, "The Rush to Move West," "How Wagon Trains Were Organized," "A Close Look at the Covered Wagon," and "Daily Life Along the Trail"). Then, have students write the first sentence of each paragraph. (Tell students to omit the paragraphs that are quotations since they amplify the main idea of another paragraph.) Finally, have students work in pairs to arrange the topic sentences under the correct categories.

AFTER READING

(✔ Reading Check)

The following are sample answers to questions on student text page 91.

1. "Oregon societies" were groups of people who met to plan their trip west in a wagon train.

2. A wagon train might consist of a thousand people, three to four thousand animals, and more than a hundred wagons.

3. The "schooners" were smaller and lighter, and they were drawn by oxen rather than horses or mules. The schooners and the Conestogas were both durable wagons made from hardwood and iron-tired wheels.

4. On a typical day, people rose to eat and pack at sunup, and the wagon train began moving at 8:00. At noon it stopped for lunch and then continued until early evening. After supper, people read, listened to sermons, or sang songs.

5. If a wagon train left in May instead of April, there would be little grass left on the trail for grazing. The wagon train might also encounter early snows in the Rockies.

Reteaching

If students have difficulty making predictions, have them preview the sidebar headings, illustrations and captions, and topic sentences of each paragraph. Then, have students work in pairs using these text features to generate questions that they would like to answer. After reading, students can answer their questions together based on information in the text.

Connecting to Language Arts

- Writing

Letter from a Pioneer Have students write a letter from the point of view of a traveler on the Oregon Trail, sending news to a friend back home on the East Coast. Students' letters should describe a day in their trip, tell of their discoveries, and express their hopes for their new homes. Encourage students to include drawings and simple maps in their letters. Ask for volunteers to read their letters to the class.

Connecting Across the Curriculum: Math

Weight Allowance Have students record how much food they eat in an average day and ask them to multiply this amount by the number of days in five months. How would they carry this much food if they were traveling west? Would they take an emergency supply of water or other items such as clothes, cooking utensils, and tools? How much would they expect these items to weigh? Students can use their calculations to design their own wagons. Display students' designs around the classroom.

Further Resources

Online

Maps, classroom activities, and further information can be found at the "In Search of the Oregon Trail" feature of the PBS Web site.

Assessment

Turn to page 130 for a multiple-choice test on the selection.

Test Answers

1. c **2.** a **3.** d **4.** c **5.** d
6. a **7.** d **8.** b **9.** c **10.** b

from The Trail of Tears

from *Cowboys & Indians*
by JOHN WADSWORTH
(student text page 92)

Reading Level: Above average

Special Considerations

Students with Native American ancestry or those interested in the history of American Indians in the western United States might find the topic of the selection a sensitive one. You may want to explore the interactions between American Indians and white settlers or discuss with students how western settlement affected American Indians.

Text Summary

This selection, a magazine article, describes the U.S. government's forced movement of the Cherokee from Georgia to Oklahoma in 1838–1839. The article explores the effects of the removal on Cherokee identity and experiences both then and now.

BEFORE READING

Make the Connection

Ask students to remember a time when their family had to move to a new town. What emotions did they struggle with? [sadness at leaving friends, apprehension about a new school, uncertainty about the future] What challenges did they face when they arrived at their new home? [feeling as though they didn't belong, making new friends, understanding unfamiliar cultural traditions of the region] Discuss with students reasons that the Cherokee removal was even more difficult. What additional issues did the Cherokee probably face? [resentment, harsh conditions, lack of supplies, erosion of certain cultural traditions, disconnectedness]

Build Background

- ### More About the Topic

The Cherokee faced formidable hardships along the trail due to a number of factors. Many felt that the government would not force them to leave their homes against their will and so did not have many possessions when the government roundup

of the Cherokee began. The first groups, totalling 2,800, left in the summer of 1838 under the supervision of the U.S. military. The death toll was particularly high because of extreme heat and drought, bad water, and disease. Many refused the government provisions of clothing and unfamiliar food. At the request of Chief John Ross, the government allowed the rest of the Cherokee to wait until the fall and oversee their own removal. However, these groups also suffered. Supplies of wild game were depleted by the first groups. Unusually heavy rains caused delays, preventing the completion of the journey before winter set in. Government supplies were inadequate. Many of the approximately 13,000 Cherokee fell victim to starvation, the cold winter, and disease.

Vocabulary Development

The following words are underscored and defined in the student text.

communal: shared; related to a community.
prophecy: a prediction about a future event believed to be given to a person by God.
encompassed: surrounded on all sides.
verdant: green.
refurbished: fixed up; made new again.
embark: to begin a journey or project.
random: without any plan or organization.
silhouette: an outline.
immaculately: perfectly.
embodies: represents; gives form to.

Before assigning the reading, you may want to introduce students to any words that could cause pronunciation or definition problems.

Vocabulary Tip

Exploring Synonyms The vocabulary of color is a rich and varied one that students may not have explored. Have students each make a pie chart listing the colors *red, orange, yellow, green, blue, indigo, violet* and challenge students to find synonyms for the color names (such as *verdant* for *green*) and for the shades in between. Ask volunteers to share their charts (and, if possible, color samples) with the class.

CONTENT-AREA VOCABULARY

Some of the following words may be unfamiliar to students. Because the words are important to understanding the text selection, you will want to introduce the words to students before they begin reading. Ask students what they predict they will read about in a selection using these words and the ones in the vocabulary-development list.

foretold: predicted.
decline*: loss of power and prominence.
comprise: make up; consist of.
descendants: a person's offspring, through the generations.
assumed*: took up.

*Although students may be familiar with other meanings of these words, the words as used in the selection have a specific meaning that pertains to the content area.

Reading Informational Material

Reading Skill
Using Prior Knowledge
Tell students that thinking about how what they are reading relates to what they already know can help them to better understand a text.

Reading Strategy
Activating and Using Prior Knowledge (Strategy 8)
To help students activate prior knowledge about the topic of the selection, you may wish to use Strategy 8 in Content-Area Reading Strategies. Have students complete the first two columns of the KWLS Chart (Graphic Organizer 7) before reading, and then complete the other columns after reading. You may wish to model this strategy by working together with the class to fill in a statement in each of the first two columns of the chart.

▶ **Teaching Tip**
Identifying Writer's Purpose Discuss with students the name of the magazine in which the article first appeared, and read the first three paragraphs aloud with the class. Encourage students to try to identify the writer's purpose and point of view. Write students' comments on the chalkboard and direct students to review their understanding of the writer's purpose and point of view after they read.

DURING READING

Differentiating Instruction
▪ Learners Having Difficulty
Students may have trouble keeping separate the views of people and events in the past with the views and events related in the present time of the article. Point out to students that one way to keep the two times separate is to pay attention to the narration. In relating the events of the present, the narrator often uses the first-person point of view: "When I asked," for example.

AFTER READING

Reteaching
If students are still having difficulty activating their prior knowledge, provide them with a general idea of the topic of the selection (i.e., "The forced removal of the Cherokee from their lands in the east to reservations was a significant event in Cherokee history."). Ask students to write predictions about the selection based on this information. Then, provide students with additional information, such as "Before the Trail of Tears ever occurred, the Cherokee Elders received a vision from the Creator." Have students brainstorm to generate questions about the text they will be reading based on their predictions and the additional information.

✔ Reading Check

The following are sample answers to questions on student text page 96.

1. The Cherokee Elders predicted that white people would want to take the Cherokee homeland and that a new home was being prepared for the Cherokee in the west.

2. According to one Cherokee member, the Trail of Tears occurred because many Cherokee did not listen to the Elders' advice and because many Cherokee had begun wanting to own things privately, as white people did.

3. They call it "The Trail Where They Cried," meaning that the onlookers cried when they saw the Indians passing by.

4. In the past, anyone who wanted to live as a Cherokee was accepted as a Cherokee.

5. Today the U.S. government defines as Indian a person whose blood is at least one-sixteenth American Indian.

Connecting to Language Arts

■ Writing

Movie Script Arrange students in groups of four and have group members work together to write a movie script of the scene in which John Ross must announce to his tribe their removal from their lands in Georgia. Suggest to students that they build on the possible conflict Ross felt in his own mind as both a friend of white Americans and the chief of the Cherokee. Group members can choose a spokesperson to present their script to the class or they may enact it.

Connecting Across the Curriculum: Science/Math

Family Tree Invite students to research their own family trees. Most students will probably find themselves a mixture of different heritages. Are there any who are "officially" American Indian? Ask for volunteers to share their findings, and remind students to be respectful and open to others' backgrounds.

Further Resources

Online

Several state-sponsored Web sites provide information about the Trail of Tears, with references to historic parks and hyperlinks. For example, for more information on the Trail of Tears as it passed over the Mississippi River, contact the Trail of Tears State Park in Cape Girardeau County, Missouri, part of the Missouri Department of Natural Resources, at 1-800-334-6946.

Assessment

Turn to page 131 for a multiple-choice test on the selection.

Test Answers

1. a	2. b	3. c	4. b	5. d
6. b	7. a	8. a	9. b	10. b
11. a	12. b	13. b	14. b	15. a

The Birthplace of Women's Rights

from *Cobblestone*
by HOWARD MANSFIELD
(student text page 97)

Reading Level: Average

Text Summary

This selection is a magazine article that describes the first efforts by Elizabeth Cady Stanton and Lucretia Mott to secure equal rights for women in the United States. The struggle took place at the Seneca Falls Convention in 1848.

BEFORE READING

Make the Connection

Discuss with students their perception of the equality of the sexes today. What has changed since women finally gained the right to vote in 1920? What has stayed the same? [Some students may point out that women are still sometimes paid less for doing the same jobs as men, although almost all occupations are now open to women. Others may suggest that some attitudes toward women are still limiting, since traditional roles are today often not accorded the same respect as more progressive roles.]

Build Background

■ More About the Topic

The achievements of the famous women listed at the end of the selection may not be familiar to students. Susan B. Anthony was a nineteenth-century reformer active in the women's and abolitionist movements. Helen Keller, though blind and deaf, was a courageous educator and author in the twentieth century. Eleanor Roosevelt, wife of President Franklin D. Roosevelt, represented the United States at the United Nations from 1949 to 1952. Amelia Earhart was the first woman to fly an airplane across the Atlantic Ocean.

Vocabulary Development

The following words are underscored and defined in the student text.

inadvertently: accidentally; thoughtlessly.
tyrannical: cruel and unjust.
adjourned: closed until a later time.
strategy: plan of action.
commemorate: to remember with honor.

Before assigning the reading, you may want to introduce students to any words that could cause pronunciation or definition problems.

Vocabulary Tip

Discovering Roots Point out to students that the same root found in the word *commemorate* is also found in the words *memorial, memory,* and *memento*. Based on the definition of the word *commemorate*, what do students think the Latin root *momor* means? [remembering]

CONTENT-AREA VOCABULARY

Although the following words are important to an understanding of the text selection, some of them may be unfamiliar to students. You will want to introduce the words to students before they begin reading. Ask students what they predict they will read about in a selection using these words. [The words are associated with meetings about voting.]

preside: to lead a meeting.
amended: added to or changed.
resolutions: formal statements made by an official group.
unanimously: without opposing votes.
suffrage: the right to cast a ballot.

(Reading Informational Material)

Reading Skill

Determining the Main Idea

Tell students that the main idea of a text is the message or central insight that is the author's focus. Other ideas and details in the text support the main idea.

Reading Strategy

Constructing Concept Maps (Strategy 4)

To help students better understand and remember the main idea and supporting ideas of the selection, you may wish to use Strategy 4 in Content-Area Reading Strategies. Provide students with a Cluster Diagram (Graphic Organizer 3) to help them organize their thoughts as they read. Have students work in pairs to complete the diagram after reading.

▶ Teaching Tip

Making Predictions Tell students that a common technique for magazine articles is to begin with an attention-getting fact or image that suggests the main idea of the article. After students read the first two paragraphs, have them predict what they think the article will be about, using evidence from the paragraphs to support their opinions.

DURING READING

Differentiating Instruction

▪ Learners Having Difficulty

Students may have trouble locating the important ideas in the article, especially since there are no subheadings or call-out quotations. Encourage students to divide the article into three parts: the introduction, or first two paragraphs; the body of the article; and the conclusion, or last two paragraphs. Each section focuses on a different time period and has a different main idea that contributes to the overall main idea of the article.

AFTER READING

✔ Reading Check

The following are sample answers to questions on student text page 101.

1. On July 19, 1848, the first Women's Rights Convention was held in Seneca Falls, New York.

2. The Declaration of Sentiments was a document that described how women's rights were being denied.

3. The ninth resolution called for women to have the vote. It was debated because some women felt that this was asking too much, too early. Others felt that without the vote women could not be truly equal to men.

4. Most newspapers said that the women were behaving foolishly. One said that women were worthless unless they were wives and mothers. Another said that giving women new rights would upset the natural order.

5. In 1979 the National Women's Hall of Fame opened in Seneca Falls.

Reteaching

If students still have difficulty determining the main idea of the article, pair students and have them work together to complete a Cloze Concept Map which you have made with a few sections already filled in. After students have completed the map, discuss with students the main idea of the selection. Based on their maps, why do students think the author organized the article as he did?

Connecting to Language Arts

- Writing/Speaking and Listening

Declaration Have students write their own declarations, based on the Declaration of Independence and focusing on one issue that is important to them. Ask for volunteers to present their declarations to the class. You may wish to have students develop their declarations into persuasive speeches that they deliver to the class.

Connecting Across the Curriculum: Social Studies

Have students research the Nineteenth Amendment to the U.S. Constitution. What groups supported or opposed its passage? How does an amendment become part of the Constitution? You can direct students' research toward designing their own amendments and drawing up plans for their passage. Have volunteers share their ideas.

Further Resources

Video

For more information on the beginnings of the women's movement, show the documentary "Not for Ourselves Alone: The Story of Elizabeth Cady Stanton and Susan B. Anthony," directed by Ken Burns (1997).

Assessment

Turn to page 132 for a multiple-choice test on the selection.

Test Answers

1. d **2.** a **3.** b **4.** c **5.** a
6. c **7.** b **8.** a **9.** a **10.** c

A Quaker Commitment to Education

from *Cobblestone*
by JUDITH FOSTER GEARY
(student text page 102)

Reading Level: Average

Text Summary

This selection is a magazine article that recounts how the religious beliefs of Quakers led them to establish the first U.S. schools to educate African Americans. The article demonstrates that by sticking courageously to their convictions a handful of people can make a great difference in the course of a nation.

BEFORE READING

Make the Connection

Tell students that people have often debated how the constitutional right to equal protection under the law applies to educational opportunities. Ask students whether they think all students are given the same educational opportunities. Why or why not? What should be done about any perceived inequality? Tell students that the selection will introduce them to a group of people who battled injustice in education in the northern states before and after the Civil War.

Build Background

▪ Motivate

Ask students to think of current causes they support or are interested in and to write a brief description of what interests them about the causes. Ask for volunteers to share with the class their causes and tell what they admire about the people who work for those causes. Point out to students that many of the rights and privileges that people enjoy today are due to the hard work of those in the past.

Vocabulary Development

The following words are underscored and defined in the student text.

abolition: the doing away with something.
restrictive: limiting.
financial: relating to money.

petitions: formal requests.
legacy: something passed down from one person or group to the next.

Before assigning the reading, you may want to introduce students to any words that could cause pronunciation or definition problems.

Vocabulary Tip

Using Context Clues Point out to students that they can often determine the approximate meaning of a word by the context in which it is used. For example, the vocabulary word *abolition* describes the view of slavery taken by a group of people who believe in equal opportunity for all. One might expect people who believe in equality to oppose slavery and want to end the practice. Therefore, *abolition* must mean "the doing away with something."

CONTENT-AREA VOCABULARY

Although the following words are important to an understanding of the text selection, some of them may be unfamiliar to students. You will want to introduce the words to students before they begin reading by putting the words on the chalkboard or on an overhead transparency and pronouncing each word. Ask students to define the words if they can. Write their definitions and add the ones given below if students have not covered those particular meanings. You may want to assign students to groups of four to write a paragraph using the words or other entries that are appropriate.

divine: godlike.
dame: a woman of authority.
Sabbath: the day of rest observed by the Jewish and Christian faiths.
Orthodox: a conservatively religious group within a sect.
faculty*: teachers.

*Although students may be familiar with other meanings of this word, the word as used in the selection has a specific meaning that pertains to the content area.

Reading Informational Material

Reading Skill
Monitoring Comprehension
Tell students that monitoring their comprehension involves thinking about what they already know about the topic of a text, reading with a purpose, and taking note of passages that they do not understand.

▶ **Teaching Tip**
Making Connections Students may view Quakers' beliefs that African Americans be given equal educational opportunities as common sense, and it may be hard for them to imagine the controversy and hardship endured by these early reformers. One way to help students is to encourage them to take the Quakers' beliefs to their logical ends, which might include the abolition of the death penalty, an end to military spending, and more government programs for those in need.

Reading Strategy
Previewing Text (Strategy 1)
To help students prepare to follow and discuss the ideas in the selection use Strategy 1 in Content-Area Reading Strategies. Provide students with a KWL Chart (Graphic Organizer 6) to complete as they work through the selection. Volunteers can share their charts with the class.

DURING READING

Differentiating Instruction
■ Advanced Learners
Students may be interested in the unpopular stands of other people throughout history who had strong convictions. One place to start is with Henry David Thoreau, the American author who went to jail for not paying his taxes in protest against the U.S. war against Mexico. Thoreau wrote that people disagreeing with their government should take a stand, no matter the penalty. His ideas influenced Dr. Martin Luther King, Jr., and Mohandas K. Gandhi. Encourage students to share their findings with the rest of the class.

AFTER READING

Reading Check
The following are sample answers to questions on student text page 105.

1. The Quakers believe there is something of God in all people. Because of this belief, Quakers work for equal opportunity for all people.

2. Many Quakers of the time allowed African Americans in their schools or formed schools specifically for African Americans.

3. Because of Nat Turner's rebellion, slavery laws became more harsh. Also, Quakers stopped supporting African American education for a time.

4. Accept any two: Crandall's neighbors opposed the school and harassed Crandall and her students; a law was passed that made it illegal to teach students from other states; the school was attacked one night.

5. The Penn School was a school and refuge for escaped slaves off the coast of South Carolina.

Reteaching
If students have difficulty monitoring their comprehension of the selection, have them take notes while re-reading the selection using INSERT symbols (Strategy 10). After students have labeled the text using the symbols, they can organize their notes using a Concept Map or a Cluster Diagram (Graphic Organizer 3).

Connecting to Language Arts
■ Writing
Commencement Speech Have students imagine they are the featured speakers at one of the pre-Civil War Quaker schools' graduation ceremonies. What would they say about the role of the school in changing society and the challenges to be met by its graduates? Have students write a speech for a graduation ceremony. Then, have them deliver their speeches to the class.

Connecting Across the Curriculum: History/Art

What might an eighteenth-century Quaker school look like? What would be the subjects taught and how would they be taught? Have students research the topic and write a description of a school of the time period. Students can accompany their descriptions with drawings or plans for a typical school.

Further Resources

Online

The Library of Congress has a Web site with information on the history of African Americans.

Assessment

Turn to page 133 for a multiple-choice test on the selection.

Test Answers

1. b   2. c   3. d   4. d   5. d
6. a   7. a   8. c   9. b   10. d

from The Birth of Modern Mexico

from The Mexican Americans
by JULIE CATALANO
(student text page 106)

Reading Level: Average

Text Summary

This selection, an excerpt from a nonfiction book, describes the causes and effects of the growth of the U.S. in the 1840s. In this important decade, the land that makes up the states of Texas, California, Nevada, New Mexico, Arizona, and parts of Utah and Colorado was added to the nation, and a growing number of Mexicans found themselves now U.S. citizens: Mexican Americans.

BEFORE READING

Make the Connection

Ask students how they would react if they found their homes suddenly claimed by another country. Ask them to imagine having to learn a different language and adapting to a new culture. Then, ask them what they already know about how the southwestern region of the U.S., including Texas and California, became part of the country. [Students may have some ideas on how the land was gained from Mexico.] Show students a map of the area and discuss the hardships the Mexican citizens there may have had to face on suddenly becoming Americans.

Build Background

- **More About the Topic**

"Remember the Alamo!" The most enduring image of Texas's war for independence was no doubt the Alamo, a small chapel in San Antonio where a group of Americans, including Davy Crockett, made a brave stand against an overwhelming Mexican force. General Santa Anna led the Mexican army in eventually capturing the building and killing all of its defenders. The Americans may have lost the battle, but "Remember the Alamo!" became their rallying cry in winning the war.

Vocabulary Development

The following words are underscored and defined in the student text.
assimilated: brought into; absorbed.
lured: attracted; tempted.
collage: a grouping of apparently unrelated parts.
ratified: approved.
aggravated: made worse.
Before assigning the reading, you may want to introduce students to any words that could cause pronunciation or definition problems.

Vocabulary Tip

Using Context Clues Point out to students that one way to determine an unfamiliar word's meaning is to see if a synonym or equivalent phrase is given in the text. In the case of the word *skirmish*, for example, the preceding phrase "armed bid for independence" gives a close approximation of the word's meaning. The following sentence in the article gives an equivalent phrase for the word *aggravated*. Have students find the phrase. ["was worsened"]

CONTENT-AREA VOCABULARY

Although the following words are important to an understanding of the text selection, some of them may be unfamiliar to students. You will want to introduce the words to students before they begin reading. Pronounce each word and ask students to define the words if they can. Write their definitions and add the ones given below and on the next page if students have not covered those particular meanings. Which of the words relates most specifically to a selection about the expansion of the United States? Why? [*ratified*, because it refers to the process of a territory being made a state]

presence: appearance; being.
primary: most important.

prominent: well-known; important.
ratified: officially recognized.
staged*: carried out.

*Although students may be familiar with other meanings of this word, the word as used in the selection has a specific meaning that pertains to the content area.

Reading Informational Material

Reading Skill
Identifying Text Structure: Cause and Effect
Tell students that a cause makes something happen and that an effect is what happens as a result of that cause.

Reading Strategy
Using Graphic Organizers (Strategy 3)
To help students diagram the causes and effects in the selection, use Strategy 3 in Content-Area Reading Strategies. Provide students with a Cause-and-Effect Chart (Graphic Organizer 2) to help them organize the events presented in the article in cause-and-effect order.

▶ **Teaching Tip**
Previewing Subheadings Preview with students the subheading given in the text of the article. Point out to students that the subheading gives an indication of the main cause and effect that will be explored in the text: the United States winning a war and gaining land.

DURING READING

Differentiating Instruction
■ **Learners Having Difficulty**
Students may have trouble following the text's treatment of many diverse geographical areas. Have students construct a three-column chart on their own paper on which to record events in the selection, labeling the first column *California*, the second column *Texas and Mexico*, and the third *The United States*. As they read, students should record the various events in the columns that correspond to the geographic regions in which they occurred.

AFTER READING

✔ Reading Check

The following are sample answers to questions on student text page 108.

1. "Manifest Destiny" was the United States's belief that it should possess the continent from coast to coast.

2. The South wanted to bring Texas into the Union because Texas shared the South's beliefs about slavery.

3. Accept any three: Mexico refused to acknowledge Texas's statehood; American settlers in California staged the Bear Flag Revolt of 1846; Mexico refused to sell the Southwest to the United States; a skirmish occurred on the Mexican-American border.

4. The Mexican War ended in 1848. Mexico surrendered to the United States what are now California, Nevada, New Mexico, Arizona, and parts of Utah and Colorado.

5. The Mexicans who lived in the new U.S. territories could either become U.S. citizens or return to Mexico.

Reteaching
If students still have difficulty linking the causes and effects in the selection, have them work with a partner to review the article backwards, starting with the last sentence. Students should ask "Why?" or "How?" the Mexicans became new U.S. citizens. This question should lead them to the cause of this event: The choice had to be made by Mexicans finding themselves on newly claimed U.S. land. Asking "Why?" or "How?" this choice had to be made will direct students to its cause: the Gadsden Purchase. Have students continue asking and answering questions in this manner for the rest of the selection, then have them draw a chain of the causes and effects they find.

Connecting to Language Arts

▪ Writing

Stump Speech Have students take a view either for or against the expansion of the United States during the 1840s and have them imagine they are politicians preparing a brief statement on the matter. How would they communicate their position and win their audience to their side? What reasons would they give? Have students write their position statements and post them on the bulletin board or a class Web page for their classmates to read.

Connecting Across the Curriculum: Math

Statistical Survey Have students research some of the statistics mentioned in the article—the ratio of Mexicans to Americans in California or Texas before those areas became part of the United States, for example, or the land area gained in the Treaty of Guadalupe Hidalgo. Encourage students to present their research in a graph or chart. Students can write a brief paragraph in which they draw conclusions based on their research and then share their visuals and conclusions with the class.

Further Resources

Book

Defending Mexican Valor in Texas: José Antonio Navarro's Historical Writings, 1853–1857, by José Antonio Navarro, edited by David B. McDonald and Timothy M. Matovina. This collection of writings offers a perspective on early Texas history from one of the first Mexican Americans, who was also a signer of the Texas Declaration of Independence and later a state senator.

Assessment

Turn to page 134 for a multiple-choice test on the selection.

Test Answers

1. b   2. a   3. d   4. c   5. c
6. b   7. a   8. a   9. b   10. c

Gold Mountain

from *The Gold Rush*
by LIZA KETCHUM
(student text page 109)

Reading Level: Average

Special Considerations

The discrimination faced by the Chinese immigrants may strike a personal chord with students. Allow students time to discuss the injustices in the text, to compare them to the prejudices still experienced by many today, and to explore how and why race relations may have improved since the times of the California gold rush.

Text Summary

This selection focuses on the experiences of Chinese immigrants to California during the gold rush who faced harsh circumstances and prejudice in seeking to make their fortunes and to better their lives in a new land.

BEFORE READING

Make the Connection

Ask students what they know about the California gold rush, and have them scan the illustrations given in the text. [Students will probably know that mining went on in the state during the mid-1800s but they might not know many details.] Then, discuss with students the excitement and chaos that must have reigned in those times, with so many people flocking to one place with aims of striking it rich there. What are some highly lucrative but risky opportunities available to fortune seekers today? [high-tech stocks, "dot com" startups] What "get rich quick" ideas have students heard of?

Build Background

- Motivate

Ask students to suggest examples of situations in which they have felt alone or alienated in a group of people very different from themselves. [Students might suggest going to a new school or moving to a different part of the country. Some students might have emigrated from other countries.] What fears did they face? [fear of not knowing what to do,

of getting lost or looking foolish] What challenges did they encounter? [trying to be understood, fitting in, adjusting to different expectations]

Vocabulary Development

The following words are underscored and defined in the student text.

census: an official count of people.
famines: widespread shortages of food.
diverted: turned in a different direction.
prosperous: yielding wealth.
taunted: ridiculed; made fun of.

Before assigning the reading, you may want to introduce students to any words that could cause pronunciation or definition problems.

┌─ *Vocabulary Tip* ─

Using Context Clues Tell students that one way to discover an unfamiliar word's meaning is to look to see if the term is explained within the text. In the case of the word *diverted* in the excerpt, an explanation is given in the same sentence: "which cut the stream in half." From the phrase, students can guess that the word *divert* means something like "to divide" or "to change the course."

(CONTENT-AREA VOCABULARY)

Although the following words are important to an understanding of the text selection, some of them may be unfamiliar to students. You will want to introduce the words to students before they begin reading. Put the words on the chalkboard or on an overhead transparency. Pronounce each word and ask students to define the words if they can. Write their definitions and add the ones given below and on the next page if students have not covered those particular meanings.

province: area or region.
banquet: large meal or feast.
chopsticks: small sticks used as eating utensils.

pulleys: system of using ropes and wheels to move large weights.

hounded: chased; attacked.

Reading Informational Material

Reading Skill
Making Predictions
Tell students that making predictions as they read the excerpt will help them to focus their reading and to remember the information in the selection.

▶ **Teaching Tip**
Identifying Text Structure Students may be confused by the interweaving of Lee Chew's story with the more general description of the Chinese immigrant experience in the selection. Point out to students that this selection describes the experiences of most Chinese immigrants to California during the gold rush, using the experience of Lee Chew as a specific example. You might ask students why a writer would choose to include one person's story or a particular event when describing a period in history. [to lend credibility to the facts being presented, to make it easier for the reader to relate to or empathize with the people of the period]

Reading Strategy
Making Predictions (Strategy 7)
To help students maintain their reading focus and increase their comprehension, use Strategy 7 in Content-Area Reading Strategies. Before reading, have students list and group in categories words about the topic of the selection. Have students use these categories to develop a Concept Map, or provide them with a Cluster Diagram (Graphic Organizer 3) to complete with their word categories. After students read the selection, have them add new information from their reading to their concept maps.

DURING READING

Correcting Misconceptions
Point out to students that prospecting for gold, laundering clothes, and cooking in restaurants were by no means the only jobs taken by Chinese immigrants in California. The three positions are emphasized because they relate to gold mining

itself or to services needed by the miners and their families.

Differentiating Instruction
■ **Learners Having Difficulty**
Tell students having difficulty associating individual words with the general topic of the selection to focus on the pictures and illustrations given with the text. Students can discuss with a partner what the art suggests about the topic of the selection before working together to create word lists.

AFTER READING

✓ Reading Check

The following are sample answers to questions on student text page 114.

1. Lee Chew decided to set out for "Gold Mountain" when a neighbor returned to China from America with pockets full of money.

2. The Chinese were packed in small, dirty cabins below deck. They were fed horrible food. They were sometimes chained or beaten.

3. Accept any four: The Chinese made money by operating restaurants, selling vegetables, working in gambling dens, opening their own laundries, or mining.

4. Accept any two: White miners became jealous of successful Chinese miners and stoned them, burned their houses, and sometimes killed them. Restaurant owners fired their Chinese cooks. People taunted the Chinese and made fun of them.

5. Lee Chew concluded that Americans were friends when people were doing well, but Americans ignored the Chinese when they were not doing so well. He also concluded that Americans' treatment of immigrants was outrageous.

Reteaching
If students are still having difficulty making predictions, provide them with a general idea of the topic of the selection (i.e., "During the gold rush many Chinese people immigrated to California to make fortunes for their poverty-

stricken families back home."). Ask students to write predictions about the selection based on this information. Then, provide students with additional information, such as "Chinese immigrants to San Francisco faced discrimination." Have students brainstorm to generate questions about the text they will be re-reading based on their predictions and the additional information.

Connecting to Language Arts

■ Writing

Letter Have students write a letter from the perspective of a Chinese immigrant in California at the time of the gold rush. Students should base their letters on the experiences outlined in the excerpt and should advise either for or against their friends' joining them in California.

Connecting Across the Curriculum: Social Studies

Have students research a specific Chinese custom or tradition and tell how it compares and contrasts with American customs and traditions. Students may choose anything from the drinking of tea and manner of dress mentioned in the reading selection to traditions of art and architecture. Have students include with their written reports a drawing of the custom they research. Assemble students' work in a book comparing and contrasting Chinese and American customs.

Further Resources

Video

For a closer look at the people of the gold rush, show the PBS documentary *The Gold Rush,* directed by Steve Boettcher and Mike Trinklei (1998).

Online Resources

Visit the "Gold Rush" section of the PBS Web site for interesting facts and classroom resources related to the gold rush.

Assessment

Turn to page 135 for a multiple-choice test on the selection.

Test Answers

1. d **2.** b **3.** b **4.** a **5.** c
6. c **7.** a **8.** d **9.** b **10.** a

The following criteria can help you evaluate each student's success in completing the activities prompted by the Cross-Curricular Activities feature in the student textbook.

*Note: Activities marked with an asterisk allow the involvement of more than one student. For these activities you may wish first to evaluate each student on his or her individual contribution and then to give groups an overall rating.

*Art/Language Arts
A Game of Chance

- The student re-reads "Into the Unknown: The Incredible Adventures of Lewis and Clark" (page 81) and takes notes on Lewis and Clark's route.
- The student works with a partner to create a board game that is based on the expedition and includes details from the selection.
- The student creates a title and writes a workable set of rules for the game.
- The game demonstrates creativity and imagination.

Science/Geography
Weather Watchers

- The student uses resources to chart the route of the Oregon Trail and to determine the average length of time required for pioneers to complete their journey.
- The student researches the climate of each region along the trail.
- The student creates a weather guide that includes information about the kind of weather pioneers should expect along the Oregon Trail.
- Writing is relatively free of errors in spelling, grammar, usage, and mechanics.

History/Art
Landscapes of Lament

- The student conducts research to locate photographs of the regions where the Trail of Tears began and ended.
- The student creates four to five pictures showing the types of landscape American Indians saw along the trail.
- The student writes a poem or group of statements to accompany the pictures. The text should be written from the point of view of an American Indian on the trail and should describe the emotions he or she feels while passing through each landscape.
- The student's artwork demonstrates creativity and imagination.

*Language Arts
Talk of the Town

- The student writes a letter to the editor of the Canterbury newspaper expressing either approval or disapproval of Prudence Crandall's boarding school.
- The student writes a second letter in response to the first, expressing the opposite viewpoint.
- The student works with a group of classmates to create two editorial pages for the set of letters, including the date and title of the newspaper. Students may choose to use a computer to design the pages.
- Writing is relatively free of errors in spelling, grammar, usage, and mechanics.

CHAPTER 4

A Nation Divided
The Civil War and Reconstruction 1860–1877

## Supplying the Armies	**CONTENT-AREA CONNECTION**
from *A Separate Battle: Women and the Civil War*	**HISTORY**
by INA CHANG	
(student text page 119)	

Reading Level: Average

Text Summary

This excerpt describes civilian war efforts in both the North and South and focuses on the women volunteers who worked to provide the armies with needed supplies. Among their many contributions were sewing uniforms, collecting and distributing donations and supplies, and staging fund-raising fairs. Presented with numerous problems, the volunteers ingeniously and enthusiastically found solutions.

BEFORE READING

Make the Connection

Brainstorm with students the various volunteer opportunities that are available in your community. Then, ask students if they have ever volunteered their services for a worthy cause. What did they do? How did it make them feel?

Build Background

▪ More About the Topic

Out of necessity, many women broke free of their traditional roles during the Civil War. With their husbands and fathers gone to battle, many women at home cared for their farms and plantations. Others saw wartime action as nurses, spies, and soldiers. Nurses not only worked in hospitals and behind the lines, but also served as medics on the battlefield. Since the Union and Confederate armies forbade the enlistment of women, a number of women disguised themselves as men to pass as soldiers. In addition, the female spies—whether disguised as men in battle, eavesdropping in social circles, or posing as slaves—provided valuable information to both armies.

Vocabulary Development

The following words are underscored and defined in the student text. Before assigning the reading, introduce students to any words that could cause pronunciation or definition problems.

frenzied: frantic; in a hurried manner.
impractical: not suitable or useful.
ornate: excessively showy or decorated.
array: display; collection.
efficiency: capability to do something with the least amount of effort and waste.
pooled: brought together for a common goal.
status: rank; position.
demoralized: corrupted; changed for the worse.
flyers: usually spelled fliers; single printed sheet circulated over a wide area.
dwindled: became less full.

Vocabulary Tip

Using Prefixes Before you introduce the vocabulary words, you may want to remind students that prefixes can help to determine a word's meaning. For example, knowing that the prefix *de–* often means "remove or undo" can help students figure out the meaning of *demoralize*, "to undo or weaken the morale of." Ask a volunteer to follow the same procedure with the other word in the list that has a prefix. [*im–* often means "not," thus *impractical* means "not practical"]

Although the following words are important to an understanding of the text selection, some of them may be unfamiliar to students. Present the list of words without definitions, and ask what many of the words have in common. [multiple meanings] Then, have students brainstorm the words' multiple meanings.

down: soft feathers, like those of a baby duck.
dashing: showy or stylish.
loud: too showy to be in good taste.
poke: to search.
depleted: used up.

Reading Informational Material

Reading Skill
Identifying Cause-and-Effect Relationships
Explain to students that a cause is a person or thing that makes something happen. An effect is something brought about by a cause. As they read, students are identifying cause-and-effect relationships when they ask such questions as "What happened?" and "What are the effects or results?"

Reading Strategy
Using Graphic Organizers (Strategy 3)
To help students identify cause-and-effect relationships, use Strategy 3 described in Content-Area Reading Strategies. With the help of a Cause-and-Effect Chart (Graphic Organizer 2), students can identify such relationships as they read.

▶ **Teaching Tip**
Cause and Effect Point out to students that this selection contains different forms of text structures. Much of the text describes the volunteers' war efforts, and portions narrate a sequence of events. Throughout the text, however, students will find many examples of cause-and-effect relationships.

DURING READING

Correcting Misconceptions
Although the Civil War offered women opportunities to display courage and resourcefulness, equality for women in American society remained elusive. The long campaign for equal voting rights illustrated this struggle. The women's suffrage movement lasted more than seventy years—from the first formal women's convention in 1848 to the adoption of the nineteenth amendment in 1920, which finally gave women full voting rights.

Differentiating Instruction
■ **Learners Having Difficulty**
To help students identify cause-and-effect relationships, write the following sentence on the chalkboard:
This happened because of that.
   (effect)   (cause)
Then, read with students the first paragraph of the selection. Discuss the cause-and-effect relationship in the paragraph, and change the sentence on the chalkboard to read
Women went to work because the armies needed to be outfitted.
Have students work through the selection in this manner, but caution students that not all paragraphs contain a cause-and-effect relationship.

■ **Advanced Learners**
Encourage students to ask questions as they read and to use the text as a springboard for satisfying their curiosity. For example, students might be interested in seeing pictures of havelocks, or they might question why the WCAR had no official status. Assure them that their outside research can benefit the entire class.

AFTER READING

✔ Reading Check

The following are sample answers to the questions on student text page 126.

1. Early in the war, the soldiers wore fancy, brightly colored uniforms. The soldiers dressed in showy costumes because they wanted to look handsome or dashing as they set off for war.

2. The foot-treadle sewing machine had a great impact on the production of supplies.

3. Elizabeth Blackwell organized the Women's Central Association of Relief. She was the first woman in the United States to earn a medical degree.

4. Accept any two: The U.S. Sanitary Commission set up hospitals and supply stations, hired nurses, collected donations, sent inspectors to Union hospitals, trained troops to cook safely and prevent the spread of disease.

5. Women at a Columbia train station provided soldiers with refreshments, a bath, a change of clothes, and a cot.

Reteaching

If students are still struggling with the concept of cause-and-effect relationships, provide a cloze graphic organizer. For many of the cause-and-effect relationships in the selection, fill in either the cause or the effect, and have students complete the relationship. [Here is a list of some of the cause-and-effect relationships: Because soldiers needed outfitting, women went to work; because the rigors of camp life were unknown, impractical items were sent with soldiers; havelocks were suggested as a useful item, so women turned out thousands of them; havelocks were not used as intended, so their production was stopped.]

Connecting to Language Arts

▪ Writing

Lady's Magazine In 1830, Louis A. Godey began publication of *Godey's Lady's Book*, one of the most popular women's magazines of the nineteenth century. During the war, the magazine provided a much needed diversion with its illustrations, fiction, editorials, poetry, recipes, nonfiction articles, and fashion and needlework patterns. Have students work in small groups to create the types of articles that might have been considered for publication in *Godey's Lady's Book*. Suggest that the class coordinate efforts to create a magazine with a varied table of contents.

Connecting Across the Curriculum: Science

Civil War Medicine The surgeons of the field hospitals did their best under adverse conditions to provide proper medical care for the soldiers. Have students research the surgical procedures and the medicines that were available during the Civil War. Suggest that students compare the treatments and medications available for certain conditions to those available today. Ask students to share their findings with the rest of the class.

Further Resources

▪ Books

The Other Civil War: American Women in the Nineteenth Century by Catherine Clinton
Civil War Sisterhood: The U.S. Sanitary Commission and Women's Politics in Transition by Judith Ann Giesberg
Mothers of Invention: Women of the Slaveholding South in the American Civil War by Drew Gilpin Faust

▪ Video

The Civil War—A Film by Ken Burns, PBS Home Video, 1997, Not Rated

▪ Web Sites

Special Collections Library, Duke University
Library of Congress American Memory Project

Assessment

Turn to page 136 for a test on the selection.

Test Answers

1. d	**2.** b	**3.** b	**4.** a	**5.** c	**6.** e
7. h	**8.** b	**9.** f	**10.** j	**11.** c	**12.** i
13. d	**14.** g	**15.** a			

from What A Foolish Boy

from *The Boys' War*

by JIM MURPHY
(*student text page 127*)

Reading Level: Average

Text Summary

This excerpt examines the hardships that were experienced by boys who volunteered to fight in the Civil War. Quotations from letters written by young men in the military emphasize the loneliness they felt being away from friends and family.

BEFORE READING

Make the Connection

Tell students to imagine that our country is on the brink of war and that young men and women are being given the opportunity to enlist in the armed services. Ask students if they would enlist, and have them explain why or why not. Ask them if they think people their age should be allowed to participate in armed combat or should be assigned other duties instead.

Build Background

■ More About the Topic

The young drummer boy was the inspiration for a number of musical compositions published during the Civil War. One such song, "The Drummer Boy of Vicksburg," or, "Let Him Sleep" was composed to honor the memory of Charles Howard Gardner, of the 8th Michigan Infantry, killed during the siege of Knoxville, Tennessee. The young musicians who played the fife and drum, calling their comrades to prepare for battle, were the subject of "The Reveille." The Battle of Shiloh in 1862 was remembered in song with "The Drummer Boy of Shiloh."

Vocabulary Development

The following words are underscored and defined in the student text.

afflicted: caused to suffer.
amass: gather together.
initial: first.

reliable: sure; stable.
allay: to reduce; give relief.

Before assigning the reading, introduce students to any words that could cause pronunciation or definition problems.

─ *Vocabulary Tip* ─────────────

Using Suffixes Before you introduce the vocabulary words, ask students to notice any suffixes that might help to determine a word's meaning. [*–able* means "able to" or "capable of," which could help with the meaning of *reliable*— "capable of being relied upon."]

─────────────────────────────

(**CONTENT-AREA VOCABULARY**)

Although the following words are important to an understanding of the text selection, some of them may be unfamiliar to students. Encourage students to discuss other meanings they know for these words. To demonstrate an understanding of a word's multiple meanings, students might create sentences with the various meanings of the word.

dry: clever but sarcastic.
wit: an example of humor characterized by clever remarks.
engaged: kept busy.
quest: a search for something important.

(**Reading Informational Material**)

Reading Strategy

Previewing Text (Strategy 1)

To help students set a purpose for reading, use Strategy 1 in the Content-Area Reading Strategies. To assist students in organizing their thoughts, use the KWL (Graphic Organizer 6). Tell students their purpose for reading may be located in their "What I Want to Know" column. They may be reading to have certain questions answered or certain predictions confirmed.

Reading Skill

Setting a Purpose

Explain to students that the reader's reason or motive for reading a text is called the purpose. Students should consider *why* they are reading: to gain information, to be entertained, and so forth. Then, suggest that once they have previewed the material, they may have some specific reasons for reading. Perhaps they will want to know about the boy of the title and why he was considered foolish.

▶ **Teaching Tip**

Variety in Previewing the Text Because not all reading selections look the same, the process of previewing the text is not always the same. Explain to students that in previewing this selection, they will look at the headnote, the title, the boldface pull-out quote, the pictures, and the Reading Check questions. Other selections, however, might have other features to preview, such as charts, graphs, boldface or italicized terms, bulleted items, and headings.

DURING READING

Using the Side-Margin Feature

■ The Great Adventure

You may want to have students brainstorm about the author's purpose in writing this feature. Ask students to consider the tone: Is it serious or ironic? Have students note the author's use of repetition to emphasize the monotony of bugling. Finally, ask students whether the author really believes joining the army is an "adventure." Have students explain their answers.

▶ **Teaching Tip**

Using Quotations Point out to students the author's use of quotations. Read the quotations aloud, and then ask students to comment on why they think the author included people's exact words. [to catch the reader's attention; to give details that support his or her main ideas; to add emotion]

Differentiating Instruction

■ English-Language Learners

Because your English-language learners might have limited knowledge about the Civil War, you may want to provide some background information. Such information will be particularly helpful if you are having students fill in the three-column

KWL chart (Graphic Organizer 6). Do not limit students, however, to writing down only what they know about the Civil War, for some could have stories and experiences from their native lands regarding young men at war.

AFTER READING

✔ Reading Check

The following are sample answers to the questions on student text page 131.

1. Boys on both sides quickly learned that soldiers spent more time marching than they did fighting.

2. Winfield Scott and George McLellan were the first two commanders of the Union army. They had decided on a defensive war.

3. Robert E. Lee was the Confederate commander. Because he had fewer troops and supplies, he used small groups of soldiers to strike at the Union army in many places and then immediately strike again.

4. Soldiers expressed their homesickness through singing and through writing down their feelings.

5. Accept any two: Young soldiers became homesick because they did not yet know how they fit into the world, they had left their families behind, their futures were uncertain, and they hadn't had time to form close friendships with their fellow soldiers.

Reteaching

If students are still struggling with setting a purpose for their reading, you may want to send them back to their KWL charts. Have them work in pairs to discuss what they listed under L. Tell them their purpose may well be related to the questions they still have. Suggest that they take one of their questions (for example, "What was life like for a person my age in the army during the Civil War?") and turn the question into a statement beginning with "My purpose is to find out . . ." (for example, "My purpose is to find out what life was like for a person my age in the army during the Civil War.")

Connecting to Language Arts

▪ Writing

Ballad A ballad is a song written in the form of a poem. It usually tells a story of some heroic deed, event in history, or romance. Ballads often contain a chorus or certain lines that are to be repeated. Have students work in pairs to write ballads about the heroic boys who served in the Civil War. Students may want to focus on one particular hero. Encourage students to do additional research to find information for their ballads. Display the completed ballads for all to enjoy.

▪ Speaking and Listening

Panel Discussion Have students work in groups of five to hold panel discussions on the issue of boys participating in the Civil War. One of the five students will be the moderator who introduces the panel members, asks them questions, and fields questions from the audience at the end of the discussion. The four other students will each play the role of an individual—such as a boy soldier, a parent, an older soldier, or commanding officer—who could appropriately comment on the subject. Before presenting the discussion to the class, each group should plan its questions and answers so that everyone has a chance to speak.

Connecting Across the Curriculum: Music

Civil War Musicians The drummers and buglers were responsible for much of the communication that went on in camp and on the battlefield. The drummers used special, recognized drumbeats and rhythms to relay information, and the buglers used various calls. Have students research these musical methods of communication and report their findings to the rest of the class. If possible, student musicians could demonstrate some of the different messages. Two books that students might use are *Following the Guidon* by Elizabeth B. Custer and *Mel Bay Presents Infantry Bugle Calls of the American Civil War* by George Rabbai.

Further Resources

Books

Everyday Life During the Civil War: A Guide for Writers, Students, and Historians by Michael J. Varhala

Berry Benson's Civil War Book: Memoirs of a Confederate Scout and Sharpshooter by Susan Williams Benson, eds. Berry Benson, Herman Hattaway

Assessment

Turn to page 137 for a multiple-choice test on the selection.

Test Answers
1. b **2.** c **3.** b **4.** a **5.** d
6. b **7.** a **8.** d **9.** b **10.** c

from **Freedom Rider**

from *Sojourner Truth and the Struggle for Freedom*
by EDWARD BEECHER CLAFLIN
(student text page 132)

CONTENT-AREA CONNECTION
HISTORY

Reading Level: Average

Text Summary

This selection examines the time period Sojourner Truth spent in Freedman's Village, an area near Washington, D.C., where ex-slaves resided. Sojourner's strength, courage, and determination helped to improve the safety, education, health, and social standing of the ex-slaves she represented.

BEFORE READING

Make the Connection

Ask students if they know an individual who seems to be a natural leader—someone to whom others are drawn in times of need. [Students may think of a relative, a favorite teacher, a student leader, an athlete, a celebrity, or even a fictional hero.] Then, ask students to think of the qualities that the individual possesses that make him or her a leader.

Build Background

■ Motivate

Ask students whether they have ever changed from one way of life to another. Have they moved from one country to another, from one city to another, or changed schools? How did they feel about their new environment? What challenges did they face? Explain to students that when the slaves were freed, they were thrown into a new way of life. They had always looked to their masters for the necessities of life, and now they had no masters. What would they have to do in order to live the life of a free man or woman?

Vocabulary Development

The following words are underscored and defined in the student text.

contraband: goods or people moved illegally from one state or country to another.
segregated: divided from the main area or group.
adrift: moving or floating in no single direction.
emancipation: freedom from slavery.

crisis: a period of great difficulty.
economy: use or management of money.
commends: recommends; presents as qualified.
defiance: daring rebellion.
industry: hard work.
menacingly: in a threatening manner.

Before assigning the reading, you may want to introduce students to any words that could cause pronunciation or definition problems.

Vocabulary Tip

Finding Related Words Ask students to brainstorm other forms of the words in the Vocabulary Development list. [*segregate, segregation, economic, economical, defy, industrious, menace*] Have student volunteers use the original and the additional forms in sentences. Point out to students that the part of speech changes as the form of the word changes.

CONTENT-AREA VOCABULARY

Although the following words are important to an understanding of the text selection, some of them may be unfamiliar to students.

barred*: kept out; excluded.
bondage: slavery.
scars*: lasting emotional effects of suffering.
preying: taking by illegal force.
*Although students may be familiar with other meanings of these words, the words as used in the selection have a specific meaning that pertains to the content area.

Before students read the selection, locate each of the above words in the text. Then, read aloud the surrounding words, sentences, or paragraphs that might give clues to the words' meanings. For example, preying (on p. 134) is explained in the second paragraph following the sentence in which preying is used. Then, have students predict what the selection might be about based on the meanings of the words in both vocabulary lists.

Reading Informational Material

Reading Skill
Drawing Conclusions

Explain to students that a conclusion is a decision, or judgment, that is made about an idea or subject in the text. Students draw conclusions by combining information in the text with experience and prior knowledge.

▶ **Teaching Tip**
Taking Notes Explain that as students take notes, they will not always find a key point in each new paragraph. Sometimes paragraphs work together to present and develop a key point.

Reading Strategy
Taking Notes (Strategy 10)

When students take notes, they often have to draw conclusions, or fill in the gaps, because the main ideas are not always directly stated. You may want to have students use a Key Points and Details Chart (Graphic Organizer 5) to take notes as they read. Remind students that they may have to draw conclusions when filling in the first column.

DURING READING

▶ **Teaching Tip**
Drawing Conclusions Explain to students that historians often must draw conclusions from their historical research. Sometimes, two historians may draw different conclusions from the same information because they apply different experiences and knowledge to the information. Encourage students to try to identify and question any conclusions drawn by writers of history.

Differentiating Instruction
▪ Learners Having Difficulty

Students might find note taking easier with the use of a Cluster Diagram. Depending on your students' abilities, you can use Graphic Organizer 3 or create a cloze cluster diagram (see Strategy 4 in Content-Area Reading Strategies) to which you have added some key words or details. Whichever you choose, model the note-taking procedure, using the first several paragraphs of the selection.

▪ Advanced Learners

To emphasize how prior knowledge and experience can influence conclusions, select a recent news article and ask interested students to jot down personal experiences or prior knowledge that comes to mind as they read it. Then, have students write conclusions based on the article. Students will probably find, when they compare their conclusions, that prior knowledge has an effect on conclusions.

AFTER READING

✔ Reading Check

The following are sample answers to the questions on student text page 137.

1. Many freed slaves headed north to Washington, D.C., because they believed it was the city of hope and because it was the home of Abraham Lincoln. (Accept either response.)

2. Many freed slaves were unable to deal with daily life because before they were freed, their owners had provided for their basic necessities and organized their lives.

3. Emancipated slaves needed to learn how to manage their household, find jobs, educate children, and ask for needed help. (Accept any two responses.)

4. Sojourner recruited some strong anti-slavery soldiers to confront the kidnappers.

5. When Sojourner was told she could to ride only the "Jim Crow" streetcar, she protested to the president of the street railroad; as a result, a streetcar law was passed that allowed African Americans to ride with whites.

Reteaching

If students are still struggling with the concept of drawing conclusions, have them create a three-column graphic organizer and label the columns "Facts," "Prior Knowledge," and "Conclusion." Walk students through the first paragraph of the selection on student text page 132. In the "Facts" column, write "could not ride streetcars with whites; were barred from all white neighborhoods; could not attend schools; could not attend the church of their choice." In the second column, write "These are privileges we generally take for granted. Everyone should have the same rights." In the last column, write "African Americans and whites were not treated equally."

Connecting to Language Arts
▪ Writing
Journal Entry Ask students to imagine they are Sojourner Truth living in Freedman's Village in 1864. Have them write journal entries covering several days in Sojourner's life. Explain that a journal entry need not chronicle the day's events from morning until night; many journal writers focus on meaningful experiences and elaborate on why the experiences affected them. Upon completion, students might want to compare journal entries.

▪ Speaking and Listening
Dramatic Presentation Ask students to act out a dramatic scene from the selection. Have them work in small groups to choose a scene and select roles within the groups. When no dialogue is available, students will need to write lines for the characters to say. Give students time to rehearse, and then have them present their scenes to the class.

Connecting Across the Curriculum: History
Black Women Freedom Fighters Explain to students that Sojourner Truth was only one of many African American women whose efforts bettered the lives of other African Americans. Have students research other freedom fighters such as Biddy Mason, Ida B. Wells-Barnett, and Mary McLeod Bethune. Have students share their findings with the class.

Further Resources
▪ Books
> *Let It Shine: Stories of Black Women Freedom Fighters* by Andrea Davis Pinkney
> *The Book of African-American Women: 150 Crusaders, Creators, and Uplifters* by Tonya Bolden

▪ Video
> *Sojourner Truth,* Schlessinger Media, 1992, Not Rated.

Assessment
Turn to page 138 for a test on the selection.

Test Answers

1. c	2. b	3. a	4. d	5. a
6. f	7. h	8. j	9. d	10. a
11. c	12. g	13. e	14. i	15. b

When I Was a Kid

from *National Geographic World*

by SANDRA FENICHEL ASHER

(student text page 138)

Reading Level: Easy

Text Summary

The effect that Louisa May Alcott's childhood had on her writing is the subject of this selection. Schooled at home with her three sisters, Louisa spent much of her time writing plays and exploring nature. She recorded her thoughts and activities in a journal. As a child, she had already determined that she would be a success at something.

BEFORE READING

Make the Connection

Ask students if they have ever used their own experiences when asked to write something fictional. Have they ever based a character on someone they know or used events in their own lives as a springboard for a story or play? Many writers keep journals in which they record impressions and events that might later prove useful. Ask students if they keep journals or diaries. If so, ask them if they have ever referred to their journals or diaries for inspiration.

Build Background

■ More About the Topic

Written in 1868 when Alcott was thirty-five years old, *Little Women* is an American classic. Based on Alcott's childhood, the story portrays four sisters growing up in New England during the Civil War. The character of Jo, one of the sisters in the story, is autobiographical. Moody and fiercely independent, tomboy Jo supports her family with the profits from her writing, just as Alcott did. Jo claims she will never marry and refuses to sacrifice herself to the domestic role of a "little woman." Louisa Alcott never married and was an advocate for women's rights.

Vocabulary Development

The following words are underscored and defined in the student text.

establish: to set up.

community: people living in a group apart from general society.

rebelled: went against authority.

criticized: made a disapproving judgment.

inspired: caused a desire.

Before assigning the reading, you may want to introduce students to any words that could cause pronunciation or definition problems.

┌─ *Vocabulary Tip* ─────────────────

Noting Usage and Pronunciation You can use *rebel*, a form of the vocabulary word *rebelled*, to demonstrate to students how a word's part of speech affects its pronunciation. As a verb, *rebel* is pronounced with the accent on the second syllable, but as a noun, it is pronounced with the accent on the first syllable. Have volunteers say aloud a sentence with each to demonstrate usage and the change in pronunciation. Then, ask students to think of other words whose pronunciations change when usage changes. [*recall, convert, export, converse, convict, record, produce, present, object, subject, intimate*]

└───────────────────────────────────

(Reading Informational Material)

Reading Skill
Main Idea

Explain to students that the main idea of the selection is the author's most important overall point. Paragraphs or sections of text also have main ideas. Some writers directly state their main ideas, while others only suggest or imply them. To identify an implied main idea, a reader must "read between the lines" to infer the author's meaning.

Reading Strategy
Constructing Concept Maps (Strategy 4)

To help your students identify the selection's main ideas, use Strategy 4 in Content-Area Reading

Strategies. A concept map can help students to visualize and organize their thoughts.

DURING READING

Using the Side-Margin Feature
- **The Transcendentalists**

The Transcendentalists were well-educated Americans, mostly New Englanders, who believed that it was time to break free from the literature of Europe. To achieve this literary independence, they created novels, poems, essays, and other writing unlike anything from England, Germany, or any other European nation. Reflecting their spiritual and social outlook, their works included Emerson's essays "Nature" and "Self-Reliance" and Thoreau's "Civil Disobedience" and *Walden, or Life in the Woods*, which is an account of his two years living simply, apart from society, and in harmony with nature.

▶ **Teaching Tip**
Use of Quotations Have students notice the author's use of quotations, and point out that the only person being quoted is Louisa. Ask students what they can learn about Louisa from the quotations. [She was a tomboy and very active; she enjoyed writing and appreciated her own space; she was determined to be successful.]

Differentiating Instruction
- **Learners Having Difficulties**

Use a pair/share approach by pairing a learner who will be challenged by the reading selection with a more able reader. Ask the students to take turns reading a small section aloud to their partners and then discussing what has been read. The focus of the discussion should be on clarification. Model the process for the whole class before pairing the students.

AFTER READING

✔ Reading Check

The following are sample answers to the questions on student text page 140.

1. The Alcott family moved from place to place when Louisa was a child because Louisa's father had a hard time finding teaching jobs.

2. Louisa's parents encouraged their children to spend time outdoors, think for themselves rather than memorize information, and keep journals. (Accept any two.)

3. Louisa disliked life in the Fruitlands community because the hard work kept her from her writing.

4. Louisa was inspired by the success of a play she wrote and performed with her sisters in the family's barn.

5. At the age of thirteen, Louisa promised herself that she would do anything to help her family and that she would be rich, famous, and happy before she died.

Reteaching

If students are still struggling with the concept of main idea, try reversing the process. First, write a statement of main idea in the center of a concept map. [For example, "Louisa had an active childhood."]

Then, ask students to provide supporting details. [She liked beating boys in races; she preferred girls who could climb trees and leap fences; her parents believed it was important for her to spend time outdoors; she wrote about running twenty miles and then going to a party.]

Connecting to Language Arts

▪ Writing

Poem Louisa expressed her sorrow in a poem that was included in this selection. Ask students to write a poem expressing something they've experienced. Point out to students that Louisa's rhyme scheme is *abcb*; however, students can use their own rhyme schemes or choose not to rhyme at all. Upon completion, display the poems in a "poet's gallery." Note: You may want to tell students in advance that the poems will be displayed; such knowledge might influence students' subject matter.

▪ Speaking and Listening

One-Act Play Have students work in small groups to prepare a script and perform a one-act play. First, have the groups choose one of Louisa May Alcott's books, such as *Little Women, Little Men,* or *Jo's Boys.* Each group should skim its chosen book to find a section that can be suitably adapted to play form. Then, ask each group to write a brief script, assign parts, practice, and perform its play for the rest of the class.

Connecting Across the Curriculum: Math

What's Your Time? Distance runners express their times in minute-miles, or the average number of minutes it takes to run a mile. Ask students to determine the number of miles Louisa could run in an hour and to figure out her running pace—or the number of minutes it took her to run a mile. [If Louisa ran twenty miles in five hours, she averaged four miles per hour; she averaged fifteen-minute miles.] In conclusion, students who are runners may want to compare their running times with hers.

Further Resources

▪ Books

The Girlhood Diary of Louisa May Alcott: Writings of a Young Author (Diaries, Letters, and Memoirs) by Louisa May Alcott
The Journals of Louisa May Alcott by Louisa May Alcott
Louisa May Alcott: A Biography by Madeleine B. Stern

▪ Videos

Little Women, Columbia-Tristar Studios, 1994, Rated PG. Movie version of Alcott's classic, starring Winona Ryder.
Little Women, Warner Studios, 1949, Not Rated. Movie, starring June Allyson and Peter Lawford.
Little Women, Warner Studios, 1933, Not Rated. Classic film version of the novel, starring Katherine Hepburn and Joan Crawford.

Assessment

Turn to page 139 for a multiple-choice test on the selection.

Test Answers
1. d **2.** b **3.** b **4.** a **5.** c
6. d **7.** a **8.** d **9.** c **10.** b

A Proud Tradition

from *Cobblestone*

by JOHN P. LANGELLIER
(student text page 141)

Reading Level: Average

Special Considerations

You may want to explain to students that prior to the Civil War, African Americans were not allowed to serve in the military and that after the war racial prejudice dictated the segregation of African American military units. Yet, the Buffalo Soldiers consistently proved themselves to be competent and praiseworthy troops. Lead a discussion about how strength, pride, and honor can help to overcome obstacles.

Text Summary

This excerpt from *Cobblestone* examines the African American army units established after the Civil War. With the passage of an 1866 law allowing African Americans to join the army, African American regiments, who came to be called Buffalo Soldiers, were formed to keep peace on the United States frontier. Men enlisted for various reasons—to find adventure, to escape an unhappy past, to make money, to get an education—and proudly proved their abilities to endure hardships and serve their country.

BEFORE READING

Make the Connection

Ask students whether they know people who have served in the armed forces. What were their duties? What inspired them to serve their country? Then, ask students whether they have ever considered joining the military. If so, have them explain their reasons for considering military service.

Build Background

- More About the Topic

The buffalo was extremely important to the Plains Indians because it supplied most of what they needed to survive. Little of the animal went to waste. The meat and some of the internal organs were eaten. The bones were carved into tools, the horns became spoons, and the rib bones were tied together to make sleds for the children. Buffalo dung was used as fuel, and the stomach served as a cooking pot. Tendons from the animal's muscles were used as sewing thread, and the hair was braided into ropes. Tepee covers, blankets, and clothing were made from the animal's hide. Even the skull found a use as part of a ceremonial altar.

Vocabulary Development

The following words are underscored and defined in the student text.

sacred: believed to be holy.
policy: course of action by a government.
merged: combined; united.
prejudice: intolerance; discrimination.
sustain: to keep up or maintain.

Before assigning the reading, you may want to introduce students to any words that could cause pronunciation or definition problems.

Vocabulary Tip

Examining Word Parts Explain to students that examining the parts of a word can sometimes help to determine the word's meaning. For example, *prejudice* can be broken down into the prefix *pre–* and the form *judice*. *Pre–* means "before," and *judice* means "judge"; therefore, *prejudice* means "a judgment or opinion formed before examining the facts."

CONTENT-AREA VOCABULARY

Although the following words are important to an understanding of the text selection, some of them may be unfamiliar to students.

cavalry: soldiers on horseback.
encountered: met with; faced.
impressive: causing admiration.

As you present this list of words and definitions, ask students to brainstorm what they already know about each word.

Reading Skill
Summarizing

Explain to students that when they summarize a reading passage, they are briefly restating the most important points of a selection.

▶ **Teaching Tip**

Summarizing Remind students that when they summarize a passage, they are trying to determine the most accurate and direct answer to the question *What is the selection (or paragraph or section) about?* Explain to students that when summarizing, they should use their own words but not their own ideas: They are simply restating the author's main ideas.

Reading Strategy
Activating and Using Prior Knowledge (Strategy 8)

To help students summarize a writer's main ideas, you may want to use Strategy 8 described in Content-Area Reading Strategies. Have students use a KWL chart (Graphic Organizer 6). Have students fill in the first two columns of the KWL before they begin to read and the third column, which requires summarizing, should be filled in after they have finished reading the selection.

DURING READING

▶ **Teaching Tip**

Recognizing Main Ideas Point out to students the author's use of a question (on p. 142) to begin the fourth paragraph of the selection. Explain that such questions are often clues signaling the paragraph's or section's main idea.

Differentiating Instruction
■ English-Language Learners

Good summaries often demand a broad vocabulary; therefore, English-language learners may struggle because of their limited knowledge of English. Pair students with more able readers who can help to make accurate word choices. Suggest the use of a thesaurus.

AFTER READING

✔ Reading Check

The following are sample answers to the questions on student text page 143.

1. American Indians felt that the buffalo was sacred because it gave them food, shelter, and clothing.

2. American Indians called African American soldiers Buffalo Soldiers because their hair resembled the matted cushion between the buffalo's horns and because their fighting spirit resembled the buffalo's courage.

3. An African American might have wanted to serve in the army in order to be a soldier, seek adventure, try something new, earn money, receive an education, or find a better life. (Accept any two.)

4. After training, African American soldiers were sent to the Great Plains, the Western mountains, or the Southwestern deserts to maintain order between American Indians and settlers, build forts and roads, patrol the borders, and protect mail coaches and railroad construction crews.

5. African American soldiers often used poor equipment, faced difficult assignments, and encountered prejudice.

Reteaching

When summarizing, students must be able to distinguish between important and unimportant information. Therefore, you may want to walk students through the process of locating the main ideas of the selection. Read aloud the first paragraph, and work with students to identify the main idea and to provide a summarizing statement. Remind students that when summarizing, they should condense the material and restate it using their own words. Continue with the next paragraphs or sections. The following are summarizing statements for the first three paragraphs.

■ The American Indians respectfully nicknamed African American troops Buffalo Soldiers because of their courage and their curly hair.

- The U.S. Army's ban on African American soldiers began to change during the Civil War.
- Special units of African American soldiers were formed after the passage of an 1866 law allowing African Americans to join the peace-time army.

Connecting to Language Arts
▪ Writing
Persuasive Letter Have students imagine they are young African American men who want to join the U.S. Army in 1866. They are convinced that the choice is a good one, but they must persuade their families to support their choice. Have students write persuasive letters in which they give valid reasons to support their enlistment.

Connecting Across the Curriculum: Social Studies
A Soldier's Life Have students find out what a typical Buffalo Soldier's life was like on the Western frontier. You might have students work with partners or in small groups to find answers to some of the following questions.
- What were frontier forts like?
- How long did most soldiers serve?
- What diseases or ailments were common among the troops?
- How did the soldiers deal with loneliness and boredom?

Further Resources
▪ Books
Black Valor: Buffalo Soldiers and the Medal of Honor, 1870–1898 by Frank N. Schubert
The Buffalo Soldiers: A Narrative of the Negro Cavalry in the West by William H. Leckie
Buffalo Soldiers and Officers of the Ninth Calvary, 1867–1898: Black & White Together by Charles L. Kenner
The Forgotten Heroes: The Story of the Buffalo Soldiers by Clinton Cox

▪ Museums
Traveling Exhibit *The Buffalo Soldiers: The African American Soldier in the US Army, 1866–1912*
Online exhibit from The International Museum of the Horse: *The Buffalo Soldiers on the Western Frontier*

▪ Videos
Buffalo Soldiers: The True Story of Our Country's First Black War Heroes, Simitar Video, 1997, Not Rated.
The Buffalo Soldiers, Goldhil Home Media, 1999, Not Rated.
Buffalo Soldiers, Turner Home Video, 1997, Not Rated. Fictionalized movie about the Buffalo Soldiers; some violence.

Assessment

Turn to page 140 for a multiple-choice test on the selection.

Test Answers

1. c	2. a	3. d	4. c	5. a
6. b	7. d	8. b	9. a	10. c

"A Few Appropriate Remarks"

from *Highlights for Children*

by NANCY NORTON MATTILA
(*student text page 144*)

Reading Level: Average

Text Summary

This magazine article examines the circumstances leading up to, the presentation of, and the responses to Abraham Lincoln's Gettysburg Address. Asked to give "a few appropriate remarks" at the dedication of the Soldiers' National Cemetery, Lincoln delivered a two-minute address that is often considered to be one of history's greatest speeches.

BEFORE READING

Make the Connection

Ask students if they have ever heard a speech that inspired or moved them. What was the occasion? Who was the speaker? Was it the speaker's words, the delivery, the reaction of the audience, or something else that especially appealed to them? Then, have students discuss what they believe are the qualities of a good speech.

Build Background

■ More About the Topic

Abraham Lincoln served as the sixteenth President of the United States from 1861 to his assassination in 1865. Although his backwoods origins were humble and he had less than one full year of formal education in his entire life, President Lincoln was a man of great insight and integrity. As President he helped to preserve the Union during the Civil War and demonstrated to the world that democracy was a viable form of government. A presidential act for which he is particularly remembered is the Emancipation Proclamation, which declared that all slaves in Confederate territory still in rebellion were free.

Vocabulary Development

The following words are underscored and defined in the student text.

dedication: setting apart for a special reason.
proclaimed: stated or declared publicly.

appropriate: suitable for a particular purpose.
reverence: high regard; respect.
orator: public speaker.

Before assigning the reading, you may want to introduce students to any words that could cause pronunciation or definition problems.

Vocabulary Tip

Using Context Clues Before students begin reading the selection, tell them that they may encounter unfamiliar vocabulary words that are not defined in the side margin or in the footnotes. Explain that many of these words have clues in the surrounding words or sentences that will help students guess their meanings. For example, in describing Lincoln's delivery of the speech, the author says "his high voice *shrilled* forth like a bugle." Even without knowing the meaning of *shrilled*, one could guess that it refers to a high-pitched or piercing sound.

CONTENT-AREA VOCABULARY

Although the following words are important to an understanding of the text selection, some of them may be unfamiliar to students.

authorized: given special power or permission.
oration: a formal speech, usually given on a special occasion.
formally: in an official way, as with a ceremony.
sacred: holy.
unity: harmony.
sacrifices: things given up for another cause.
elegant: with tasteful richness.

Point out to students that suffixes often offer clues to usage and meaning. For example, an *–ed* ending, as in *authorized*, often indicates that the word is a verb (*sacred* is an exception). An *–ion* ending, as in *oration*, and a *–y* ending, as in *unity*, usually indicate a noun. The *–ly* ending, as in *formally*, generally indicates an adverb.

Reading Informational Material

Reading Skill
Identifying Chronological Order

Explain to students that selections that are written in chronological order present events in the order in which they occurred.

▶ **Teaching Tip**

Sequence of Events Explain to students that although the author of this selection presents a series of events in chronological order, the first paragraph is actually a flashforward. In order to give background information and add interest, writers often deviate from telling the sequence of events in a story in the same order as they actually occurred.

Reading Strategy
Understanding Text (Strategy 2)

To help students identify the text structure, use Strategy 2 described in Content-Area Reading Strategies. To assist students in recognizing the chronology of events, suggest that they use a Sequence and Chronological Order chart (Graphic Organizer 10).

DURING READING

Using the Side-Margin Feature
- **The Final Act**

Students might find it interesting to learn that Lincoln's assassination may have been part of a conspiracy to weaken the government and provide the South with a measure of revenge. Booth, a Confederate sympathizer, and a group of co-conspirators may have planned to assassinate simultaneously President Lincoln, Vice-President Andrew Johnson, and Secretary of State William Seward. Booth did assassinate Lincoln, successfully carrying out his portion of the plan, but no apparent attempt on Johnson's life was made. Seward was stabbed, but he managed to survive.

▶ **Teaching Tip**

Using Descriptive Details Point out to students the author's use of descriptive details, particularly sensory details—those that can be observed using the senses. For example, note the description of the way Lincoln looks, moves, and sounds as he's about to give his speech. Have students find other examples of sensory details.

Differentiating Instruction
- **Learners Having Difficulties**

Displaying in the classroom a list of chronological order signal words can help students to identify sequence in the text structure. Besides those listed in Reading Strategy 2 in Content-Area Reading Strategies, point out to students specific time markers in the text, such as "two weeks before," and "at 2 P.M."

AFTER READING

✔ Reading Check

The following are sample answers to the questions on student text page 147.

1. Abraham Lincoln delivered his Gettysburg Address at the dedication of the Soldiers' National Cemetery.

2. Lincoln decided to go to Gettysburg to give the speech because he thought it was a good opportunity to say something important about the war and to persuade people to continue to fight.

3. Everett's speech was approximately two hours long; Lincoln's speech was about two minutes long.

4. Lincoln's choice of words was influenced by his love of poetry, the Bible, and Shakespeare.

5. The audience's response to Lincoln's address was lukewarm.

Reteaching

To reteach chronological order, provide students with the following list of events, but scramble the order. Allow students to refer to the selection as they reorder the events. Remind students to look for transitional words and phrases to help them locate the events.

- Lincoln received an invitation to speak at a cemetery dedication in Gettysburg.
- With a partly finished speech, Lincoln boarded a train to Pennsylvania.
- The presidential party arrived at the Wills' house.

- Dinner was served, and Lincoln met Everett.
- Lincoln spoke to a crowd outside the Wills' house.
- Lincoln finished his speech in his room.
- Everett gave his speech.
- Lincoln gave his speech.
- Lincoln lay back with cold towels covering his eyes.
- Lincoln received a complimentary letter from Everett.

Connecting to Language Arts

- **Writing**

News Story Have students assume the role of a reporter whose assignment is to cover President Lincoln's speech in Gettysburg. They can find most of the information they need in the reading selection, but encourage students to go beyond the selection for additional details. Upon completion, create a "Reporter's Wall" in the classroom where the news stories can be displayed.

- **Speaking and Listening**

Debate When Abraham Lincoln ran against Stephen A. Douglas for the U.S. Senate in 1858, he challenged Douglas to a series of debates. The most important issue of these debates was the expansion of slavery in the territories. Have students work in groups to stage debates about issues that are important to them. First, have the groups locate and study information about the debating procedure. Then, have them plan their debates and present them to the rest of the class.

Connecting Across the Curriculum: History

Presidential Danger Abraham Lincoln was the first U.S. President to be assassinated but not the last. Three additional Presidents have been assassinated while in office, and numerous unsuccessful attempts on other Presidents have been made. Have interested students delve deeper into this dark chapter of American history. Students may want to carry their research further and examine the role of the Secret Service in protecting U.S. Presidents.

Further Resources

- **Books**

The Lincoln Forum: Abraham Lincoln, Gettysburg, and the Civil War, John Y. Simon, ed.
Abraham Lincoln's Gettysburg Address: Four Score and More by Barbara Silberdick Feinberg

- **Videos**

The Civil War – A Film by Ken Burns, PBS Home Video, 1997, Not Rated.
An Evening with Abraham Lincoln, with Gene Griessman, 2001, Unrated.
The Speeches of Abraham Lincoln, 1990, Not Rated.
Touring Civil War Battlefields, Questar, 1988.
Biography – John Wilkes Booth, A&E Entertainment, 1998, Not Rated.

Assessment

Turn to page 141 for a multiple-choice test on the selection.

Test Answers
1. d   2. d   3. b   4. a   5. c
6. b   7. a   8. a   9. c   10. d

Reenactment of War Is Far Too Civil

from *the Los Angeles Times*
by JON LOVE
(student text page 148)

Reading Level: Average

Text Summary

The author of this newspaper article takes a stand against Civil War reenactment. After witnessing the re-creation of the 1863 Chickamauga battle, he professes that warfare should not be glorified by playacting. He believes that reenactment belittles the sacrifices made by soldiers and sends young people a false message—that being a soldier is fun.

BEFORE READING

Make the Connection

Ask students to brainstorm topics about which they have strong opinions. For example, do they think wearing bicycle helmets should be mandatory, that lunch periods should be longer, or that parents should monitor their children's Internet usage? Discuss with students the fact that everyone has opinions, but to get someone else to agree with those opinions, good reasons and valid evidence must be given to support the opinions.

Build Background

■ More About the Topic

The actual reenactment of a Civil War battle or event is only part of a reenactor's experience. Preparing for the event can be daunting. First, an individual must choose the character he or she intends to be, such as a Union or Confederate civilian or soldier, an officer, a cook, or a doctor. Then, to ensure a costume's authenticity, research must be done. The actual re-enactment usually has a set of rules and restrictions to facilitate its progress and to help guarantee the absence of anachronistic or inappropriate items. For example, all visible equipment must be suitable for the time period. Even non-period snack food is forbidden. Reenactors hope to replicate as closely as possible the historic experience.

Vocabulary Development

The following words are underscored and defined in the student's text.

authentic: real.
industrial: relating to manufacturing.
impending: approaching.
replica: a copy.
ironic: meaning the opposite of what one would expect.

Before assigning the reading, you may want to introduce students to any words that could cause pronunciation or definition problems.

Vocabulary Tip

Understanding Denotation and Connotation
Explain to students that a word's dictionary definition is its denotation. A word's connotation is a feeling or association suggested by the word. For example, the words *sham* and *pretend* have similar denotative meanings, but they suggest different ideas because *sham* usually has a negative connotation. Writers of persuasion often use connotative words to stir their reader's feelings. Have students look for words in the selection that have either a negative or positive connotation. [warrior, impending, terror, scorn, sank in, tortured]

CONTENT-AREA VOCABULARY

Although the following words are important to an understanding of the text selection, some of them may be unfamiliar to students.

artillery: the unit in the army that is in charge of the large mounted guns.
cavalry: soldiers mounted on horses.
drafted: taken into military service.
draftees: people who have been chosen to serve in the military.
sham: not genuine; pretend.

After you introduce the words and definitions to students, ask what most of the words in the list have in common. [All except *sham* deal with warfare.]

Reading Informational Material

Reading Strategy

Visualizing Information (Strategy 5)

To help students make predictions based on text features, use Strategy 5 described in Content-Area Reading Strategies. Suggest that students use a Key Points and Details Chart (Graphic Organizer 5) to record their thoughts.

▶ **Teaching Tip**

Using Text Features As students are making predictions based on text features, point out that the callout on page 149 presents the author's opinion statement. The words "I think" designate an opinion. This statement presents both the issue and the author's point of view.

Reading Skill

Making Predictions Based on Text Features

Explain to students that many informative texts include features such as headings, subheadings, titles, callouts, and illustrations. Because writers often use these text features to highlight important information, students can use the text features to predict the kind of information the text will contain.

DURING READING

Differentiating Instruction

■ English-Language Learners

Because of its conversational tone and its persuasive nature, the selection might be more accessible to students if it is read aloud. You or one of your more able readers can read the selection aloud or record it beforehand and play it as students follow along in the text. In addition, suggest that students use self-adhesive notes to mark any part of the selection that raises questions or seems confusing. Then, after the reading is completed, the questions can be addressed.

▶ **Teaching Tip**

Recognizing Persuasive Writing Explain to students that writers of persuasion appeal to a reader's logic by using various types of evidence to support their opinions. Point out the author's use of supporting facts, statistics, expert opinions, and examples. In addition, persuasive writers often include details that have emotional appeal—that elicit such feelings as guilt, fear, or happiness. Help students recognize that Jon Love uses a mixture of logical and emotional appeals in his article.

AFTER READING

✔ Reading Check

The following are sample answers to questions on student text page 152.

1. This selection describes the reenactment of the battle of Chickamauga, a Civil War battle.

2. The author is opposed to reenacting battles. He writes that "Warfare isn't a game, and I don't think it should be glorified."

3. According to the author, this event will give young people the mistaken idea that it is fun to be a soldier.

4. The article is about American soldiers who killed Korean civilians in the Korean War. Some people now want to hold the soldiers responsible for these deaths.

5. The author quotes William T. Sherman's words—"War is hell"—because they support the author's argument that war is not a game.

Reteaching

To foster an understanding of making predictions based on text features, find a newspaper or magazine article that you think will be of interest to students. Eliminate all text features, such as boldfacing, italicizing, titles, headings, and illustrations. Then, work with students to determine what the author might use as text features. Discuss why these added features would help readers with their predictions.

Connecting to Language Arts

▪ Writing

Editorial   Newspaper editorials provide citizens with a public forum for their opinions. Have students write editorials about issues that are important to them. You may want to provide the editorial section of several newspapers for students to peruse for style and subject matter. Post the completed editorials in the classroom, or suggest that students submit them to the school or local newspaper.

▪ Speaking and Listening

Interview   Pair students to create an interview with a Civil War reenactor. One student will play the role of the interviewer who asks questions about the reenactor's experience. The other student will play the role of the reenactor and answer the questions. After the student pairs have prepared and practiced their interviews, have them present their interviews to the rest of the class.

Connecting Across the Curriculum: History

Living History   Have students research periods in history besides the Civil War that offer reenactment opportunities. Then, ask students to choose one of the specific periods or events and to prepare a brief report on the reenacting experiences available. (The Internet will provide detailed information that can be found by entering the keyword *reenactment.*) Students can combine their reports into a classroom directory of historical reenactment.

Further Resources

▪ Books

Past into Present: Effective Techniques for First-Person Historical Interpretation by Stacy Flora Roth.

Charley Waters Goes to Gettysburg by Susan Sinnott, illustrated by Dorothy Handelman. Photo essay told from point of view of eight-year-old boy.

Assessment

Turn to page 142 for a multiple-choice test on the selection.

Test Answers

1. d   2. c   3. b   4. a   5. b
6. a   7. c   8. d   9. a   10. b

The following criteria can help you evaluate each student's success in completing the activities prompted by the Cross-Curricular Activities feature in the student textbook.

Art/Language Arts
Dandy Duds
- The student conducts research on the various Civil War uniforms.
- The student creates detailed sketches of two of these costumes.
- The sketches accurately represent the uniforms and reflect the student's research.
- The student includes a descriptive paragraph for each costume that explains the costume's history, tells who wore it, and describes its various components.
- The student presents his or her sketches and findings to the class.
- The student's presentation is clear and effective.

Speech
Women's Work
- The student conducts research to find Sojourner Truth's speech, usually known as the "Ain't I a Woman" speech, or another famous speech of the period.
- The student performs a dramatic reading of the speech for the class.
- The student utilizes appropriate body language, facial expressions, and vocal tones to communicate the speech effectively.
- The student's performance is relatively free of performance errors.

Language Arts/History
Labors of Love
- The student researches various occupations available during the Civil War.
- The student writes a poem or series of journal entries written from the point of view of a young person performing one of these jobs.
- The poem or entries accurately describe the work involved in the student's chosen occupation and also describe the worker's feelings about the job and about the war.
- The student's work demonstrates imagination and creativity.
- The poem or entries are relatively free of errors in spelling, grammar, usage, and mechanics.

Art/Design
Stamp of Greatness
- The student chooses a person or a member of a group mentioned in Chapter 4, "A Nation Divided," and conducts research to find out what important contributions the person or group made to society.
- The student designs a postage stamp that commemorates the person or group.
- The student's postage stamp accurately represents the contributions of the person or group.
- The student's postage stamp demonstrates imagination and creativity.

A Nation Transformed
The Industrial Era 1877–1914

Cielito Lindo

from *Songs of the Wild West*

Commentary by ALAN AXELROD
Arrangements by DAN FOX
(student text page 157)

CONTENT-AREA CONNECTIONS

HISTORY ●
MUSIC ●
WORLD LANGUAGES ●

Reading Level: Average

Text Summary

Through Spanish terminology and a well-known song in the traditional Spanish style, the historical origins of the working cowboy and the singing cowboy of the movies are traced to the Indian ranch workers on early Spanish missions.

BEFORE READING

Make the Connection

Ask students to tell why some people like to work to music and give examples of work-related songs. [Music can provide a rhythmic pace for work; music can provide a soothing background for work. One example might be "I've Been Working on the Railroad."]

Build Background

▪ More About the Subject

"Cielito Lindo," composed by the Mexican musician Quirino Mendoza y Cortés in the 1930s, is in the tradition of the love songs sung by the vaqueros. One of many English translations is: "From the brown mountain range a pair of black eyes are stealing away. Sing and don't cry because we know that singing gladdens the heart."

▪ More About the Time Period

The Spaniards who colonized the area that is now Texas called unbranded cattle *mesteños*. Later this word became *mustangs* in English and eventually also described wild horses. The lifestyle of the American Indians in the West and Southwest changed after the first horsemen arrived from Spain. Initially afraid of the strange animals, Indians soon became skilled riders and acquired their own mounts. This enabled some groups of American Indians to switch from farming to the nomadic following of the bison herds.

Vocabulary Development

The following words are underscored and defined in the student text.

pedigree: origin; history.

stoic: seeming unaffected by pain or suffering.

Before assigning the reading, you may want to introduce students to any words that could cause pronunciation or definition problems.

┌─ *Vocabulary Tip* ─────────────

Using Multiple Meanings No one knows where the word *duds* came from, but it has been around for hundreds of years. In this selection duds means clothes, but it can also mean personal possessions that are not valuable, ragged and tattered clothing, and a useless or inefficient person or thing. Examples of the latter are a counterfeit coin or an unexploded bomb. Three hundred years ago a dud-man was a scarecrow, dressed in rags and set out in a field.

Stanley Lucero: From synopsis of "Cielito Lindo" lyrics written by Stanley A. Lucero from *Dos Voces-Un Espiritu,* at *http://www.lucerito.net/dosvoces.htm,* accessed June 4, 2001. Copyright © 1999 by Lucerito's Music (Madera, California).

Although the following words are important to an understanding of the text selection, some of them may be unfamiliar to students.

mission*: religious, teaching, and living center for Spanish missionaries in Spain's colonies.

colonial: having to do with a colony; that is, an area under the control of the government of a distant country.

enslaved: made the property of and bound to work for others.

duds*: clothing.

ancestry: people from whom a person is descended.

*Although students may be familiar with other meanings of these words, the words as used in the selection have a specific meaning that pertains to the content area.

Reading Informational Material

Reading Skill
Using Prior Knowledge

Explain to students that asking questions and thinking about ideas while reading help them understand and remember text.

▶ **Teaching Tip**
Using the Spanish Language This selection includes and explains some Spanish words as well as Spanish song lyrics. Remind students that among Spanish-speaking cultures pronunciation can vary, that words set to music in any language often change somewhat to fit the melody, and that the pronunciation of words adopted from one language into another often changes to suit speaking styles.

Reading Strategy
Activating and Using Prior Knowledge (Strategy 8)

To help students build on their knowledge of cowboys and cowboy songs, use Strategy 8 described in Content-Area Reading Strategies. Have them set as a goal to find out how cowboys, including the "singing cowboys" of television and film, are connected to early Spanish *vaqueros*. You may wish to provide students with a KWL Chart (Graphic Organizer 6) to help them organize what they know about cowboys and what they want to know about the topic.

You will want to have students return to the chart to fill in the last column when they have completed their reading.

DURING READING

Correcting Misconceptions
Speakers of English may have difficulty understanding how the word *vaquero*, starting with a *v*, could have developed into the *b* word *buckaroo* in English. Have students notice where their lips and teeth are positioned as they pronounce the words *very* and *berry*. Point out that a slight movement of the lower lip makes these sounds distinct in English.

Using the Side-Margin Feature:
▪ On a Mission

Ask students to name early Spanish missions with which they are familiar. Students may mention the Alamo (San Antonio de Valero) or Nuestra Señora del Carmen in Texas, or Santa Barbara and San Juan Capistrano in California.

Differentiating Instruction
▪ Advanced Students

You may wish to have advanced students who are studying Spanish collaborate on their own English translation of "Cielito Lindo" for the class, or invite students who have firsthand knowledge of these lyrics to share what they know about the song's origin, meaning, and melody.

AFTER READING

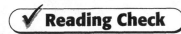 **Reading Check**

The following are sample answers to the questions on student text page 159.

1. Spanish mission priests began to train American Indians as horsemen because the cattle herds became too large for the priests to manage alone.

2. A *vaquero* is a cowboy.

3. The word *buckaroo* comes from the Spanish word *vaquero*, spoken as it sounded to people who did not speak Spanish.

4. The repeated message in the song "Cielito Lindo" is "Sing and don't cry."

5. The main idea in this selection is that the image of the western cowboys and their clothing, working tools, and songs can be traced to the American Indians who worked on the Spanish missions.

Reteaching

Have students fill in the "What I *Learned*" column of their KWL Chart. Then, if they are still having difficulty integrating the new information with their prior knowledge, have them construct a Cowboy concept map (Reading Strategy 4 in Content-Area Reading Strategies), either independently or as a class activity. Students could then write a short summary of what they learned about cowboys.

Connecting to Language Arts

- Writing

I've Been Workin'... Brainstorm and write on the chalkboard the different kinds of work that people now do. Then, ask students to pick either one type of work or a category that includes several different types of work and write a job description. This should include the tasks involved, salary, benefits, and so forth. Have students exchange job descriptions and write a job application. Display these on a Work bulletin board, along with illustrations, sheet music for songs to accompany work, photos of workers, and cartoons and comic strips about work.

- Speaking and Listening

Sing Along Have groups of three or four students identify and select several cowboy songs or at least two singers well known for singing cowboy songs. Then, have students do the research on the songs or the singers and organize the information for a group presentation to the class. The group presentation should include visual aids, such as a poster, photos, or videos; recordings; and a short informative speech.

Connecting Across the Curriculum: Social Sciences

Missions as Museums Ask students to select and do research on one of the missions still standing in Texas, New Mexico, Arizona, or California. Then, ask them to create a brochure that will encourage people to visit that mission. The brochure should include the history of the mission—in particular, details of the hardships and lifestyles of the earliest ranch workers. The brochure can be illustrated with a floor plan of the mission, photos or drawings of it as it was in the past and as it is now, and details of particularly interesting events in the past or modern events in which tourists might be interested. The brochures can be presented to the class and then placed in the resource center.

Further Resources

- Book

Songs of the Wild West, commentary by Alan Axelrod; arrangements by Dan Fox. The Metropolitan Museum of Art in association with the Buffalo Bill Historical Center.

- Video

The Alamo. A&E, 1995. Not rated. An overview of the decisive battle which eventually led to independence for Texas.

Assessment

Turn to page 143 for a multiple-choice test on the selection.

Test Answers

1. c 2. d 3. b 4. c 5. a
6. b 7. b 8. c 9. d 10. a

The Great Bicycle Experiment

from *Cobblestone*
by TONI A. WATSON
(student text page 160)

Reading Level: Average

Text Summary
In the late 1800s, bicycles were put to the test as replacements for horses in the military.

BEFORE READING

Make the Connection
Have students assign an order of priority to the following requirements soldiers might have for their means of transportation: dependability, economy, safety, simplicity.

Build Background
■ More About the Time Period

James Moore, an Englishman, won the first recorded bicycle race in a park in 1868. In 1869, he also won the first road race, which covered a distance of 83 miles from Paris to Rouen, France. His solid-tire bike is reported to have weighed 160 pounds, and his winning time was 10 hours and 25 minutes.

■ More About the Subject

The Twenty-fifth Infantry was composed mainly of African American men, known as the Buffalo Soldiers.

Vocabulary Development
The following words are underscored and defined in the student text.

consisted: was formed or made up of.
horizontally: in a position parallel to the horizon; not vertically.
expedition: a journey for a specific purpose.
incentive: something that encourages someone to perform a certain task or work toward a goal.
escorted: accompanied to show honor or respect.
Before assigning the reading, you may want to introduce students to any words that could cause pronunciation or definition problems.

Vocabulary Tip
Using Word Origins There is nothing childish about the soldiers in the infantry despite the fact that the word *infantry* originated with a Italian word meaning "a very young person." Infantry is related historically to *footman, groom, knight,* and *lad.*

CONTENT-AREA VOCABULARY

Although the following words are important to an understanding of the text selection, some of them may be unfamiliar to students.

reliable: able to be depended on.
corporal*: a military rank below that of a sergeant.
enlightenment: increased knowledge.
infantry: soldiers that fight on foot.
puncture: a small hole made with something sharp, such as a nail or tack.
utility*: intended to be used for work.
body*: group.

*Although students may be familiar with other meanings of these words, the words as used in the selection have specific meanings that pertain to the content area.

Reading Informational Material

Reading Skill
Using Chronology

Explain to students that noticing how the writer organizes the information in the selection can help them understand the bicycle experiment and its outcome.

▶ **Teaching Tip**
Using Visuals To help students visualize times past, this selection includes a reproduction of an original newspaper article about the military experiment led by Moss. Have students suggest why other visuals, such as photos or diagrams, might be used

in an article about an experiment. [Photos and diagrams add details to our impressions, especially to impressions that require scientific accuracy.]

Reading Strategy
Using Graphic Organizers (Strategy 3)
To help students place the events of the bicycle experiment in sequence, use Strategy 3 described in Content-Area Reading Strategies. Provide students with a Sequence and Chronological Order Chart (Graphic Organizer 10) to help them record information in chronological order.

DURING READING

Differentiating Instruction
■ **Learners Having Difficulty**
To help students establish chronological order, allow pairs to jot down events that occurred during the bicycle experiment and number them in the order that they occurred. They can then transfer this information to the graphic organizer.

AFTER READING

 **Reading Check**

The following are sample answers to the questions on student text page 162.

1. Bicycles were a better form of transportation than horses because bicycles do not have to be fed and watered.

2. The first test ride was to Lake McDonald in western Montana and back to Fort Missoula.

3. Problems riders testing the bicycle faced were the difficulties of rough weather and land and frequent flat tires, broken pedals, and lost chains.

4. The first long-distance test ride was from Fort Missoula in Montana to St. Louis, Missouri, a distance of nineteen hundred miles.

5. One possible reason bicycles were never adopted by the military was the ease with which the enemy could puncture the tires. Other reasons suggested in the text are the lack of protection from weather given the rider of the bicycle; the

effort needed to ride a bicycle over rough terrain while carrying weapons, tent, and rations; and the fact that a bicycle can break down easily.

Reteaching
If students are still struggling to place events in the bicycle experiment in sequence, write on the chalkboard the question "What happened first?" Then, ask for volunteers to give a quote from the selection that helps answer the question and record this on the chalkboard. Continue with the question, "What happened next?" and record quotes from the selection.

Connecting to Language Arts
■ **Writing**
"Through heavy rain and deep mud, the valiant . . ." In groups of three or four, have students write a script for a radio dramatization of the Great Bicycle Experiment. Before breaking into groups, lead a class discussion and list on the board the main elements students will have to keep in mind when writing for the radio. [the need for a commentator to connect the parts of the drama, the fact that dialogue will have to be written for the actors, and the use of sound rather than visuals to tell the story] Groups may record their dramas on audiotape for the entire class to play.

Connecting Across the Curriculum: Science
Bicycles for Health and the Environment Have students investigate the safe use of bicycles for recreation or for transportation. Suggest that they ask school health and science teachers about resources for learning the safety risks and health benefits of bicycling. Have them use keywords such as *transportation* and *bicycles* in an Internet search. When students complete their investigation, ask them to create a flier or poster to share their information with the class or school at large.

Further Resources
■ **Video**
Bicycle Corps: America's Black Army on Wheels. PBS Home Video, 2000. Not rated.

Assessment
Turn to page 144 for a multiple-choice test on the selection.
Test Answers
1. c 2. d 3. c 4. a 5. d
6. c 7. d 8. a 9. b 10. d

How the Wealthy Lived

from *Cobblestone*

by HELEN WIEMAN BLEDSOE
(student text page 163)

Reading Level: Average

Text Summary

The lifestyle of the wealthy in the United States after the Civil War demonstrates the extremes people went to in order to impress others.

BEFORE READING

Make the Connection

Ask students to tell how they would spend a million dollars. List answers on the chalkboard and then discuss headings for categories of expenses. [Clothes, Cars, Travel, Houses, Education, Recreation, Business, Charity, and so forth.]

Build Background

■ More About the Subject

Gilding is the process of covering an object with a thin layer of gold. Egyptians gilded royal mummy cases. The Chinese decorated wood, pottery, and textiles with gold. Both the Greeks and the Romans gilded masonry and marble statues. The Romans even embellished temples and palaces with the gilding process.

Vocabulary Development

The following words are underscored and defined in the student text.

gilded: covered in a thin layer of gold.

elaborate: detailed and complicated.

lavish: more than is needed; overly generous.

rigid: fixed; inflexible.

obligatory: necessary; required.

Point out to students that all of these words are adjectives. Ask them to suggest a noun for each adjective. Write these phrases on the chalkboard. Then, have students conduct a round-robin story-composing session, with each student adding a sentence that uses one of the adjectives and its noun to the story. Tape-record the story as students create it.

Vocabulary Tip

Developing Word Lists To help students realize the power of words, ask them to create a similar list of words about another group in society, such as homeless people, poor people, movie and TV personalities, or soldiers.

CONTENT-AREA VOCABULARY

Although the following words are important to an understanding of the text selection, some of them may be unfamiliar to students. You may want to ask students what they predict they will read about in a selection using these words.

incomes: money earned or inherited over a period of time.

social: having to do with the activities of a particular group of people.

season*: time period for a set schedule of social activities.

hostess*: woman who gives a party.

socialites: people who are the leaders in a fashionable group.

ball*: a party with dancing.

yachts: small sailing boats.

estates*: extensive areas of land which are privately owned.

elite*: group most socially prominent.

*Although students may be familiar with other meanings of these words, the words as used in the selection have specific meanings that pertain to the content area.

Reading Informational Material

Reading Skill
Supporting Ideas

Explain to students that words such as *another, in addition, important,* and *first* tell the reader that the text is descriptive, giving a number of details about the subject.

▶ Teaching Tip
Identifying Signal Words Have students work informally in pairs to list details of a school function or widely observed holiday for which special preparations are made and traditions observed. Ask each pair to share from their list and identify signal words. Write these on the chalkboard.

Reading Strategy
Understanding Text (Strategy 2)

To help students recognize signal words for descriptive texts, use Strategy 2 described in Content-Area Reading Strategies. Ask students to use the Cluster Diagram (Graphic Organizer 3) to record details from the text.

DURING READING

Correcting Misconceptions
Students may be unaware of this particular period of time in the United States, when an entire income class lived lifestyles similar to the leisurely lives of aristocracy in other countries. Invite students to share their views on what would be appealing, dull, rewarding, or challenging to live as a member of, or to work as an employee for, a wealthy family during the Gilded Age.

▶ Using the Sidelight Feature
- "Four Hundred"

Have students share with one another the characteristics of group behavior, such as that of teenagers. [dress, speech, activities, attitudes, music, body language] Ask them to decide how the behavior of the "Four Hundred" was different from or the same as the behaviors they have listed. Students may want to use a Venn Diagram (Graphic Organizer 11) to organize their lists.

▶ Teaching Tip
Taking Notes As students read, have them keep a three-column chart with the headings "Mrs. Vanderbilt," "Mrs. Mills," and "Mrs. Astor." Under these names have them list details about each woman's lavish indulgence of herself or her guests.

Differentiating Instruction
- Advanced Students

Have students who understand the principles of satire draw cartoons depicting the excesses of socialites described in the article. Invite all students to search newspapers and magazines for cartoons depicting self-indulgence.

AFTER READING

✔ Reading Check

The following are sample answers to the questions on student text page 165.

1. Autumn—New York, Spring—Europe, Summer—Rhode Island.

2. Details of lavish spending on dinner parties include cigars wrapped in hundred-dollar bills as party favors and black pearls hidden inside oysters.

3. In the "Coach Parade," well-dressed ladies rode in horse-drawn carriages and discussed one another's clothing and vehicles.

4. Wealthy people managed their households by employing large staffs of servants that included maids, valets, butlers, chefs, footmen, and stable hands.

5. Mark Twain is credited with coining the phrase "the Gilded Age."

Reteaching
If students are still struggling to recognize the descriptive details presented throughout the article, divide the class into four groups, each responsible for listing the most startling details under one of the following categories: "Money Spent," "Fashion Requirements," "Travel Abroad," "Parties and Invitations." Have members of each group

skim the article for the descriptive details for their category.

Connecting to Language Arts
- Writing

"You are cordially invited..." Have students look at examples of friendly letters, invitations, and thank-you notes. Ask them to write their own version of some or all of these social documents as they might have appeared during the Gilded Age. Remind students to include details such as time, proper dress, entertainment enjoyed, and so forth.

- Speaking and Listening

Coach Parade and Party Chat Have students work with one or two partners to create a conversation that might have taken place during one of the era's social functions. Ask students to make the dialogue exchanges brief so that they can present their Gilded Age conversations without reading from their draft. Remind students that ad-libbing and body language can convey meaning as well as dialogue. Allow a volunteer to role-play Caroline Astor's comments as she decides which of these fictional personalities are to be invited to her next party.

Connecting Across the Curriculum: Social Sciences

What Did the Common Folk Do? Have students investigate a variety of resources to discover details about other socioeconomic groups during the same time period. Since the difference between industrial and agrarian economies affected lifestyles of ordinary workers, divide the various regions of the United States among students. Some students may find details about the lives of the country's newest immigrants at the time to contrast starkly with those of the social elite. If they have access to the Internet, students may find that the keywords *Gilded Age* provide them with details to share.

Further Resources
- Videos

The 1900 House. PBS Home Video, 2000. Not rated.

The American Experience—America 1900. PBS Home Video, 1999. Not rated.

Sears Roebuck's Impact on Life. Koch Vision/Shanachie Video, 1996. Not rated.

Assessment

Turn to page 145 for a multiple-choice test on the selection.

Test Answers

1. b 2. c 3. b 4. c 5. a
6. a 7. c 8. d 9. a 10. b

The Great Galveston Hurricane

from *Weatherwise*

by PATRICK HUGHES

(student text page 166)

Reading Level: Average

Special Considerations

Students may feel more comfortable reading the graphic details of life and property loss in this article at a time when their own geographical area is not subject to threatening weather.

Text Summary

Details of the deadliest weather disaster in United States history underscore the importance of advancements in storm-warning techniques made since 1900.

BEFORE READING

Make the Connection

Ask students to discuss any dangerous weather situations they have experienced. Then, have them share what they know about modern weather prediction techniques and safety steps to be taken in the face of dangerous weather conditions.

Build Background

- **More About the Topic**

An ocean storm becomes a hurricane when its winds are over seventy-four miles per hour. Hurricanes that hit North America develop over warm tropical water and usually move from east to west. All of these hurricanes eventually turn northward, where the air is colder and less moist. As they pass over land, the storms begin to weaken in intensity. The average duration of a hurricane is three to fourteen days.

Vocabulary Development

The following words are underscored and defined in the student text.

debris: wreckage; pieces of things that have been destroyed.

submerged: placed under the surface of a body of liquid.

benevolent: kindly; characterized by doing good deeds.

habitable: able to be lived in.

maimed: severely wounded or injured; crippled.

disintegrating: falling apart.

estimated: judged or determined to be nearly accurate.

capsized: turned over.

protruding: sticking out from.

barricade: a barrier put up quickly for protection. Before assigning the reading, you may want to introduce students to any words that could cause pronunciation or definition problems. Point out the prefixes *sub–* (under), *dis–* (not), and *pro–* (forward), and have students brainstorm a list of words using these prefixes.

Vocabulary Tip

Using Suffixes Reread the paragraph on page 168 that describes Captain Simmons' experience with the barometer. Have students identify other weather forecasting instruments and their functions. [thermometer: measures temperature; rain gauge: measures amount of rain fallen] Call students' attention to the suffix *–meter* and its meaning. [an instrument that measures]

CONTENT-AREA VOCABULARY

Although the following words are important to an understanding of the text selection, some of them may be unfamiliar to students. You will want to introduce the words to students before they begin reading and ask students what they predict they will read about in a selection using these words.

(in) vain*: without hope of a positive outcome.

rubble: pieces of what is destroyed.

institutions*: buildings occupied by a public organization.

barometer: device that measures the pressure of the atmosphere.

surge*: strongly moving water.

breakers*: waves of water that become foam when they hit the shore.

en route: on the way to a destination.

torrents: heavy, wavelike wind or rain.

missiles*: objects that move as if shot from a gun.

pall: something that covers.

*Although students may be familiar with other meanings of these words, the words as used in the selection have a specific meaning that pertains to the content area.

Reading Informational Material

Reading Skill
Predicting Outcomes

Explain to students that details about the weather and testimony about the natural disaster will lead them to predict steps taken afterward to prevent a recurrence of the destruction of the city.

▶ **Teaching Tip**

Establishing Safety Measures Ask students to list on the chalkboard or an overhead transparency the safety steps their school has in place for threatening situations such as a tornado alert, a fire alarm, or a dangerous intruder. Ask students to use school handouts or bulletins to verify the steps they have listed and add any safety measures they may have omitted.

Reading Strategy
Building Background Information (Strategy 6)

To help students predict the outcomes of events described in the selection, use Strategy 6 described in Content-Area Reading Strategies. Provide students with a Predicting and Confirming Activity (Graphic Organizer 8). Have students fill in the first two columns now and the others while and after reading.

DURING READING

Using the Side-Margin Feature
■ Weather on the Wire

Have a volunteer student or student pair investigate how messages were sent by Morse code over the telegraph. Most encyclopedias will contain an article explaining the code for each letter of the alphabet. Ask students to list the Morse code for several brief messages such as *hello, SOS,* and *all*

clear. Let student investigators report to class, and then have their classmates predict whether the Morse code is entirely obsolete today or whether it is still used to communicate in some instances.

Viewing the Art
■ Photographs

Have students look closely at the photographs for this selection. Ask what surprises or interests them about the photos that show the destruction in Galveston after the hurricane. Then, ask students to look at the photo of the Galveston seawall and to speculate about the outcome of the storm had the protective barrier been in place before the great hurricane. Volunteers may want to research subsequent hurricanes and the damage they have done since the wall was put up. Students could use a Venn diagram to compare lives lost, property damaged, and cost in current dollar value between the hurricane of 1900 and a later one.

Differentiating Instruction
■ English-Language Learners

Have students make a two-column chart for vocabulary words in the selection that have strong associations with "Water" and words that are just as likely to be found in "Other" contexts. Consider pairing some students while they read so that they can more easily list words such as *torrents, submerged, submerging, capsized, flooded, moorings,* and *drown* correctly in the *Water* category.

AFTER READING

✓ Reading Check

The following are sample answers to the questions and student text page 172.

1. At least 8,000 people were killed in Galveston by the 1900 hurricane.

2. Galveston had been a city of splendid homes, clean wide streets, good schools and churches, as well as resort and port buildings.

3. The last words wired were, "Gulf rising rapidly; half the city now under water. Great loss of life must result."

4. The Cline brothers huddled with their backs to the wind and the children in front of them, while holding planks behind them as protection against flying debris.

5. The barricade of wreckage acted as a partial shield against flood waters. This gave them the idea of building a seawall.

Reteaching

If students find that their predictions did not match up well with the outcomes presented in the selection, have them turn some of their predictions into questions for further reading. Questions such as the following can be investigated in the school library, on the Internet, or with the help of a science teacher:

- How often are citizens in North America asked to evacuate their homes prior to a hurricane strike?
- In what cities besides Galveston have seawalls been constructed to hold back water surges?
- What are the most modern methods of communicating warnings to people in danger from storms?
- What improvements in the construction of buildings have some coastal communities made to strengthen their resistance to hurricane-force winds?

Connecting to Language Arts

- **Writing**

Personal Accounts Have students write a short first-person narrative about the hurricane from one of two points of view—*Someone Lucky* or *Someone Lost*. Ask them to use details of the weather and the destruction in the city, as well as the style of factual first-person accounts in the selection, to develop a single-page account of the events. Have the class collect these short narrative passages in a scrapbook along with pictures of hurricanes or photos of Galveston.

- **Speaking and Listening**

Evacuation In small groups, ask students to write the dialogue for an exchange between an evacuation crew and a family that is reluctant to leave home before a dangerous hurricane hits. Remind the students to include details similar to those mentioned in the selection. After a brief rehearsal, have some or all groups present their skits to the class.

Connecting Across the Curriculum: Earth Sciences

Storms and More Disasters Have each student research one of the following: hurricanes, typhoons, tornadoes, earthquakes, volcanoes, or tidal waves. Students should focus on the success or failure of warning and evacuation practices that have been adopted by at-risk areas in modern times. Then, have students pool their information to create a wall chart of the information.

Further Resources

- **Videos**

  Great San Francisco Earthquake. Time-Life Video, 1988. Not rated.
  Hurricane Force—A Coastal Perspective. U.S. Geological Survey, 2000. Rated G.

- **Books**

Bronson, William. *The Earth Shook, the Sky Burned: A Photographic Record of the 1906 San Francisco Earthquake and Fire.* Chronicle Books, 1997.

Duey, Kathleen and Karen A. Bale and Bill Dodge (Artist). *Survival! Fire, Chicago, 1871.* Aladdin, 1998.

Gallagher, Jim. *The Johnstown Flood (Great Disasters and Their Reforms).* Chelsea House, 2000.

Gibbons, Gail. *Weather Forecasting.* Econo-Clad Books, 1999.

Murphy, Jim. *The Great Fire.* Scholastic Trade, 1996.

Assessment

Turn to page 146 for a multiple-choice test on the selection.

Test Answers

1. b	**2.** c	**3.** b	**4.** b	**5.** a
6. a	**7.** a	**8.** b	**9.** b	**10.** a
11. a	**12.** b	**13.** a	**14.** b	**15.** a

from The Maple Leaf Club

from *Scott Joplin*

by KATHERINE PRESTON
(student text page 173)

Reading Level: Average

Text Summary

The selection examines the influence of African American musician Scott Joplin on ragtime music.

BEFORE READING

Make the Connection

Have students list styles of music. [folk, rock, country, classical, jazz, rhythm and blues, salsa, alternative] Then, ask students to suggest which of these types of music originated in the United States. [country western, jazz, rhythm and blues, rock] Tell students that they will be learning about a musician in the United States who influenced a musical style related to jazz.

Build Background

■ More About the Topic

Scott Joplin, who was born in Texarkana, Texas, grew up in a musical household. His father played the fiddle, and his mother sang and played banjo. During his teens Joplin played at African American churches, gatherings, and bars because racial discrimination made other venues inaccessible. Joplin composed a number of waltzes, marches, and even ragtime operas. In 1976, years after his death, he was awarded a Pulitzer Prize for his musical accomplishments.

Vocabulary Development

The following words are underscored and defined in the student text.

integrated: open to people of all races.
lofty: impressive.
indisputable: unable to be challenged.
dominated: overwhelmed or overshadowed by.
amiably: in a friendly, easygoing manner.
commotion: noisy disturbance or confusion.
improvise: to make up or create without any preparation.
respectable: considered acceptable and proper by society.

diligence: persistence.
legitimate: recognized or approved.

Before assigning the reading, you may want to introduce students to any words that could cause pronunciation or definition problems. Point out the use of the prefix *in–*, meaning "not," in the word *indisputable*. Have students brainstorm a list of words that use the prefix *in–* in this way.

┌─ *Vocabulary Tip* ─

Examining Word Origins The word *hallmark* comes from the name of the assay, or metal testing, office at Goldsmith's Hall in London. The mark from the authorities in the Hall meant that the gold or silver articles were legal and could be sold. Later the word came to mean any sign, or mark, of something genuine or of a high quality.

CONTENT-AREA VOCABULARY

Although the following words are important to an understanding of the text selection, some of them may be unfamiliar to students. You will want to introduce the words to students before they begin reading. Put the words on the chalkboard or on an overhead transparency. Pronounce each word, and ask students to define the word if they can. Write their definition and add the ones given below if students have not covered those particular meanings. You may want to assign students to groups of four to write a paragraph using the words, or to write another entry that is appropriate.

rousing: sparking enthusiasm.
incorporating*: mixing in together.
hallmark*: characteristic feature.
oblige: to agree to.
rendition: version of a musical piece.

*Although students may be familiar with other meanings of this word, the word as used in the selection has a specific meaning that pertains to the content area.

Reading Informational Material

Reading Skill
Finding the Main Idea

Explain to students that the main idea is the overall topic being developed in an article or in part of an article.

▶ **Teaching Tip**
Finding the Main Idea This selection is from a book. Remind students that because of its length, a book does not have one main idea. Point out that this selection has two main sections [the life of Scott Joplin and the style of music he helped develop] and that each section has its own main idea.

Reading Strategy
Taking Effective Notes (Strategy 10)

To help students think about what they are reading and respond to it by recording valuable information in note form, use Strategy 10 in Content-Area Reading Strategies. You may ask students to use the Key Points and Details Chart (Graphic Organizer 5) to help them organize their thoughts about the main ideas as they move through the reading process. Tell them that they will have an opportunity to go back over their charts after they finish reading.

DURING READING

Correcting Misconceptions
Many high schools and middle schools in the United States provide practice and lessons in a variety of styles of music, including ragtime. Students may not realize that it took perseverance on the part of early artists and enthusiasts to make ragtime music widely acceptable and that ragtime had a significant impact on the development of jazz. Ask students if they know the names of contemporary musicians who helped popularize ragtime or jazz. Many students will recognize names such as Ella Fitzgerald, Charlie Parker, and Miles Davis.

Using the Side-Margin Feature
▪ Rhythm Relations

Have students in small groups find examples of ragtime and another style of music and make notes for a comparison-contrast chart. The chart can be decorated with images of composers, musicians,

musical instruments, and performers, and displayed for the class. The groups can select examples of the two styles of music and either perform them on instruments or play recordings for the class.

▶ **Teaching Tip**
Taking Effective Notes Point out to students that their notes will be more effective if they ask themselves these questions: Is this point important? Is this detail descriptive and clear? Does this example help me understand the text? Is what this person says important?

Differentiating Instruction
▪ Learners Having Difficulty

Have students work in pairs, each reading to the other a key point from his or her notes and the details that support the point. Then, ask the students to explain how they figured out that the details lead to the key point. Tell students that by explaining, or thinking out loud, they may find that they want to change some details or key points, and that they should do so.

AFTER READING

✔ Reading Check

The following are sample answers to the questions on student text page 177.

1. Even though membership was limited to African Americans, a racially mixed crowd gathered to hear the music.

2. As Joplin played a tune, he would improvise and play each verse differently, using a "ragged" rhythm.

3. Musicians would often stay after the club had closed to play music together and exchange musical ideas.

4. Some people did not like the ragged rhythm of standard pieces, and others were not pleased with the vulgar words of the songs.

5. Joplin liked ragtime music because he felt it captured the charm of the era and because he thought its beauty made it worth composing and playing.

Reteaching

If students are still struggling to determine the main idea, have them form small groups, skim through the selection, and discuss what they think are the main ideas. Then, ask the group to decide the most important idea about Scott Joplin [his composing and playing ragtime music helped make it acceptable] and the most important idea about ragtime music. [it contributed to the development of jazz] As each group presents its findings, record them on the chalkboard and lead a class discussion that settles on two final main ideas.

Connecting to Language Arts

▪ Writing

Music Review Play for students several examples of ragtime music. Then, as a class, have them discuss their reactions to the music as you record these comments on the chalkboard. Ask students to choose one musical selection and write a review, giving background on the style, commenting about the performer(s) and the performance, describing innovations and special sections of the music, and finishing with their own comments. Post the music reviews on a bulletin board, along with photographs of performers and examples of sheet music.

▪ Speaking and Listening

Commentary Have students view a video segment about Scott Joplin and ragtime music or listen to several selections of ragtime music. Then, ask students to discuss in small groups why they think the music and the musician attracted integrated audiences, what the importance of such audiences was to the integration process, and how integration has affected our present appreciation of music. Ask each group to present their findings in a panel discussion, with questions from the audience.

Connecting Across the Curriculum: Social Sciences

Freedom in Music Scott Joplin is introduced in the selection as the son of a former slave. In pairs, have student consult a variety of research resources to learn what they can about the music of pre–Civil War African Americans in the United States. Then, have them use the information to create one of the following.

- a newspaper ad for a live musical performance
- a flier announcing the performance
- an actual staged performance of the music

Further Resources

▪ Book

Jasen, David A. and Gene Jones. *That American Rag: The Story of Ragtime from Coast to Coast.* Schirmer, 2000.

▪ Audio

Dave Tucker, *Tickled Ragtime & Novelties.* Audio CD, 2001.

▪ Video

Scott Joplin. Universal Studios, 2001. Rated PG. Movie tells the life story of the composer.

Assessment

Turn to page 147 for a multiple-choice test on the selection.

Test Answers

1. b	**2.** a	**3.** b	**4.** d	**5.** c
6. b	**7.** a	**8.** b	**9.** a	**10.** b
11. b	**12.** a	**13.** b	**14.** a	**15.** b

from The Railroad Unites America

from *The Iron Horse: How Railroads Changed America*

by RICHARD WORMSER
(student text page 178)

Reading Level: Easy

Special Considerations

The selection includes a description of the scalping of a railroad worker by an American Indian. You may wish to emphasize to students that the conflict between the American Indians and the western expansion of settlers and industry was prolonged and bloody. Remind students that descriptions of attacks by white soldiers on defenseless American Indian families would prove equally gruesome.

Text Summary

The article explores opposing perspectives on the construction of a transcontinental railroad after the Civil War. Emphasis is on both the broken promises and shattered lifestyle suffered by American Indians and the dangers encountered by railroad workers as they crossed through Plains Indians' territory.

BEFORE READING

Make the Connection

Ask students to consider how a new road or means of public transportation might make travel more convenient for members of their community. Then, have students suggest how such a change might be viewed by people whose houses, land, or businesses would be in the path of the new construction.

Build Background

- **More About the Time Period**

In 1854, American Indians signed away part of their territory when the Kansas-Nebraska Act was passed by Congress. Further pressure was brought on the Plains Indians when Congress passed the Homestead Act of 1862, which gave white settlers 160 acres of public land if they lived on it for five years and improved it. In 1887, Congress passed the General Allotment Act, which broke up certain sections of the land set aside for Indian reserva-

tions and allowed the acreage to be sold by individual Indians to white settlers at extremely low prices.

Vocabulary Development

The following words are underscored and defined in the student text.

subdued: defeated; brought under submission.

plundered: robbed, usually as part of an attack.

notorious: well known in a negative way.

massacres: cruel, large-scale killings of people.

retaliation: the return of one harmful act with another.

Before assigning the reading, you may want to introduce students to any words that could cause pronunciation or definition problems.

Vocabulary Tip

Using Prefixes Introduce students to the prefix *trans–*, and write these three meanings on the chalkboard: "on or to the other side of, across;" "to change;" and "above, beyond." Have students brainstorm words for each definition, write them on the chalkboard, and ask for sentences using the words. [transatlantic, transpacific, transcribe, transcultural, transfigure, transform, transliterate, translocation, transmigrate, transpersonal, and so forth]

CONTENT-AREA VOCABULARY

Although the following words are important to an understanding of the text selection, some of them may be unfamiliar to students.

transcontinental: crossing the entire continent.

gigantic: enormous; very large.

ambushed: attacked by surprise.

surveyors: people who measure and determine the boundaries of land areas.

miraculously: happening as if by an act of God.

Because the words are important to understanding the

text selection, you will want to introduce the words to students before they begin reading

Reading Informational Material

Reading Skill
Making Inferences

Explain to students that people's beliefs and attitudes can often be inferred by their actions. From actions described in the selection, students will be able to infer some of the attitudes American Indians and white settlers had toward one another.

Reading Strategy
Anticipating Information (Strategy 9)

To help students build on evidence in the selection, use Strategy 9 described in Content-Area Reading Strategies. A question such as "Do you think it was fair for railroad builders in the late nineteenth century to lay tracks on the American Indians' land?" may help students develop opinions that they can reevaluate after reading the selection. You may want students to use an Anticipation Guide (Graphic Organizer 1).

DURING READING

Correcting Misconceptions

While the title of the selection is "The Railroad Unites America," from the perspective of people of both American Indian and white ancestry, the building of the railroad caused great pain and hardship and created an almost insurmountable division between the two groups of people.

Using the Side-Margin Feature
- The Golden Spike

Certain actions and incidents can be seen as symbolic of a larger situation. Ask students to speculate on the symbolism of the failure of the golden spike to be hammered in the first time. What might this say about the larger claim that the railroad was uniting the country?

Differentiating Instruction
- Advanced Students

Have students write a short play about a meeting between American Indian leaders and U.S. government officials as they try to negotiate a treaty. Be sure to have students portray individuals on both sides of

the conflict who are honest and optimistic, as well as distrustful or aggressive. You may want students to turn their collaborative effort in as a written play script or to perform their drama for the class.

AFTER READING

✔ Reading Check

The following are sample answers to the questions on student text page 182.

1. The Plains Indians did not mind people hunting on or traveling through their land, but they were angered by the greed and dishonesty of railroad companies and saw the railroad as an end to their way of life.

2. Railroad companies argued that American Indians were dangerous and needed to be defeated or totally wiped out.

3. The Indians killed two of the crew and scalped Thompson, who played dead. After the attack he took the scalp to a doctor, hoping it could be sewn back on. When the attempt was unsuccessful, he donated his scalp to an Omaha library, where it was put on exhibit.

4. Colonel George Custer led some of the worst attacks against the American Indians, who struck back by wrecking trains, killing crews, and eventually killing Custer at the Little Big Horn.

5. While the railroad was being built, hunters, soldiers, and railroad passengers slaughtered around twelve million buffalo, which were a major food and clothing source for American Indians.

Reteaching

If students are still having difficulty inferring beliefs and attitudes of people on both sides of the railroad conflict, have them list five specific actions taken by American Indians and five specific actions taken by railroad builders or government officials. Then, have students state for each action which was valued more—progress or maintaining traditional lifestyles. Next, have students evaluate each action and suggest whether keeping promises or promoting one's own needs was considered more important. Then, ask whether peace or resistance was valued more. Finally, rephrase the question, and ask students to name three or four values that they infer American Indians held highest, and three or four values white settlers felt were most important.

Connecting to the Language Arts

■ Writing

Diaries Discovered Have students make at least five diary entries for one of the following characters who lived during the transcontinental railroad era: an American Indian teenager, an immigrant from Ireland, a railroad engineer, a member of Congress, an American Indian chief, a tourist riding on the train, a train crew member, or a family member of any of these people. Ask students to vary the amount of time—days weeks, months—so that the character's response to change is shown. Students may wish to collect their writing in a binder or post some of their work on a bulletin board.

■ Speaking and Listening

Final Speeches Have students locate public speeches made by American Indians during and after the period of the transcontinental railroad construction. Ask student volunteers to read selections from these speeches to the class. Ask students to identify sentiments expressed in the speeches that are similar to quotations found in the selection.

Connecting Across the Curriculum: Socia Studies

Reservations Today Select various regions of the United States, and have students look for information about American Indian reservations in these regions today. Ask students to note information about land quality, means of achieving self-sufficiency, standard of living, and political spokespersons for people living on the reservations. Students may be able to locate on the Internet information about recent legislation affecting American Indian life. Ask students to present the information in the form of a poster or map.

Further Resources

■ Books

Durbin, William. *The Journal of Sean Sullivan: A Transcontinental Railroad Worker (My Name is America)*. Scholastic Trade, 1999.

Fraser, Mary Ann. *Ten Mile Day: And the Building of the Transcontinental Railroad*. Henry Holt, 1996. Story of the record set on ten miles of track of the transcontinental railroad as the result of a bet.

U.S. maps of various kinds from different time periods.

Pamphlets or brochures from states with a significant Native American population.

Assessment

Turn to page 148 for a multiple-choice test on the selection.

Test Answers

1. c **2.** b **3.** a **4.** b **5.** c

6. c **7.** d **8.** d **9.** c **10.** c

Rubrics for *Cross-Curricular Activities*

The following criteria can help you evaluate each student's success in completing the activities prompted by the Cross-Curricular Activities feature in the student textbook.

History/Mathematics
Off to Work We Go

- The student conducts a poll to determine whether a group of twenty-five to fifty fellow students agree that it should be illegal for students to work full time.
- The student writes questions for the poll that are related to the topic and require only brief answers.
- The student creates a visual that clearly, accurately, and neatly represents the results of the poll.

Language Arts/History
Full Steam Ahead?

- The student conducts research to learn about the culture of one of the Plains peoples of the Southwest during the time of the Indian Wars.
- The student writes a human-interest story for a newspaper of the time that describes how the building of the transcontinental railroad would affect the Indians' way of life.
- The student's article reflects his or her research and includes adequate supporting details.
- The newspaper page that the student designs demonstrates imagination and creativity.
- The student's article is relatively free of errors in spelling, grammar, usage, and mechanics.

Science
My Significant Five

- The student conducts research to find out about the inventions and inventors of the Industrial Age.
- The student chooses the five most important inventions of the period and writes a report in which he or she describes the invention, its inventor, and its effect on American society.
- The student presents his or her findings to the class in an oral presentation.
- The student's presentation is clear and well organized.
- The student's presentation is relatively free of performance errors.

Science
A Storm Is Born

- The student writes a report describing either a recent tornado or hurricane or the ways in which the tragedy of the Galveston hurricane could have been minimized using modern storm-tracking equipment.
- The report includes two or three written paragraphs and one or more maps or diagrams.
- The report is clear and well organized.
- The report is relatively free of errors in spelling, grammar, usage, and mechanics.

CHAPTER 6

American Issues
The United States from 1914 to the Present

A Gentleman's Agreement

from *Shadow Ball: The History of the Negro Leagues*

by GEOFFREY C. WARD AND KEN BURNS, WITH JIM O'CONNOR
(student text page 187)

CONTENT-AREA CONNECTIONS

PHYSICAL EDUCATION •

HISTORY •

Reading Level: Average

Special Considerations

Nearly one hundred years after the 1919 Chicago riot described in the selection, race riots are still not a thing of the past. Some students may find the racial attitudes and segregationist policies in this selection disturbing.

Text Summary

An excerpt from a nonfiction book about the history of the Negro baseball leagues, this selection focuses on the determined efforts of Rube Foster to build an African American baseball league at a time when African Americans were barred from playing on professional teams.

BEFORE READING

Make the Connection

Ask students to name their favorite sports stars, and write the names on the chalkboard. Then, circle the name of every African American mentioned by students, and ask them to imagine that none of the circled players are allowed to play. How would such a ban change sports? How would people react? [Students may say that almost every sport, from golf to football, would be strongly affected. People would be angry and outraged.] Remind students that at one time in the United States, African Americans were not allowed to play professional sports.

Build Background

▪ More About the Topic

Prominent African American athletes include Jackie Robinson, who in 1947 became the first African American to play major league baseball; Jesse Owens, who won four gold medals in track and field at the 1936 Olympics in Germany (an event the German leader Adolf Hitler had hoped would showcase his "master race"); and Muhammad Ali, a heavyweight boxing champion of the 1960s and '70s known for his hard hitting and quick wit.

Vocabulary Development

The following words are underscored and defined in the student text.

confirmed: proved that something was true.
aggressive: active; forceful.
baffled: confused.
enraged: angered.
prevailed: triumphed.

Before assigning the reading, you may want to introduce students to any words that could cause pronunciation or definition problems.

Using Context Clues Tell students that one way to discover the meaning of an unfamiliar word is to see if the word's meaning is restated or explained in the surrounding text. In the case of the word *confirmed* in the first paragraph, the meaning can be determined from the statement that the "worst fears" were proved true. Remind students that this process of looking for clues to meaning in the surrounding words and sentences is called using context clues.

CONTENT-AREA VOCABULARY

Although the following words are important to an understanding of the text selection, some of them may be unfamiliar to students.

racism: discrimination against a particular group of people on the basis of race alone.

assert: stand up for (oneself).

concrete*: real; able to be seen.

crafty*: clever.

belted*: hit very hard.

strategy*: plan of action.

change-up*: a pitch thrown at a slower speed.

braved: faced with fearless determination.

*Although students may be familiar with other meanings of these words, the words as used in the selection have a specific meaning that pertains to the content area.

Reading Informational Material

Reading Skill
Finding the Main Idea

Explain to students that the main idea is the central opinion, insight, or message being developed in a text.

▶ **Teaching Tip**
Using Text-Structure Clues Remind students that the selection is an excerpt from a longer work—a section with its own subheading given at the beginning of the piece. Keeping the subheading in mind and paying attention to the pull-out quotation on page 189 will help students focus on the main idea of the selection.

Reading Strategy
Previewing Text (Strategy 1)

To help students maintain their reading focus and increase their comprehension, use Strategy 1 described in Content-Area Reading Strategies. Provide students with a KWLS Chart (Graphic Organizer 7) to help them list what they know and what they would like to know before reading the selection. Tell students that they will be filling out the remainder of the chart as they read and after they finish reading the selection.

DURING READING

Using the Side-Margin Feature
- Baseball Roundup

You can use the side-margin feature on the origins of baseball to interest students in researching their own favorite games. Ask students to share their findings with the class in an informal report.

Differentiating Instruction
- Learners Having Difficulty

Some students may have difficulty keeping straight the dates, names of the various leagues, and so on as they read. Have students create a two-column chart on their own paper and write in the left-hand column the years 1919, 1920, 1922, 1923, 1924, 1926, and 1930. Direct students to look for the dates as they read and record the significant events that happened in these years in the right-hand column of the chart.

AFTER READING

✔ Reading Check

The following are sample answers to the questions on student text page 191.

1. One positive result of the 1919 race riots was that African Americans began to assert themselves.

2. Rube Foster organized the Negro National League to ensure African American ownership of the league and to help African American players make as much money as their white counterparts.

3. Baseball in the Negro National League was faster and more aggressive than in the white leagues.

4. A group of white businessmen started the Eastern Colored League. They were interested in making a profit from African American baseball.

5. Rube Foster suffered a nervous breakdown in 1926 and was confined to a mental hospital.

Reteaching

If students still have difficulty determining the main idea of the article, pair students and have them work together to complete a Cloze Concept Map (see Strategy 4). You will need to fill in some of the key words and phrases for students. After students have completed the map, discuss with students the main idea of the selection.

Connecting to Language Arts

▪ Writing

Business Plan Put yourself in Rube Foster's place and write a letter inviting investors to join him in forming the Negro National League. Tell students that their letters should include at least two main points explaining why the league would be a good idea, supported by facts and details. Their letters should also end with a persuasive call to action. Have volunteers read their letters to the class.

▪ Speaking and Listening

Poetry Slam Ask students to write a poem about their favorite sports star, concentrating on the sensory details—how it probably feels to perform, how it looks to a bystander, and the sounds and smells that accompany the action. Students can read their poems to the class and then post them on a Poetry Slam bulletin board, along with illustrations of the sport and the star.

Connecting Across the Curriculum: Social Studies

Breaking Barriers Have students research an African American who broke the color barrier in a field other than sports—art, music, dance, science, politics, or civil rights. You can incorporate students' reports into a class Black History Day scrapbook.

Further Resources

▪ Video

Baseball: A Film by Ken Burns. 1994. Not rated. The section on Jackie Robinson is informative.

▪ Online Resource

The Negro Leagues Baseball Museum in Kansas City, Missouri, has a Web site with more information.

Assessment

Turn to page 149 for a multiple-choice test on the selection.

Test Answers

1. d **2.** b **3.** d **4.** a **5.** b
6. a **7.** c **8.** a **9.** b **10.** a

from "You're Under Arrest"

from *Rosa Parks: My Story*

by ROSA PARKS WITH JIM HASKINS
(student text page 192)

Reading Level: Easy

Text Summary

An excerpt from the autobiography of Rosa Parks, the selection focuses on Parks's fateful decision to remain in her bus seat although the law required her to make room for a white passenger. Parks's action contributed significantly to the beginning of the civil rights movement in the United States.

BEFORE READING

Make the Connection

Write the word *segregation* on the chalkboard and ask students to tell what the word means and what role it played in American history. [Segregation is separation by race, and it was the law in many parts of the United States for approximately a century after the Civil War.] Discuss with students what areas might have been segregated. [schools, buses, trains, parks, churches, and public facilities] Ask students for their opinions on such a system.

Build Background

■ More About the Topic

Rosa Parks was only one of a number of brave civil rights leaders in the fight against racial discrimination in the United States. Probably the most famous was Martin Luther King, Jr., who championed nonviolent ways of making people aware of the injustice of segregation. King helped organize the march of hundreds of thousands of protesters on Washington, D.C., in 1963. It was here that he made his famous "I Have a Dream" speech. In 1964, King was awarded the Nobel Peace Prize. In the same year, the Civil Rights Act passed by Congress made the practice of segregation illegal.

Vocabulary Development

The following words are underscored and defined in the student text.

vacant: empty.
complied: did as ordered.
segregation: separation of people into different groups or locations according to race.
resurgence: return.
violations: actions that break or ignore laws.

Before assigning the reading, you may want to introduce students to any words that could cause pronunciation or definition problems.

Vocabulary Tip

Using Prefixes Point out to students that the prefix *se–* in the word *segregate* is the same as in *secede*, which means to separate. That is what the southern states did when they tried to break from the Union before the Civil War. The root of *segregate* comes from the Latin for "herd." If *segregate* literally means "to separate from the herd," can students use that knowledge to guess the meaning of a word with the same root, *gregarious*? [sociable, or "herdlike"] Have students also explore the meaning of the prefix *re–* ["go back to former condition," "again," "become like new"] and list words that use this prefix [see dictionary for extensive list of these words].

CONTENT-AREA VOCABULARY

Although the following words are important to an understanding of the text selection, some of them may be unfamiliar to students.

boarded*: got on a vehicle.
marshals: law-enforcement officials.
manhandled: wrestled; shaken about.
apprehensive: fearful.

*Although students may be familiar with other meanings of this word, the word as used in the selection has a specific meaning that pertains to the content area.

Reading Informational Material

Reading Skill

Identifying Text Structure: Cause and Effect

Tell students that a cause makes something happen and that an effect is what happens as a result of that cause.

▶ **Teaching Tip**

Text Organization Alert students to the fact that the text uses not only cause-effect organization but also comparison and contrast. For example, Rosa Parks describes the ways in which the United States has progressed and the ways in which it has remained the same. In addition, in recounting the events of the fateful day, Parks narrates the events in chronological order. Students may find themselves on the lookout for two or three separate sets of transition words and using two or three different graphic organizers to take notes.

Reading Strategy

Understanding Text (Strategy 2)

To help students identify causes and effects in the selection, use Strategy 2 described in Content-Area Reading Strategies. Have students use a Cause-and-Effect Chart, a Venn Diagram, and a Sequence or Chronological Order Chart (Graphic Organizers 2, 11, and 10). Have students write the transition words between events on the sequence chart.

DURING READING

▪ Using the Side-Margin Feature

Other Bridges to Cross Use the feature on six-year-old Ruby Bridges to pique student curiosity about lesser-known heroes of the civil rights movement in the United States. Students can research a figure and draw portraits or action scenes of their heroes, with captions listing the people's accomplishments. Display students' work on a classroom Wall of Fame.

Differentiating Instruction

▪ Learners Having Difficulty

If students are getting bogged down in the details of the selection, have them work in pairs to take notes on the text as they read. Students should construct a two-column chart, labeling the left-hand column

Key Ideas and the right-hand column *Details*. Have students read through the selection together, pausing at each paragragh to note its main idea and record supporting facts or examples in the corresponding column.

AFTER READING

✔ Reading Check

The following are sample answers to the questions on student text page 197.

1. Rosa recognized the driver as the same one who had removed her from a bus twelve years earlier.

2. Rosa Parks did not move from her seat because she was tired of giving in to injustice.

3. Accept any three: People can register to vote without being intimidated; there are no declared segregated areas; African Americans have achieved high positions in public office and politics; laws against segregation have been passed.

4. Accept any two: Many white people are still prejudiced against African Americans; the Supreme Court has made it harder to prove discrimination in employment; the national government does not seem interested in pursuing civil-rights violations; white supremacy is an idea that still attracts supporters; and there are more incidents of racial violence on college campuses.

5. According to Parks, the best way to overcome hatred and racism is through love and brotherhood.

Reteaching

If students still have difficulty understanding the cause-and-effect structure in the text, make copies of the excerpt and allow students working in groups to color-code the three types of signal words on their copies. Then, each student in the group should choose a structure (cause-effect, comparison-andcontrast, or sequence) and tell how the text fits that structure. Have a class discussion in which students can share their findings.

Connecting to Language Arts

■ Writing

Proclamation Do students know of another civil-rights hero or some leader of their own acquaintance who deserves a day in his or her honor? If students are not aware of such leaders, give them specific suggestions, such as Julian Bond, John Lewis, or James Farmer, to research. Have students write an official proclamation of such a day, listing the reasons for the person's recognition. Students may also want to present their proclamations as speeches to the class.

■ Speaking and Listening

Speech Have students research Martin Luther King, Jr.'s famous "I Have a Dream" speech and write speeches that reflect their own dreams of a future without racial discrimination or hatred. How can such a world be realized? Ask volunteers to present their speeches to the class.

Connecting Across the Curriculum:
World History

Heroes Around the World Have students research the achievements of champions for civil rights around the world, such as Nelson Mandela in South Africa or Mahatma Gandhi in India. Students could also research from recent decades another important event in the struggle for human rights, such as the collapse of the Berlin Wall or the protests in China's Tiananmen Square. Students can present their reports to the class in the form of news stories.

Further Resources

■ Videos

Martin Luther King, Jr.: I Have a Dream. MPI Home Video, 1986. Not rated.
Small Steps, Big Strides: The Black Experience in 1997. Twentieth Century Fox, 1997. Not rated.
Buffalo Soldiers: the True Story of Our Country's First Black Heroes. Simitar Video, 1997. Not rated.

Assessment

Turn to page 150 for a multiple-choice test on the selection.

Test Answers
1. c **2.** d **3.** c **4.** b **5.** a
6. a **7.** c **8.** b **9.** d **10.** a

The New Immigrants

from *Junior Scholastic*

by NAOMI MARCUS
(student text page 198)

Reading Level: Easy

Special Considerations

The immigrants' stories may prompt discussion of students' own experiences as newcomers to the United States, or it may spark remarks about the immigrants' expectations or manners of expression. Alert students, whatever their remarks, to be especially considerate of experiences, cultures, and opinions that are different from their own.

Text Summary

The selection is a magazine article that discusses today's immigrants to the United States. By allowing these new young citizens to describe their experiences in their own words, the article offers insight into the changing face of American society.

BEFORE READING

Make the Connection

Draw a rough map of the world on the chalkboard, or display at the front of the room a map with bright-colored pins in it. Ask students if any of them have knowledge of the original homes of their ancestors. If so, from what lands did students' families come? Mark the places on the map, and discuss with students the diversity of the places marked. What problems can such diversity present? What benefits? [Students may say that such diversity might cause clashes in culture and communication, but that a society with such a broad foundation is bound to be a strong and vital one.]

Build Background

■ More About the Topic

The Statue of Liberty From 1892 to 1943, Ellis Island in New York City's harbor was the chief immigration station for the country, and the statue there, a gift from France in the nineteenth century, greeted millions of newcomers. The following lines from American poet Emma Lazarus's "The New Colossus" are inscribed upon its base.

Give me your tired, your poor,
Your huddled masses yearning to breathe free,
The wretched refuse of your teeming shore,
Send these, the homeless, tempest-tossed, to me:
I lift my lamp beside the golden door.

Vocabulary Development

The following words are underscored and defined in the student book.

customs: traditions and practices of a group of people.

residents: people who live in a place.

profile: overview or general picture of a person, group of people, or thing.

flee: escape.

stability: the state of being steady or unlikely to change.

Before assigning the reading, you may want to introduce students to any words that could cause pronunciation or definition problems.

┌─ *Vocabulary Tip* ─────────────

Using Roots Students may be interested to learn that the root of the word *profile*, like that of the word *file*, comes from the Latin word for "thread." The root word got its present connotations from the French, in which *file* used to mean, literally, "to attach important papers to a string or wire." Ask students how a profile is like a string of important papers. [For example: A profile is a collection of detailed views of someone.]

└────────────────────────────────

(CONTENT-AREA VOCABULARY)

Although the following words are important to an understanding of the text selection, some of them may be unfamiliar to students.

native: original; ancestral.
Muslim: a follower of the Islamic religion.
Hindi: the chief language in India.

Arabic: relating to the region that includes the Middle East and part of northeast Africa.

documents*: official identity papers.

*Although students may be familiar with other meanings of this word, the word as used in the selection has a specific meaning that pertains to the content area.

Reading Informational Material

Reading Skill
Forming Opinions
Tell students to be alert to forming opinions as they read through this series of interviews. Forming opinions will engage them in the text and give them a purpose for reading.

▶ Teaching Tip
If You Want My Opinion . . . Students may have difficulty keeping separate the opinions and experiences shared by the young people interviewed in the selection. One approach is to focus not only on the similarities between the interviewees, but also the differences. Tell students to ask themselves of each interview section: *What is it about this person's experiences that sets him or her apart from the others?* Provide students with Venn Diagrams (Graphic Organizer 11).

Reading Strategy
Anticipating Information (Strategy 9)
To help students maintain their focus and purpose while reading, use Strategy 9 in Content-Area Reading Strategies. Provide students with an Anticipation Guide (Graphic Organizer 1) in which they can comment on statements before and after reading the text. Students can meet in small groups to share their opinions and explanations.

DURING READING

Differentiating Instruction
■ Learners Having Difficulty
Students may find it easier to form opinions if they pay close attention to the conclusions drawn by the writer in the first part of the selection. Tell students to focus especially on the two paragraphs before the first of the immigrants' statements. Do students find support for the writer's statements in the comments made by the immigrants themselves? Allow students to meet in small groups to search for supporting or contradictory evidence.

AFTER READING

✔ Reading Check
The following are sample answers to the questions on student text page 202.

1. Accept any two: Today's immigrants are mostly from Asia and Latin America, rather than Europe; they are more likely to be fairly well-educated; they are usually more prosperous; they maintain closer ties to their homelands.

2. Many immigrants come to the U.S. to flee from war, to make better lives for their children, and to find stability.

3. One example is Judith Paredes's mother who worked two jobs and was separated from her children for five years before she could afford to bring them into the country.

4. Judith Paredes expected life to be much easier in America, but she has had trouble communicating with others and misses many of the customs of her homeland.

Reteaching
If students still have difficulty forming opinions on the subject covered by the selection, provide them with statements of your own before students re-read the article. Give students a statement that might fit in with their own notions, but which is contradicted by the reading. For example, "Immigrants to the United States are usually so happy to be in such a great country they never think of their old homes again," or "Immigrants to the United States must quickly adapt to new ways and leave their old customs behind."

Connecting to Language Arts
■ Writing
Anecdote Have any of your students experienced hardships adapting to a new life in the United States? Do they know anyone who has? Have students write an anecdote, or a brief story, of their own or someone else's experience—one that illustrates a specific difficulty. If students use someone

else's experience, make sure they have the other person's permission and that they report the experience accurately—if possible, in that person's own words.

Connecting Across the Curriculum: Social Studies

Important New Person Have students research the life of a prominent immigrant to the United States and present his or her experiences and accomplishments in a biographical sketch or a monologue. Students should focus on only two or three events in the person's life and tell what the person thought of his or her new home. Did coming to the United States help the person accomplish what he or she is famous for doing or make it difficult?

Further Resources

▪ Video

U.S. Immigrants: A Multicultural Journey. TMW/Media Group, 1998. Not rated.

Assessment

Turn to page 151 for a multiple-choice test on the selection.

Test Answers

1. a   **2.** d   **3.** a   **4.** b   **5.** c
6. a   **7.** b   **8.** d   **9.** c   **10.** c

from A Girl Among the Whales

from *Storyworks*

by EVE NILSON
(student text page 203)

Reading Level: Average

Text Summary

In an original composition, a young girl describes her experiences with whales in Alaska and gives a rare glimpse of their natural habitat.

BEFORE READING

Make the Connection

Have students share their most memorable experiences of nature, whether from city parks, beaches, or hikes in remote wildernesses. What is the most unusual or striking thing students have seen in nature?

Build Background

■ Motivate

Whales and their songs have been the subject of nature documentaries shown on television. If possible, play for the class a videotape of part or all of one such program. First, make students curious about the topic by turning off the classroom lights and playing a recording of a whale's song. Don't tell students what it is beforehand. Let the eerie sounds spark the students' imaginations.

Vocabulary Development

The following words are underscored and defined in the student text.

marine: having to do with the sea or the ocean.
cooperative: working together toward a common goal.
technique: a method of doing something.
condensed: reduced in volume by evaporation of water content.
breached: broke through the surface.

Before assigning the reading, you may want to introduce students to any words that could cause pronunciation or definition problems.

┌─ *Vocabulary Tip* ─────────────────┐

Using Roots The Greek root of the word *technique, technē,* is present in many useful terms. It means "art" or "craft" and is often used to indicate the skillful way pieces are put together. Can students think of another word that indicates skill from the Greek root in putting pieces together and has the root *technē?* [technology, technical]

└────────────────────────────────────┘

(**CONTENT-AREA VOCABULARY**)

Although the following words are important to an understanding of the text selection, some of them may be unfamiliar to students.

passage*: a sea route between land masses.
arcs: curving lines.
glaciers: great masses of ice that slowly move down from mountains, often carving valleys in the process.
startle: frighten.
cherish: value highly.

*Although students may be familiar with other meanings of this word, the word as used in the selection has a specific meaning that pertains to the content area.

(**Reading Informational Material**)

Reading Skill
Adjusting Reading Rate

Tell students that their reading rate is the speed with which they read a particular text. Alert students that they may need to slow down their rate of reading in dense passages of description or technical details to avoid skipping over details.

Reading Strategy
Visualizing Information (Strategy 5)

To help students fully comprehend the text, use Strategy 5 described in Content-Area Reading Strategies. Have students choose a descriptive piece in the text and draw a picture of the action or scene described. Students may also organize the information using a Cluster Diagram (Graphic Organizer 3), filling in as many levels as they need and adding circles when appropriate. After students finish reading, ask for volunteers to share their sketches or concept maps with the class.

DURING READING

Differentiating Instruction
- Learners Having Difficulty

Students may benefit from more visuals than are given with the selection. Bring to class videos, books, or magazine articles on whales. Allow students time to view and discuss the images in the materials. Students can use these samples as models when making their own visuals.

AFTER READING

 **Reading Check**

The following are sample answers to the questions on student text page 206.

1. The author's mother is a marine biologist who studies humpback whales in Alaska each summer.

2. The whales swim to Alaska to eat enough food to live on for the rest of the year.

3. The author hopes her essay will inspire readers to visit the wilderness areas of Alaska and to help protect these areas and their creatures.

4. Once, a whale calf playing close to the author's boat allowed the author to touch its fin. The author stared into one of the calf's eyes and felt that it trusted her.

5. Dinoflagellates are tiny marine creatures that light up when touched.

Reteaching

If students still have difficulty visualizing the selection's information, such as the migration of the humpback whales or their method of cooperative feeding, pair these students with students who are having trouble with other parts of the text.

Students can use diagrams, drawings, or gestures to explain the sections they understand to their partners. Have students share particularly helpful explanations with the class.

Connecting to Language Arts
- Writing

Sketchbook Have students choose a natural setting and sit quietly, observing for a time. What interesting things do they see? Ask students to write a brief description of their observations, using as many sensory details as possible except taste. If they want, students can include drawings with their descriptions. Ask for volunteers to share their observations with the class.

Connecting Across the Curriculum: Science

My Favorite Animal . . . Have students research the behavior of an animal they find interesting—one they have seen or one they would like to see someday. Students can write their own informative articles on their animals, including at least one appropriate photograph or drawing.

Further Resources
- Videos

Alaska's Whales and Wildlife. NTSC format, 1990. Not rated.

IMAX—Whales: An Unforgettable Journey. E-Realbiz.Com, 1988. Not rated.

Real Animals: A Day With Whales. Warner Studios, 1995. Not rated.

Assessment

Turn to page 152 for a multiple-choice test on the selection.

Test Answers

1. c **2.** c **3.** a **4.** d **5.** b
6. d **7.** a **8.** c **9.** a **10.** b

Is Anyone Else Out There?

from *The Planet Hunters: The Search for Other Worlds*
by DENNIS BRINDELL FRADIN
(student text page 207)

Reading Level: Average

Text Summary

The selection is an excerpt from a nonfiction book that discusses the possibility of intelligent life outside Earth's solar system. The excerpt examines how we might make contact with extraterrestrial beings and how such contact might change the course of human history.

BEFORE READING

Make the Connection

Students will probably have seen TV programs or movies on the subject of human contact with extraterrestrial life. Ask students to describe these programs and movies and to give their own opinions on how such contact might happen and what it would mean for humans. Encourage students to give reasons to support their opinions. Write students' opinions on the chalkboard so they can see if their views change after they have read the selection.

Build Background

- More About the Topic

In 1961, scientist Frank Drake of Cornell University devised the following formula for determining the probable number of civilizations in the galaxy capable of communicating with other civilizations: $N = R^* f_p n_e f_l f_i f_c L$. The symbols stand for the number of new stars formed in the galaxy each year (R^*); the fraction of stars that have planets (f_p); the average number of planets in such systems that can support life (n_e); the fraction of planets on which life occurs (f_l); the fraction of planets on which intelligent life occurs (f_i); the fraction of planets on which intelligent beings learn how to communicate with other civilizations (f_c); and, finally, the average lifetime of such a civilization (L). Multiply together all of these estimates to find the number. Needless to say, the formula gives a wide range of possible answers.

Vocabulary Development

The following words are underscored and defined in the student text.

temporarily: for a limited period of time.
skeptical: doubtful.
emitted: sent out; transmitted.
simultaneously: happening at the same time.
intercept: to stop or catch on the way from one place to another.

Before assigning the reading, you may want to introduce students to any words that could cause pronunciation or definition problems.

Vocabulary Tip

Using Context Clues Point out to students that often the meaning of an unfamiliar word can be determined from the word's context. Sometimes the meaning of the word is restated within the same sentence. Such is the case with the term *abducted* on the second page of the selection, after which is given the restatement "or temporarily kidnapped."

CONTENT-AREA VOCABULARY

Although the following words are important to an understanding of the text selection, some of them may be unfamiliar to students.

atmospheres: the combinations of gases that surround planets.
remote*: distant.
cosmic: relating to the cosmos, or universe.
observatory: a building designed to hold telescopes for observing the stars.
"wanderers"*: the literal meaning of the word *planets*, from their movement across the sky.

*Although students may be familiar with other meanings of these words, the words as used in the selection have a specific meaning that pertains to the content area.

Reading Informational Material

Reading Skill
Using Problem and Solution

Tell students that the selection focuses on a question that could also be termed a problem: *Is there intelligent life elsewhere in the universe, and if so, how can humans come into contact with these beings?* Students should pay attention both to the solutions the author proposes for this problem and to the effects the author suggests will come from the solutions.

▶ **Teaching Tip**

Using Contextual Clues Point out to students that since the selection is an excerpt from a longer work, some of the terms at the beginning, such as "Planet Finder," may be unfamiliar. The first paragraph may also seem like an abrupt introduction. Tell students to be patient as they begin to read the text and to be alert to the context to explain meanings (as the phrase "or another instrument" explains "Planet Finder").

Reading Strategy
Using Graphic Organizers (Strategy 3)

To help students follow and comprehend the main idea in the text, use Strategy 3 in the Content-Area Teaching Strategies. Have students use the Problem and Solution Chart (Graphic Organizer 9) or a similar organizer of their own devising.

DURING READING

Differentiating Instruction
■ Learners Having Difficulty

Students may benefit from making sketches from the text as well as using diagrams and other graphic organizers. Students having difficulty understanding the text can also work with a partner or small group to read the selection collaboratively. Partners or group members can stop reading after each paragraph to discuss its meaning.

AFTER READING

✔ Reading Check

The following are sample answers to the questions on student text page 212.

1. The simplest way to contact intelligent life on other planets is to exchange radio signals with them.

2. SETI stands for "Search for Extraterrestrial Intelligence."

3. There are millions of places in the sky from which signals may originate, and each place could take thousands of years to study.

4. Extraterrestrials might help humans end world hunger, cure cancer, and clean up pollution; they might teach us how to avoid war; they might teach us how to travel to the stars.

5. The vastness of space is one obstacle to interstellar travel; another obstacle is the lack of knowledge about where to go.

Reteaching

If students still have difficulty following the problem-solution and cause-effect structures of the selection, give students plastic overlays to put over the text page and draw arrows to show the relationships between the paragraphs. Students should then write on the overlay appropriate labels such as "First Possible Way to Communicate with Extraterrestrials" and "Effects of Contact."

Connecting to Language Arts
■ Writing

Ship's Log Have students imagine they are the captain of the spaceship that makes the first human contact with extraterrestrial life. Ask students what they would say to the alien beings. How would such contact come about? Students should address their reports to their superiors and peers— and, of course, to the historians who will study their words for centuries to come. Students should also include sensory details.

Greetings Astronomers have already sent an audio message into space with greetings in many Earth languages. Have students imagine that scientists are preparing a videotaped broadcast to send to a newly detected planet that may host intelligent life, and students are in charge of writing the message. What would they say to the alien beings? Have students deliver their messages to the class. Direct students to keep their messages brief and to the point.

Connecting Across the Curriculum: Social Studies

Take Me to Your Leader Point out to students that one way humans can prepare for possible contact with extraterrestrial life is to study past meetings between unfamiliar groups of humans. [Columbus, or another European explorer, and American Indians; colonists and American Indians] Have students choose a documented meeting between two such groups and conduct research to find both problems and solutions. What can we learn from the meeting? What can we be sure to do or not to do when speaking for the first time to intelligent beings from outside our solar system? Ask volunteers to present their findings and their results to the class.

Further Resources
▪ Videos

Phantom Quest: The Search for Extraterrestrials. National Geographic, 1999. Not rated.
Understanding Extraterrestrials. Discovery Home Video, 2000. Not rated.

Assessment

Turn to page 153 for a multiple-choice test on the selection.

Test Answers
1. d **2.** a **3.** b **4.** b **5.** d
6. b **7.** c **8.** c **9.** c **10.** c

The following criteria can help you evaluate each student's success in completing the activities prompted by the Cross-Curricular Activities feature in the student textbook.

*Note: Activities marked with an asterisk allow the involvement of more than one student. For these activities you may wish first to evaluate each student on his or her individual contribution and then give groups an overall rating.

Language Arts/Drama
Face to Face

- The student conducts research to find out how a current civil rights leader has helped improve the lives of African Americans.
- The student writes a script in which the leader and Rosa Parks discuss issues in today's society and explain their own contributions.
- The dialogue reflects the student's research and is accurate and believable.
- The student performs the dialogue for the class with a partner, effectively conveying the personalities and achievements of both characters.
- The student's performance is well prepared and relatively free of performance errors.

Language Arts
Listen and Learn

- The student writes a list of eight to ten questions in preparation for interviewing an immigrant to the United States or a student new to the school.
- The questions are designed to elicit meaningful responses (rather than *yes* or *no*) and cover both good and bad aspects of the new experience.
- The student conducts the interview.
- The student neatly transcribes the interview on paper and sends a copy to the interviewee.
- The student includes a note to the interviewee explaining what he or she learned from and enjoyed most about the interview.

Science
Critters Aren't Quitters

- The student conducts research about an endangered species in his or her region.
- The student creates a public-service brochure that presents the plight of the species, including facts, statistics, tips to help save the species, illustrations, and resource books.
- The student's brochure reflects his or her research and displays imagination and creativity.

Visual Arts
Facts on Film

- The student writes a proposal for a documentary based on one of the selections in *The United States: Change and Challenge.*
- The proposal summarizes what the documentary should be about and reflects an understanding of the selection.
- The student sketches important scenes that would be included in the documentary.
- The student's choice of scenes demonstrates imagination and creativity.

*Art
On the Wall

- The student creates a design for a mural illustrating important social movements of the twentieth century.
- The mural reflects the student's research of the various social movements and is arranged in a logical order.
- The student's work demonstrates neatness and creativity.

Selection Test

Droughts Played Major Role in Jamestown, "Lost Colony" Tragedies
from *William and Mary News*
by PEGGY SHAW

COMPREHENSION QUESTIONS

Circle the letter of the best answer to each of the following items. *(50 points)*

1. Researchers from the College of William and Mary worked with researchers from
   a. the University of Virginia
   b. the College of Roanoke
   c. the University of Arkansas
   d. the University of North Carolina

2. The period of disease and death endured by the early Jamestown settlers was known as the
   a. "starving time"   c. "drought"
   b. "bad time"   d. "dying time"

3. The Roanoke settlers' disappearance
   a. was expected
   b. is unexplained
   c. was temporary
   d. was linked to an epidemic

4. How many settlers of Jamestown died between 1607 and 1625?
   a. 4,800 out of 6,000   c. 550 of 10,000
   b. 38 of 104   d. 280 of 500

5. The dates of the Jamestown droughts match perfectly with
   a. the colonists' requests for the king's help
   b. four documented witch trials
   c. settlers' attempts to relocate their colony
   d. the dates of two Anglo-Indian wars

VOCABULARY

Using your knowledge of the underlined word, circle the letter of the word or phrase that best completes each statement. *(50 points)*

6. A person implicated in a crime could expect to
   a. be cleared of all wrongdoing
   b. sue for damages against the person responsible for the crime
   c. win the case for the prosecution
   d. be questioned and possibly charged with the crime

7. If a message is enigmatic, that means it is
   a. mysterious and puzzling
   b. clear and concise
   c. wordy but well written
   d. grammatically incorrect

8. If you are interested in archaeology, you are probably fascinated by
   a. modern construction techniques
   b. poems written in classical languages
   c. the aerodynamics of flying
   d. ancient human cultures

9. A person farming for his or her subsistence is doing so in order to
   a. enjoy a favorite hobby
   b. write a report for a magazine or newspaper
   c. live
   d. learn more about farming

10. A city that has been decimated has been
    a. destroyed or washed away
    b. rebuilt after a fire
    c. modeled after a famous city
    d. occupied by an invading army

Selection Test

from "The Time of Most Distress"
from *William Bradford: Rock of Plymouth*
by KIERAN DOHERTY

COMPREHENSION QUESTIONS

Circle the letter of the best answer to each of the following items. *(50 points)*

1. All of the following features were characteristic of the land the Pilgrims chose as the site of their settlement **except**
   a. a river bend that was a natural barrier to Indian attack
   b. a convenient freshwater supply
   c. land ready for planting
   d. a small hill to be used for defense

2. Each person got land measuring
   a. 100 square feet
   b. 40 acres
   c. 8 feet by 50 feet
   d. 1 acre

3. Once ashore in New England, the Pilgrims were forced to change their diet to
   a. all fruits and vegetables
   b. beef, wheat bread, and beer
   c. nuts and wild berries
   d. shellfish and game birds

4. By the summer of 1621, what percentage of the original Pilgrim settlers had died?
   a. 99 percent
   b. 10 percent
   c. 35 percent
   d. almost 50 percent

5. At what age were children in the seventeenth century considered "little adults"?
   a. sixteen or seventeen
   b. twelve or thirteen
   c. nine or ten
   d. six or seven

VOCABULARY

Using your knowledge of the underlined word, circle the letter of the word or phrase that best completes each statement. *(50 points)*

6. An <u>enduring</u> legend is one
   a. in which the hero overcomes obstacles
   b. that is told and retold over many years
   c. that takes a long time to tell
   d. in which good conquers evil

7. <u>Allocating</u> money is a way to
   a. save in case of a sudden emergency
   b. assign a value to it
   c. set aside funds for a certain purpose
   d. stabilize its rate of exchange

8. Which of the following would be a <u>scourge</u> to a young settlement?
   a. plentiful water
   b. surplus grain
   c. few good tools
   d. disease

9. A person <u>vehemently</u> denying a charge would speak in what kind of manner?
   a. intense and forceful
   b. crafty and elusive
   c. elegant and graceful
   d. deceitful and two-faced

10. Helping a friend <u>install</u> a basketball goal would involve
    a. setting up the goal in the best place
    b. tearing down the goal
    c. repairing the goal
    d. building the goal from spare lumber

Selection Test

from Smallpox

from *Invisible Enemies: Stories of Infectious Disease*
by JEANETTE FARRELL

COMPREHENSION QUESTIONS

Circle the letter of the best answer to each of the following items. *(50 points)*

1. In which year was Boston struck by the worst smallpox epidemic in its history?
   a. 1701
   b. 1721
   c. 1764
   d. 1776

2. How many particles of the virus had to be inhaled in order to contract smallpox?
   a. one
   b. twenty
   c. one thousand
   d. one million

3. When Dr. Boylston inoculated his own son in 1721, the inhabitants of Boston
   a. begged the doctor to inoculate them
   b. declared the doctor a local hero
   c. were outraged he endangered his son
   d. were glad someone finally took action

4. What was the result of Cotton Mather's inoculation of his son Sammy?
   a. the boy survived
   b. the boy died
   c. the boy survived but killed his father by passing on the disease
   d. the boy died, along with everyone else in the household

5. Where did the practice of having inoculation parties begin?
   a. Boston
   b. Philadelphia
   c. England
   d. Turkey

VOCABULARY

Using your knowledge of the underlined word, circle the letter of the word or phrase that best completes each statement. *(50 points)*

6. A person immune to a particular disease
   a. is likely to catch the disease
   b. is not afraid of the disease
   c. is suffering from the disease
   d. cannot catch the disease

7. Declaring an epidemic in a city would probably cause its inhabitants to
   a. worry about catching a disease
   b. celebrate with a parade
   c. ask for police assistance
   d. hold epidemic parties

8. A distraction in an air traffic control tower
   a. helps air traffic controllers to concentrate
   b. could cause an accident
   c. is essential for maintaining the equipment
   d. would require medical assistance

9. Intervening in an argument between two people means
   a. avoiding the argument
   b. taking one side and fighting fiercely
   c. trying to settle the matter
   d. ignoring them

10. A virus is a
   a. method of preventing disease
   b. raised, pus-filled bump on the skin
   c. scratch or mark on the skin
   d. tiny living particle that causes disease

Name _____ Class _____ Date _____

Selection Test

The Young Witch Hunters
from *Muse*
by RHODA BLUMBERG

COMPREHENSION QUESTIONS

Circle the letter of the best answer to each of the following items. *(50 points)*

1. In which year did the Salem witch trials take place?
   a. 1492
   b. 1592
   c. 1692
   d. 1792

2. Where did the Salem villagers get their fear of witches?
   a. from European superstitions brought over by settlers
   b. from destructive conflicts with real native witches
   c. from stories told by the Indians of strange forest spirits
   d. from storybooks

3. The witch scare began in the home of the town
   a. constable
   b. minister
   c. storyteller
   d. mayor

4. After examining Betty and Abigail, Dr. Griggs, a local physician, declared
   a. "The Devil made them do it"
   b. "The Evil Hand is upon them"
   c. "They are suffering from guilt"
   d. "They are suffering from smallpox"

5. Suspects were tested by touching the girls. They were deemed guilty if the girls
   a. felt pain
   b. felt an unseen hand
   c. fell down asleep
   d. could not feel their touch

VOCABULARY

Using your knowledge of the underlined word, circle the letter of the word or phrase that best completes each statement. *(50 points)*

6. An example of something supernatural is
   a. an earthquake
   b. a chemical additive
   c. a well-trained horse
   d. a ghost

7. A contagious disease is one
   a. that may be spread to another person
   b. for which there is no known cure
   c. that cannot harm humans
   d. for which a vaccine has been found

8. An epidemic is the quick spread through a community of
   a. a temporary fad
   b. an irrational fear
   c. exciting news
   d. a disease

9. You might call an event "bizarre" if it is
   a. highly publicized
   b. surprising and incredible
   c. historically important
   d. sad and depressing

10. Someone accused of a crime is
    a. charged with the crime
    b. secretly suspected of the crime
    c. convicted of that crime
    d. officially innocent of the crime

Selection Test

The Slave Ship
from *The Kidnapped Prince:*
The Life of Olaudah Equiano
by OLAUDAH EQUIANO, ADAPTED BY
ANN CAMERON

COMPREHENSION QUESTIONS

Circle the letter of the best answer to each of the following items. *(50 points)*

1. Once on board, Equiano was so terrified he says he would have traded places with
   a. the lowest slave in his own country
   b. one of those who had already died
   c. a dead bird
   d. a flying fish

2. All of the following were sources of amazement for Equiano **except**
   a. the whites' complexion and hair
   b. the effects of a glass of alcohol
   c. the ship itself
   d. the whites' strange clothes

3. When he refused to eat, Equiano was
   a. beaten
   b. taken to the ship's doctor
   c. given different food
   d. allowed to walk freely

4. Africans in the hold of the ship suffered all of the following conditions **except**
   a. extreme heat   c. poor air
   b. chains   d. lack of food

5. When a white sailor shows him a quadrant, Equiano is
   a. mystified   c. excited
   b. surprised   d. sad

VOCABULARY

Using your knowledge of the underlined word, circle the letter of the word or phrase that best completes each statement. *(50 points)*

6. You can judge a person's <u>complexion</u> by looking at his or her
   a. bank account   c. hair
   b. clothes   d. face

7. Someone willing to trade his or her <u>lot</u> is tired of his or her
   a. situation in life   c. residence
   b. profession   d. job

8. A person would probably react with <u>consternation</u> to
   a. a sad movie
   b. a nice birthday gift
   c. an elephant bursting through the door
   d. a spectacular play by a favorite sports figure

9. A <u>flogging</u> is an extreme form of
   a. reward
   b. punishment
   c. consternation
   d. skiing

10. One would probably describe as <u>fetid</u>
    a. a crisp fall day
    b. a rotten apple
    c. an underinflated basketball
    d. a blooming rose

Name _____ Class _____ Date _____

Selection Test

Lacrosse Yesterday and Today
from *Cobblestone*
by STANLEY A. FREED

COMPREHENSION QUESTIONS

Circle the letter of the best answer to each of the following items. *(50 points)*

1. Lacrosse was the favorite sport of North American Indian tribes
   a. on the East Coast
   b. in the Midwest
   c. in the Pacific Northwest
   d. in the Southwest

2. In American Indian tribes, lacrosse served all of the following purposes **except**
   a. punishment for criminals
   b. training for war
   c. a religious festival
   d. entertainment

3. Southeastern tribes called lacrosse the
   a. "test of men"
   b. "ball-and-stick game"
   c. "little brother of war"
   d. "mother of all great games"

4. The night before a lacrosse game, Choctaw Indians
   a. danced and sang throughout the night
   b. did not eat or drink anything
   c. reviewed their strategies for the game with their coaches
   d. drank an herbal tea supposed to have energizing qualities

5. The American Indian team that competed in the 1990 World Cup Lacrosse Championship was
   a. Choctaw   c. Iroquois
   b. Sioux   d. Cherokee

VOCABULARY

Using your knowledge of the underlined word, circle the letter of the word or phrase that best completes each statement. *(50 points)*

6. A film <u>modified</u> for television has been
   a. discounted   c. banned
   b. sold   d. changed

7. A player who shows great <u>agility</u> is
   a. courageous and resourceful
   b. a natural leader
   c. strong and tough
   d. quick and graceful

8. Someone with incredible <u>stamina</u> might be expected to
   a. run very fast
   b. run gracefully and effortlessly
   c. run a great distance without tiring
   d. run a short distance each day

9. An event at which a <u>procession</u> might take place is
   a. a funeral   c. a soccer game
   b. a charity run d. a family picnic

10. An act of <u>mayhem</u> might result in all of the following **except**
    a. injury
    b. exhaustion
    c. arrest by the police
    d. rest and relaxation

Selection Test

from Inventor and Scientist
from *Benjamin Franklin: The New American*
by MILTON MELTZER

COMPREHENSION QUESTIONS

Circle the letter of the best answer to each of the following items. *(50 points)*

1. Science came naturally to Benjamin Franklin because
   a. his father was a scientist
   b. he needed to know the why and how of everything he came across
   c. he wrote scientific articles in the *Gazette*
   d. as a child he read many science books

2. Benjamin Franklin is credited with all of the following inventions **except**
   a. the Franklin stove
   b. the flue
   c. the light bulb
   d. a candle made from whale oil

3. Franklin's many inventions were the result of
   a. pressure from the American Philosophical Society
   b. his desire for fame

   c. his desire to improve the quality of life
   d. his need for additional income

4. Benjamin Franklin founded the American Philosophical Society so its members could
   a. compete with the Royal Society
   b. continue publishing the *Gazette*
   c. raise money to fund scientific research
   d. share information regarding science

5. Franklin's scientific method was based on
   a. experiments
   b. electricity
   c. library research
   d. the work of others

VOCABULARY

Using your knowledge of the underlined word, circle the letter of the word or phrase that best completes each statement. *(50 points)*

6. A person who is an <u>amateur</u>
   a. makes a lot of money
   b. performs poorly
   c. patents an invention for profit
   d. takes part in an activity for enjoyment

7. When Benjamin Franklin demonstrated <u>inventiveness</u>, he
   a. was able to make something new that did not exist before
   b. wanted to be the center of attention
   c. improved on what someone else had done
   d. made others follow his lead

8. If you are <u>analytic</u>, you are
   a. afraid of enclosed places

   b. able to study carefully
   c. able to remain calm
   d. unwilling to be curious

9. When Sir Francis Bacon spoke of <u>genius</u> throughout the world, he was referring to
   a. a species of plant life
   b. human intellectual and creative powers
   c. a code of behavior
   d. a group of scientists who met regularly

10. If you are <u>voracious</u>, you
   a. talk excessively
   b. are generous with your time and money
   c. have an enormous appetite
   d. make friends easily

Selection Test

The Women of the American Revolution
from *Who Were the Founding Fathers?*
Two Hundred Years of Reinventing American History
by STEVEN H. JAFFE

COMPREHENSION QUESTIONS

Circle the letter of the best answer to each of the following items. *(50 points)*

1. Elizabeth Ellet wrote *The Women of the American Revolution* because
   a. her mother fought in the Revolutionary War
   b. she wanted to help women gain the right to vote
   c. she wanted to help the women's families receive pensions
   d. she wanted to tell about the brave deeds of a forgotten group

2. According to Ellet's book, women advanced the Revolutionary War cause in all of the following ways **except**
   a. publishing war-related stories
   b. raising money for the army
   c. counseling important politicians
   d. boycotting British goods

3. Mercy Warren had to teach herself because
   a. she lived far from a women's university
   b. she hoped to work for the government
   c. higher education for women was not encouraged
   d. she wanted to be a teacher

4. Public recognition for the women who served their country in the Revolutionary War came in the form of
   a. a letter   c. promotion
   b. a medal   d. a pension

5. This selection concludes that the role women played in the American Revolution helped to prove that
   a. women were superior to men
   b. women deserved equal rights
   c. women won the war
   d. a woman's place is in the home

VOCABULARY

Using your knowledge of the underlined word, circle the letter of the word or phrase that best completes each statement. *(50 points)*

6. A soldier in a skirmish is participating in
   a. a ceremony   c. a fight
   b. an activity   d. a surrender

7. Stereotypes are
   a. oversimplified ideas or beliefs
   b. scientific discoveries
   c. rumors
   d. stories

8. Women played crucial roles in the war that were
   a. of no concern
   b. assigned by the army

   c. very important
   d. intended for men

9. To revive something is to
   a. destroy it
   b. hide it
   c. to bring it to mind
   d. fight over it

10. Your exploits are your
    a. travels   c. hobbies
    b. brave acts   d. plans

Selection Test

from Ground Truth
. . . . from *Breaking Ground, Breaking Silence:*
The Story of New York's African Burial Ground
by JOYCE HANSEN and GARY McGOWAN

COMPREHENSION QUESTIONS

Circle the letter of the best answer to each of the following items. *(50 points)*

1. Osteologists at the burial site concluded all of the following information about the skeleton **except**
   a. age
   b. sex
   c. race
   d. family history

2. Archaeologists are particularly careful when cleaning a skeleton's chest cavity because
   a. it may contain contagious diseases
   b. valuable information can be learned from the surrounding soil
   c. the bones are less sturdy than other bones in the body
   d. valuables are often hidden there

3. The "ground truth" of Burial #6 will help to set straight the history of
   a. British Revolutionary War leaders
   b. New York cemeteries
   c. African Americans in the Revolutionary War
   d. burial rites

4. In cleaning and analyzing the artifacts from Burial #6, the archaeologists used all of the following equipment **except**
   a. an electric drill
   b. dental picks
   c. aspirators
   d. microscopes

5. From this selection, you can conclude that identifying and classifying articles from burial sites
   a. is something anyone can do with the right tools
   b. requires permission from the government
   c. is rarely done in a laboratory
   d. is a long, involved process

VOCABULARY

Match each word in the left-hand column with its meaning from the right-hand column.

_____ 6. particles   a. obstacles

_____ 7. corroded   b. related to living things

_____ 8. phase   c. easily changed

_____ 9. organic   d. small pieces

_____ 10. critical   e. stage

           f. important

           g. rusted

_____ 11. extracted   a. dead

_____ 12. immersed   b. prove

_____ 13. eroded   c. changed

_____ 14. deceased   d. dipped completely into

_____ 15. verify   e. dried

           f. taken out

           g. worn away

Selection Test

Your Rights and Mine
from *Give Me Liberty! The Story of the Declaration of Independence*
by RUSSELL FREEDMAN

COMPREHENSION QUESTIONS

Circle the letter of the best answer to each of the following items. *(50 points)*

1. According to the Declaration of Independence, governments are created to
   a. establish tyrannies
   b. ensure the happiness of individuals
   c. secure the rights of individuals
   d. make everyone equal

2. Jefferson made all of the following charges against King George III except
   a. taxing without consent
   b. waging war
   c. removing the right of trial by jury
   d. selling slaves

3. Individuals from the northern states freed their slaves based on the values set forth by
   a. Martin Luther King, Jr.
   b. the Intolerable Acts
   c. the Declaration of Independence
   d. King George III

4. Abraham Lincoln believed that the Declaration of Independence
   a. expressed few of history's most important political truths
   b. was outdated
   c. did not spell out that all individuals are created equal
   d. should be rewritten

5. The Declaration of Independence
   a. was welcomed by the British government
   b. continues to affect the lives of individuals
   c. took years to write
   d. provided a model for other governments

VOCABULARY

Using your knowledge of the underlined word, circle the letter of the word or phrase that best completes each statement. *(50 points)*

6. When a passage of the Declaration of Independence was eliminated, it was
   a. published   c. read aloud
   b. added   d. gotten rid of

7. If you make an indictment, you make
   a. an accusation   c. a presentation
   b. a compliment   d. a request

8. To abolish slavery is to
   a. continue it
   b. do away with it
   c. make it widespread
   d. punish a slave

9. If you listen to an affirmation, you listen to
   a. a statement or declaration that something is true or right
   b. a request for goods or services
   c. an opinion stated angrily
   d. a speech in someone's honor

10. If a passage of the Declaration of Independence denounced slavery, the passage
    a. declared it necessary
    b. condemned it as wicked or wrong
    c. recommended that it be continued
    d. weighed its good points against its bad points

Selection Test

Benjamin Banneker
from *Pioneers of Discovery (Profiles of Great Black Americans)*
edited by RICHARD RENNERT

COMPREHENSION QUESTIONS

Circle the letter of the best answer to each of the following items. *(50 points)*

1. Throughout childhood, Benjamin Banneker's favorite activity was
   a. farming
   b. reading
   c. fishing
   d. inventing

2. Banneker led a lonely life because
   a. he was a free black
   b. his mother had been a slave
   c. he disagreed with Thomas Jefferson
   d. he did not enjoy the company of others

3. From this selection, you can infer that Banneker's letter to Jefferson
   a. angered Jefferson
   b. prompted Jefferson to end slavery
   c. encouraged Jefferson to publish an almanac
   d. impressed Jefferson

4. All of the following accomplishments can be credited to Benjamin Banneker except
   a. helping to survey the land on which the nation's capitol stands
   b. teaching himself astronomy
   c. becoming secretary of state
   d. publishing an almanac

5. Banneker's many achievements helped to prove that
   a. astronomy was more important than mathematics
   b. blacks were as intelligent as whites
   c. fewer slaves were needed in the Colonies
   d. self-teaching was more important than schooling

VOCABULARY

Using your knowledge of the underlined word, circle the letter of the word or phrase that best completes each statement. *(50 points)*

6. If you are a surveyor, you are a person who
   a. grows tobacco
   b. studies the stars and planets
   c. measures the size and shape of a piece of land
   d. makes a great deal of money from investments

7. Five years of servitude is five years of
   a. labor
   b. education
   c. vacation
   d. travel

8. If you are interested in statistics, you are interested in
   a. the study of the location of the sun, moon, stars, and planets
   b. helping others to find employment
   c. freeing slaves
   d. facts or data collected as numbers and arranged so as to give information

9. Censure of African Americans is
   a. blame or disapproval
   b. freedom
   c. traditions
   d. complimentary remarks

10. A contemplative person is one who
    a. shows anger
    b. is thoughtful
    c. talks a lot
    d. makes friends

Selection Test

from Thomas Jefferson
from *Science in Colonial America*
by BRENDAN JANUARY

COMPREHENSION QUESTIONS

Circle the letter of the best answer to each of the following items. *(50 points)*

1. Thomas Jefferson believed that the study of science should
   a. be useful and serve mankind
   b. be reserved for philosophers
   c. be controlled by the Europeans
   d. happen only on planned expeditions

2. In Jefferson's attempts to reject the Europeans' theory that North America was inferior, he did all of the following **except**
   a. write notes on the State of Virginia
   b. display a moose skeleton in a hotel
   c. criticize European scientists
   d. organize a fossil-hunting expedition

3. You can infer from this selection that Thomas Jefferson was
   a. embarrassed to live in the colonies
   b. lonely and depressed
   c. a good President
   d. proud of his country

4. Jefferson was honored in France for
   a. contributing to France's fossil collection
   b. writing the Declaration of Independence
   c. organizing the Lewis and Clark Expedition
   d. his membership in the American Philosophical Society

5. The main purpose of the Lewis and Clark expedition was to
   a. find a woolly mammoth
   b. find fossils of extinct animals
   c. explore northwestern United States
   d. recapture land claimed by the British

VOCABULARY

Using your knowledge of the underlined word, circle the letters of the word or phrase that best completes each statement. *(50 points)*

6. If a place is <u>inferior</u>, that place is
   a. lower in rank   c. popular
   b. for sale   d. expensive

7. The study of <u>geology</u> is the study of
   a. mathematics   c. the structure of the earth
   b. the human body   d. the stars and planets

8. A scientist looks at <u>specimens</u> for
   a. a series of patterns
   b. a system of books
   c. examples or classification
   d. animal behavior

9. Something that is <u>impressive</u> is
   a. unimportant   c. humorous
   b. has a strong   d. out of date
      effect

10. If Jefferson <u>sponsored</u> an event, he
    a. organized or   c. joked about it
       supported it   d. stopped it
    b. attended it

Selection Test

Into the Unknown: The Incredible Adventures of Lewis and Clark

from *National Geographic World*
by MARGARET McKELWAY

COMPREHENSION QUESTIONS

Circle the letter of the best answer to each of the following items. *(50 points)*

1. Lewis and Clark began transporting supplies for their trip from
   a. St. Louis in 1804
   b. North Dakota in 1812
   c. Washington, D.C., in 1800
   d. Louisiana in 1801

2. The land acquired from the French was called the
   a. Canadian Region
   b. Louisiana Territory
   c. Napoleon Purchase
   d. Dakota Land

3. Sacagawea was all of the following **except**
   a. the wife of a French fur trader
   b. one of the expedition's translators
   c. the sister of the Shoshone chief
   d. the inventor of the canoe

4. All of the following were obstacles along the journey **except**
   a. crossing the mighty Mississippi
   b. rapids on the Columbia River
   c. the Rocky Mountains
   d. waterfalls on the Missouri River

5. The expedition led by Lewis and Clark traveled a total of approximately
   a. 8,000 miles in 28 months
   b. 3,000 miles in 3 years
   c. 1,000 miles in 11 months
   d. 30,000 miles in 48 months

VOCABULARY

Using your knowledge of the underlined word, circle the letter of the word or phrase that best completes each statement. *(50 points)*

6. One might best acquire a watch by
   a. hoping to be given one
   b. polishing it carefully every day
   c. buying one
   d. smashing it with a hammer

7. To be commissioned to do something is to be
   a. given an assignment
   b. forbidden to do something
   c. encouraged to look into the matter
   d. warned against it

8. A family reunion is an event in which family members
   a. meet with lawyers in order to settle their differences
   b. circulate a family newsletter through the mail
   c. pay their taxes
   d. see one another again after being separated

9. An example of a road obstacle is
   a. a highway entrance sign
   b. a huge pothole
   c. the yellow stripe down the middle of the street
   d. asphalt

10. A treacherous trail is one that is
    a. dangerous
    b. easy to follow
    c. a dead end
    d. slightly hilly

Name _____ Class _____ Date _____

Selection Test

from **The Oregon Trail**
by LEONARD EVERETT FISHER

COMPREHENSION QUESTIONS
Circle the letter of the best answer to each of the following items. *(50 points)*

1. Scouts who knew the Oregon Trail were called
   a. guides   **c.** pilots
   b. leaders   **d.** lieutenants

2. The selection focuses on wagon trains that traveled in the
   a. 1840s and '50s
   b. 1720s and '30s
   c. 1860s and '70s
   d. 1880s and '90s

3. The settlers used lighter wagons so that
   a. they could float the wagons across rivers
   b. they could carry the wagons if the mules died
   c. they could quickly take apart and reassemble them
   d. they could lower the wagons from cliffs

4. Wagon trains traveled an average of how many hours a day?
   a. three hours
   b. five hours
   c. seven hours
   d. twelve hours

5. Supply wagons for the wagon trains usually carried all of the following **except**
   a. food
   b. weapons
   c. medicine
   d. extra oxen

VOCABULARY
Using your knowledge of the underlined word, circle the letter of the word or phrase that best completes each statement. *(50 points)*

6. An <u>emigrant</u> is someone who
   a. has recently left one country for another
   b. moves around constantly
   c. gives things to others
   d. is newly arrived to the country

7. You would probably describe as a <u>multitude</u>
   a. the number of bananas in a small bunch
   b. around a dozen or so objects
   c. two elephants
   d. a crowd of people

8. An example of a <u>maneuver</u> is
   a. jumping at the sight of a large snake
   b. a motorcycle stunt
   c. a graduation party
   d. snapping one's fingers

9. A <u>durable</u> backpack is one
   a. that looks good
   b. that is of a medium size
   c. that lasts a long time
   d. is very heavy and awkward

10. <u>Brackish</u> water can be described as
   a. full of twigs and leaves
   b. foul tasting or sickening
   c. slightly tangy
   d. fresh

(130) The United States: Change and Challenge

Copyright © by Holt, Rinehart and Winston. All rights reserved.

Selection Test

from The Trail of Tears

from *Cowboys and Indians* by JOHN WADSWORTH

COMPREHENSION QUESTIONS

Circle the letter of the best answer to each of the following items. *(50 points)*

1. The Cherokee originally lived in
   a. the Appalachian region
   b. the Pacific Northwest
   c. Oklahoma
   d. Maine

2. Where is the capital of the Western Band of Cherokee?
   a. Clingman's Dome, North Carolina
   b. Tahlequah, Oklahoma
   c. Cherokee, North Carolina
   d. Red Clay, Tennessee

3. How long is the Trail of Tears auto route?
   a. 100 miles
   b. 500 miles
   c. 900 miles
   d. 1,200 miles

4. The memorial in Red Clay, Tennessee is called
   a. "The Trail Where They Cried Memorial"
   b. "The Eternal Flame of the Cherokee Nation"
   c. "The Sacred Home of the Cherokee"
   d. "The Meeting of the Elders"

5. All of the following statements about Chief John Ross are true **except**
   a. He was one-eighth Cherokee
   b. He grew up in Georgia
   c. He fought with General Andrew Jackson in the War of 1812
   d. He agreed to leave Georgia for a sum of money

VOCABULARY

Using your knowledge of the underlined word, circle the letter of the word or phrase that best completes each statement. *(50 points)*

6. A <u>communal</u> garden is one
   a. designed for meditation and retreat
   b. owned by the entire community

7. A woman who claims she has received a <u>prophecy</u> is claiming to
   a. have been given a prediction about the future
   b. have won a major settlement in court

8. A city block is usually <u>encompassed</u> by
   a. streets
   b. trees

9. An example of something that is usually <u>verdant</u> is
   a. a shiny new coin
   b. a well-watered lawn

10. A <u>refurbished</u> computer is one that
    a. is brand new
    b. has been fixed up

11. <u>Embarking</u> on a voyage means
    a. beginning it
    b. continuing it

12. A <u>random</u> number is one that
    a. has been planned out
    b. has been arrived at without planning

13. An example of a <u>silhouette</u> is
    a. a story passed down from one's ancestors
    b. a shadow in a window

14. An <u>immaculate</u> room is
    a. extremely messy and unorganized
    b. perfectly clean and well-kept

15. An example of something <u>embodied</u> is
    a. a concept or idea such as freedom
    b. an area of water such as the Pacific Ocean

Name _____ Class _____ Date _____

Selection Test

COMPREHENSION QUESTIONS

Circle the letter of the best answer to each of the following items. *(50 points)*

1. All of the following happened in 1848 **except**
   a. Elizabeth Cady Stanton organized a convention
   b. A Seneca Falls minister opened his church to the convention
   c. The first Women's Rights Convention took place
   d. Women were given the right to vote

2. The women's rights movement followed the strategies of
   a. the antislavery and temperance movements
   b. the Civil Rights movement
   c. the French Women's Rights movement
   d. the antislavery, but not the temperance, movement

3. The convention's first order of business was Stanton's reading of
   a. the Declaration of the Rights of Women
   b. the Declaration of Sentiments
   c. the Declaration of Independence
   d. the Declaration of Suffrage for Women

4. The ninth resolution, which called for women to have the vote,
   a. was unanimously approved
   b. was debated but defeated
   c. was debated but approved
   d. was unanimously defeated

5. Belva Lockwood, the first woman candidate for U.S. president, ran for election in
   a. 1884
   b. 1920
   c. 1966
   d. 1984

VOCABULARY

Using your knowledge of the underlined word, circle the letter of the word or phrase that best completes each statement. *(50 points)*

6. Inadvertently locking your friend's keys in her car is an example of
   a. meanness
   b. good humor
   c. thoughtlessness
   d. mischievousness

7. A tyrannical boss is
   a. fair and even-handed
   b. cruel and unjust
   c. kind and gentle
   d. imposing but harmless

8. To adjourn a meeting means
   a. to close it until a later time
   b. to continue it after its planned finish
   c. to cancel it
   d. to begin it anew

9. An example of a strategy is
   a. waiting for the open shot in basketball
   b. having to sit out a game with an injury
   c. not noticing time had expired
   d. asking the referee when the game is to begin

10. Commemorating a person's accomplishments in a certain field would probably mean
    a. accusing the person of misconduct
    b. signing a petition
    c. placing a plaque in a public place honoring that person
    d. suing that person in a court of law

Name _____ Class _____ Date _____

Selection Test

A Quaker Commitment to Education
from *Cobblestone* by JUDITH FOSTER GEARY

COMPREHENSION QUESTIONS

Circle the letter of the best answer to each of the following items. *(50 points)*

1. Another name for Quakers is the
   a. Community of Courageous Idealists
   b. Religious Society of Friends
   c. Assembly of Alternative Thinkers
   d. Spiritual Society of Activists

2. Coffin's school in North Carolina taught slaves how to read
   a. Shakespeare   c. the Bible
   b. horn books   d. the Constitution

3. Nat Turner's rebellion
   a. started the Civil War
   b. helped many slaves escape
   c. was a nonviolent one
   d. led to the murder of more than fifty white southerners

4. Prudence Crandall's school was located in
   a. Alabama
   b. Georgia
   c. Virginia
   d. Connecticut

5. By the 1920s, leadership of most Quaker-founded schools passed into the hands of
   a. the U.S. government
   b. abolitionists
   c. Levi Coffin
   d. African Americans

VOCABULARY

Using your knowledge of the underlined word, circle the letter of the word or phrase that best completes each statement. *(50 points)*

6. People working for the abolition of nuclear missiles
   a. oppose the weapons' development
   b. support the use of the weapons
   c. are working to develop the weapons further
   d. cautiously approve of the weapons' use in certain circumstances

7. A more restrictive law governing drivers' licenses
   a. would raise the minimum age to 25
   b. would lower the minimum age to 14
   c. would list the drivers' car model on the license
   d. would allow one to renew one's license on the Internet

8. A person looking to improve his or her financial situation would probably
   a. pay more attention to his or her clothing
   b. study harder
   c. save money and look for a job
   d. go on vacation

9. A petition is a
   a. temporary wall   c. situation or stance
   b. formal request   d. a kind of fence

10. What is a fitting legacy of a person committed to establishing equal rights in a country?
    a. the persons obtaining a position in the government
    b. a newspaper article written about the person
    c. a cash award given to the person
    d. an award for civil rights work given in the person's name

Name _____ Class _____ Date _____

Selection Test

COMPREHENSION QUESTIONS

Circle the letter of the best answer to each of the following items. *(50 points)*

1. Kentucky mountain men had traveled out west by the early 1840s because of the
   a. discovery of gold
   b. trapping trade
   c. cheap price of land
   d. war with the Mexicans

2. What about California lured Americans there in the 1840s?
   a. reports of its wealth and magnificence
   b. it was a steppingstone to Hawaii
   c. the trapping trade
   d. the war with the Mexicans

3. The belief that the U.S. should possess the continent from coast to coast was called
   a. "A Greater Union"   c. "Bear Flag Politics"
   b. "The Big Collage"   d. "Manifest Destiny"

4. Which U.S. president declared war on Mexico in 1846?
   a. James Madison
   b. Andrew Jackson
   c. James Polk
   d. Abraham Lincoln

5. The treaty that ended the Mexican War in 1848 was called
   a. the Treaty of Tears
   b. the Gadsden Treaty
   c. the Treaty of Guadalupe Hidalgo
   d. the Treaty of the Alamo

VOCABULARY

Using your knowledge of the underlined word, circle the letter of the word or phrase that best completes each statement. *(50 points)*

6. Early American settlers in California may have assimilated into Mexican society by
   a. ridiculing Mexican traditions
   b. speaking Spanish and learning about Mexican culture
   c. buying land and selling it for a profit
   d. claiming surrounding lands for the U.S.

7. Someone lured by a bowl of ripe grapes on a side table at a party probably
   a. is hungry and likes grapes
   b. hates the taste of grapes
   c. is too excited to think about food
   d. is feeling ill

8. A piece of art called a collage is composed of
   a. different materials assembled together
   b. finely chiseled and polished marble
   c. a single piece of carved wood
   d. a simple framed photograph

9. An example of a skirmish is
   a. a brightly colored skirt
   b. a brief battle along a border
   c. a traditional dance
   d. an elaborately played song

10. One could aggravate a minor ankle sprain by
   a. having the sprain treated by a doctor
   b. not putting weight on the foot
   c. ignoring the sprain and running anyway
   d. placing a bandage on the ankle

Selection Test

Gold Mountain
from *The Gold Rush*
by LIZA KETCHUM

COMPREHENSION QUESTIONS

Circle the letter of the best answer to each of the following items. *(50 points)*

1. Many Chinese referred to California with the Cantonese *Gum San*, which meant
   a. "Land to the East"
   b. "Place Across the Waters"
   c. "Land of Devils"
   d. "Gold Mountain"

2. Most Chinese immigrants planned
   a. to spend the rest of their lives in the U.S.
   b. to return to China as soon as they made their fortunes
   c. to open a chain of restaurants on their arrival in California
   d. to claim California as a Chinese territory

3. Americans and Europeans referred to the Chinese as
   a. the Foreign Devils   c. the Gold Diggers
   b. the Celestials   d. the Mine-Men

4. The Chinese water wheel was
   a. a series of buckets operated by pulleys
   b. a method for diverting streams
   c. the first successful Chinese mine
   d. a method of torture

5. When someone was told he "didn't have a Chinaman's chance," it meant
   a. his chances were good
   b. the odds were fifty-fifty
   c. his situation was hopeless
   d. his situation was up in the air

VOCABULARY

Using your knowledge of the underlined word, circle the letter of the word or phrase that best completes each statement. *(50 points)*

6. A government might undertake a census in order to
   a. conquer new territory
   b. make peace with one's neighbors
   c. count the country's inhabitants
   d. open new opportunities to immigrants

7. Someone suffering in a famine would probably be
   a. hungry and malnourished
   b. quarantined to stop the spread of disease
   c. attacked by a hostile army
   d. left homeless from the floods

8. Diverting the path of a spaceship would mean
   a. stopping it
   b. starting it moving
   c. sending it back home
   d. turning it in a different direction

9. Extracting gold means
   a. polishing it   c. weighing it
   b. digging it up   d. hiding it away

10. A prosperous business is one that
    a. makes money   c. breaks even
    b. loses money   d. is bankrupt

Selection Test

Supplying the Armies
from *A Separate Battle: Women and the Civil War*
by INA CHANG

COMPREHENSION QUESTIONS

Circle the letter of the best answer to each of the following items. *(50 points)*

1. All of the following statements regarding women's wartime production of havelocks are true **except**
   a. a northern newspaper suggested their use
   b. thousands were produced in all colors and sizes
   c. soldiers did not use them for sun protection as was intended
   d. havelock production continued until the end of the war

2. Dr. Elizabeth Blackwell formed the Women's Central Association of Relief because
   a. all of the women knew how to knit
   b. the Union army needed help distributing supplies
   c. the sewing machine had not yet been invented
   d. the Confederate soldiers needed medical supplies

3. The U.S. Sanitary Commission educated citizens about
   a. handling firearms
   b. the types of supplies to send the troops
   c. the war's progress
   d. how to correspond with the troops

4. The major purpose of the "sanitary fairs" was to
   a. raise money for transporting army supplies
   b. entertain the soldiers
   c. display newly designed uniforms
   d. educate citizens about health hazards

5. What is the main idea of this selection?
   a. women wanted to be soldiers
   b. Dr. Blackwell started the WCAR
   c. women made valuable contributions during the Civil War
   d. the armies' uniforms were made by women

VOCABULARY

Using your knowledge of the vocabulary words, choose the letter of the matching word or phrase that best defines the vocabulary word. *(50 points)*

_____ 6. impractical

_____ 7. pooled

_____ 8. efficiency

_____ 9. status

_____ 10. demoralized

_____ 11. dwindled

_____ 12. flyer

_____ 13. frenzied

_____ 14. ornate

_____ 15. array

a. display

b. the capability to do something with the least amount of effort or waste

c. became less full

d. frantic

e. not suitable or useful

f. rank or position

g. excessively showy

h. brought together for a common goal

i. single printed sheet circulated over a wide area

j. corrupted

Selection Test

from What A Foolish Boy
from *The Boys' War*
by JIM MURPHY

COMPREHENSION QUESTIONS

Circle the letter of the best answer to each of the following items. *(50 points)*

1. According to the selection, soldiers spent most of their time
   a. fighting
   b. marching from place to place
   c. singing
   d. writing letters to friends and family

2. After the boys joined the army, what did they realize about the duration of the war?
   a. the war would end in ninety days
   b. the war would be fought in Texas for six months
   c. the war would last a long time
   d. the war would end when President Lincoln said it would

3. According to the selection, soldiers became homesick for all of the following reasons **except**
   a. they were unsure of their futures
   b. they missed their bosses and co-workers
   c. their families had been left behind
   d. they had not developed lasting friendships with other soldiers

4. The war lasted longer than expected because
   a. both sides were stalling until more troops were enlisted
   b. the weather was so bad
   c. roads needed to be built
   d. both sides were waiting for assistance from British soldiers

5. From this selection, you can conclude that the war experience for most boys was
   a. fun
   b. a dream come true
   c. easy
   d. difficult

VOCABULARY

Using your knowledge of the underlined word, circle the letter of the word or phrase that best completes each statement. (*50 points*)

6. An <u>initial</u> call for troops would be a call that is
   a. urgent
   b. first
   c. the most successful
   d. ignored

7. If something is <u>reliable</u>, it is
   a. stable
   b. left behind or forgotten
   c. difficult to believe
   d. worth a lot of money

8. A soldier who has been <u>afflicted</u> by a disease has been
   a. pleased with it
   b. able to recover from it
   c. killed by it
   d. caused to suffer by it

9. If you <u>allay</u> your fears, you
   a. make them worse, or intensify them
   b. reduce them, or get relief from them
   c. ignore them
   d. announce them, or say them aloud

10. To <u>amass</u> troops is to
    a. train them
    b. praise them for their accomplishments
    c. gather them together
    d. give them their marching orders

Selection Test

from Freedom Rider
from *Sojourner Truth and the Struggle for Freedom*
by EDWARD BEECHER CLAFLIN

COMPREHENSION QUESTIONS

Circle the letter of the best answer to each of the following items. *(50 points)*

1. Escaped slaves who fled to Washington, D.C., were allowed to
   a. ride streetcars with whites
   b. live in all white neighborhoods
   c. settle in the area called "Murder Bay"
   d. attend the church of their choice

2. Which of the following statements best describes the situation of the inhabitants of Freedman's Village?
   a. their conditions improved daily
   b. they had to learn to be free
   c. they needed no help
   d. they welcomed their comfortable lifestyle

3. Slave traders preyed upon the people of Freedman's Village because
   a. slavery was still legal in Maryland

   b. the Confederate states offered rewards for ex-slaves
   c. Washington's leaders wanted to be rid of the ex-slaves
   d. Sojourner Truth asked them to

4. When a law was passed giving blacks the right to ride streetcars with whites,
   a. a "Jim Crow" car was added
   b. racial relationships improved
   c. whites refused to ride on streetcars
   d. the law was ignored

5. From this selection, you can conclude that Sojourner Truth was
   a. energetic   c. selfish
   b. shy   d. easily discouraged

VOCABULARY

Using your knowledge of the vocabulary word, circle the letter of the word or phrase that best defines the vocabulary word. *(50 points)*

_____ 6. adrift

_____ 7. defiance

_____ 8. segregated

_____ 9. crisis

_____ 10. contraband

_____ 11. emancipation

_____ 12. menacingly

_____ 13. economy

_____ 14. industry

_____ 15. commends

a. something or someone moved illegally from one state or country to another

b. recommends; presents as qualified

c. freedom from slavery

d. a period of great difficulty

e. the use or management of money

f. moving in no single direction

g. in a threatening manner

h. daring rebellion

i. hard work

j. set apart from the main area or group

Name _____ Class _____ Date _____

Selection Test

When I Was a Kid
from *National Geographic World*
by SANDRA FENICHEL ASHER

COMPREHENSION QUESTIONS

Circle the letter of the best answer to each of the following items. *(50 points)*

1. You can infer from the selection that as a child Louisa was
   a. extremely happy   c. slow to learn
   b. prim and proper   d. athletic

2. As children, Louisa and her sisters were educated
   a. by neighbors from Fruitlands
   b. at home
   c. in a local public school
   d. at a boarding school

3. The Alcott children spent much of their childhood
   a. in museums
   b. outdoors
   c. at Fruitlands
   d. volunteering for worthy causes

4. Louisa was happy about moving to Concord, Massachusetts, because
   a. she could write in her own room
   b. her best friend lived there
   c. she could attend the theater
   d. the weather was agreeable

5. At the age of thirteen, Louisa
   a. wrote *Little Women*
   b. became very ill
   c. was already determined to be a success
   d. stopped writing in her journal

VOCABULARY

Using your knowledge of the underlined word, circle the letter of the word or phrase that best completes each statement. *(50 points)*

6. If something inspired Louisa to write, it
   a. made her sad
   b. earned money
   c. brought good luck
   d. caused a desire

7. To establish a new home is to
   a. set it up
   b. break it apart
   c. examine it carefully
   d. tear it down

8. When Louisa rebelled, she
   a. wrote plays
   b. studied with her sisters
   c. behaved respectfully
   d. went against authority

9. When Louisa's family criticized her, they
   a. encouraged her writing
   b. loved her dearly
   c. made a disapproving judgment
   d. praised her accomplishments

10. Moving to a new community is moving to a place where
    a. everyone does an equal amount of work
    b. people are living in a group apart from general society
    c. the people educate their children at home
    d. all the homes look alike

Selection Test

A Proud Tradition
from *Cobblestone*
by JOHN P. LANGELLIER

COMPREHENSION QUESTIONS

Circle the letter of the best answer to each of the following items. *(50 points)*

1. Which two characteristics of the African American soldiers reminded American Indians of the buffalo?
   a. dark skin and intelligence
   b. large heads and good appetites
   c. fighting spirit and curly hair
   d. intelligence and courage

2. After the Civil War, the U.S. Army formed special units of African American soldiers as a result of
   a. a law passed by Congress
   b. pressure from African American citizens
   c. a request from the American Indians
   d. the army's desire for fairness

3. African Americans joined the military after the Civil War for all of the following reasons **except**
   a. to find adventure
   b. to earn money
   c. to learn to read and write
   d. to become better farmers

4. After a period of training, African American soldiers were
   a. sent to officers' training school
   b. given medals of honor
   c. sent to the West and Southwest
   d. allowed to go home for two months

5. According to Professor Rayford Logan, African Americans at the turn of the century had
   a. pride in African American cavalry and infantry units
   b. determined that military careers were impractical
   c. successfully integrated all branches of the military
   d. a museum dedicated to the Buffalo Soldiers

VOCABULARY

Using your knowledge of the underlined word, circle the letter of the word or phrase that best completes each statement. *(50 points)*

6. If two or more regiments of African American soldiers <u>merged</u>, they were
   a. honored
   b. combined; united
   c. broken apart; disbanded
   d. sent to the frontier

7. To change a <u>policy</u> is to change
   a. directions when traveling
   b. your mind about something important
   c. a daily schedule
   d. a course of action by a government

8. To <u>sustain</u> faith in yourself, you must
   a. reject your faith
   b. keep up, or maintain, your faith
   c. share your faith with others
   d. ignore your faith

9. When the buffalo soldiers faced <u>prejudice</u>, they encountered
   a. intolerance and discrimination
   b. bad weather
   c. good will and kindness
   d. a difficult training schedule

10. Since the buffalo was <u>sacred</u> to the Plains Indians, it was
    a. considered bad luck
    b. worth a great deal of money
    c. believed to be holy
    d. something to be feared

Selection Test

"A Few Appropriate Remarks"

from *Highlights for Children*
by NANCY NORTON MATTILA

COMPREHENSION QUESTIONS

Circle the letter of the best answer to each of the following items. *(50 points)*

1. All of the following points were an objective of Lincoln's Gettysburg Address **except**
   a. to convince Northerners to continue fighting in the war
   b. to explain that a Union victory would bring national harmony
   c. to honor the soldiers who had suffered at Gettysburg
   d. to campaign for a second presidential term

2. From the selection, you can conclude that when writing a speech, Lincoln needed
   a. help from others
   b. a noisy, crowded place
   c. the use of a library
   d. a quiet place

3. According to the author, to shape the wording of his speech, Lincoln definitely used all of the following sources **except**
   a. poetry   c. the Bible
   b. encyclopedias   d. Shakespeare

4. After his speech Lincoln was disappointed because
   a. the crowd didn't seem excited by his words
   b. he had to go back to Washington
   c. he hadn't given a very good speech
   d. no one shook his hand

5. The Gettysburg Address has been labeled one of history's greatest speeches because it
   a. quoted Shakespeare
   b. was so popular with the Gettysburg crowd
   c. was short and simple but very meaningful
   d. honored the soldiers who had died in battle

VOCABULARY

Using your knowledge of the underlined word, circle the letter of the word or phrase that best completes each statement. *(50 points)*

6. If remarks are <u>appropriate</u>, they are
   a. embarrassing
   b. suitable for a particular purpose
   c. meant to be kept secret
   d. stated publicly

7. Edward Everett was an <u>orator</u>, or
   a. a public speaker
   b. a presidential candidate
   c. a soldier receiving honors
   d. an assistant to the President

8. To attend a <u>dedication</u> is to witness a
   a. setting apart for a special reason
   b. political rally
   c. humorous or entertaining event
   d. heated debate

9. President Lincoln looked for ways to express <u>reverence</u>, because he wanted to portray
   a. disappointment; frustration
   b. humor; lightheartedness
   c. high regard; respect
   d. anger; resentment

10. When the Gettysburg Address is <u>proclaimed</u> as a great speech, its greatness is
    a. memorized
    b. universally praised
    c. occasionally mentioned
    d. stated or declared publicly

Selection Test

Reenactment of War Is Far Too Civil
from *the Los Angeles Times*
by JON LOVE

COMPREHENSION QUESTIONS

Circle the letter of the best answer to each of the following items. *(50 points)*

1. After studying the reenactment at Chickamauga, the author determined the problem to be that
 a. the uniforms were not authentic
 b. too little time was spent reenacting the battle
 c. too many children were present
 d. the Union soldier that he was watching seemed too happy

2. The author believes that war should
 a. be reenacted for the thrill of the battle
 b. never happen
 c. not be glorified
 d. help the economy

3. The author relates a story about American soldiers shooting Korean civilians to prove his point that
 a. soldiers are trigger-happy
 b. our society looks down on soldiers until they are needed

 c. civilians should stay clear of all battle-grounds
 d. other wars besides the Civil War have produced casualties

4. To support his opinion that war is not a game, the author uses all of the following details **except**
 a. a child's quotation about learning history through reenacting it
 b. General Sherman's quotation about war
 c. a newspaper article about soldiers on trial
 d. the number of casualties at Chickamauga

5. What change to reenactments do you think the author would like to see?
 a. more interaction between the actors and the audience
 b. less emphasis on the battles
 c. fewer women and children
 d. more authentic weapons

VOCABULARY

Using your knowledge of the underlined word, circle the letter of the word or phrase that best completes the statement. *(50 points)*

6. If the North had a strong industrial base, it had a base relating to
 a. manufacturing **c.** farming
 b. trading **d.** mining

7. A replica of a rifle is a
 a. picture **c.** copy
 b. plastic toy **d.** sculpture

8. Items that are authentic are
 a. not for sale **c.** priceless
 b. imaginary **d.** real

9. If a situation is ironic, it
 a. has the opposite meaning of what one would expect
 b. has never really happened
 c. causes great embarrassment
 d. should be kept a secret

10. A battle that is impending is
 a. never going to happen
 b. approaching
 c. the result of a surrender
 d. a standoff

(Selection Test)

Cielito Lindo
from *Songs of the Wild West*
Commentary by ALAN AXELROD
Arrangements by DAN FOX

COMPREHENSION QUESTIONS

Circle the letter of the best answer to each of the following items. *(80 points)*

1. Many Americans grew up with mistaken ideas about the looks and lifestyles of cowboys because of
   a. mistakes in books
   b. newspaper photos
   c. movies and TV
   d. pop songs

2. Early cattle herding was done mostly
   a. on large ranches
   b. on agricultural farms
   c. in horse corrals
   d. around religious centers

3. The earliest cowboys were probably
   a. Western Anglos **c.** escaped slaves
   b. mission Indians **d.** European immigrants

4. The Hollywood idea of a singing cowboy wearing chaps and throwing a lariat originated from
   a. mission priests **c.** vaqueros
   b. Mexican soldiers **d.** Anglo farmers

5. The tone of the song "Cielito Lindo" is
   a. emotional **c.** merry
   b. humorous **d.** angry

6. The reading selection implies that Anglo ranch workers prided themselves in being
   a. poetic **c.** religious
   b. tough **d.** young

7. Missions were established to spread Christianity and to help Spain
   a. teach grammar and usage
   b. keep control of territory
   c. experiment with architecture
   d. promote its songs

8. A refrain in "Cielito Lindo" or in any song is a line that is
   a. the same as the title
   b. the first line
   c. a repeated line
   d. the longest line

VOCABULARY

Using your knowledge of the underlined word, circle the word or phrase that best completes each statement. *(20 points)*

9. The <u>pedigree</u> of the singing cowboys will tell you their
   a. enemies
   b. songs
   c. friends
   d. history

10. To be <u>stoic</u> you would have to be able to endure through to the end of
    a. hard times
    b. professional careers
    c. an unpleasant afternoon
    d. spending a large amount of money

Name _____ Class _____ Date _____

Selection Test

COMPREHENSION QUESTIONS

Circle the letter of the best answer to each of the following items. *(50 points)*

1. General Miles wanted to replace the horse with the bicycle because
   a. he was allergic to animals
   b. bicycles were faster
   c. horses needed food and water
   d. bicycles provided more exercise

2. Which of the following tested the bicycle for military use?
   a. U.S. Navy
   b. U.S. Marines
   c. U.S. Air Force
   d. U.S. Army

3. All of the following were advantages of the safety bike **except**
   a. easier to mount   c. easier to clean
   b. easier to handle   d. easier to stop

4. What was the total number of miles traveled by the bicycle corps on their first test ride?
   a. 252 miles   c. 1,252 miles
   b. 3 1/2 miles   d. 800 miles

5. A possible reason the military finally decided not to use the bicycle was that
   a. horses were loyal
   b. the soldiers could not ride well
   c. the bicycle became too expensive
   d. bikes did not have puncture-proof tires

VOCABULARY

Using your knowledge of the underlined word, circle the word or phrase that best completes each statement. *(50 points)*

6. On the trip to Lake McDonald and back, part of the load each soldier carried <u>consisted</u> of
   a. a bicycle
   b. a knapsack, a blanket, and a tin cup
   c. bandages for injuries
   d. a cannon and ammunition

7. The fact that the soldiers carried their rifles <u>horizontally</u> means that the weapons were positioned
   a. straight up and down
   b. pointing down
   c. at an angle
   d. level with flat ground

8. When the bicycle corps led by Moss went on an <u>expedition</u>, they
   a. went on a purposeful journey
   b. went on a vacation
   c. entered a race
   d. fought for freedom

9. One <u>incentive</u> to redesign early bikes could have been
   a. receiving a reward for bigger bikes
   b. the need for safer bikes
   c. that there was a lot of money to be won in races
   d. that there was a demand for prettier bikes

10. If riders on bicycles <u>escorted</u> soldiers who were on foot, the bicycle riders
   a. left the foot soldiers behind
   b. rode in circles around the foot soldiers
   c. ran into the foot soldiers
   d. accompanied the foot soldiers

Selection Test

How the Wealthy Lived
from *Cobblestone*
by HELEN WIEMAN BLEDSOE

COMPREHENSION QUESTIONS

Circle the letter of the best answer to each of the following items. *(50 points)*

1. The very rich spent large sums of money on all of these **except**
   a. traveling
   b. public education
   c. parties
   d. mansions

2. By today's money standards, a party back then could cost
   a. billions of dollars
   b. several hundred dollars
   c. over a million dollars
   d. trillions of dollars

3. According to this article, the rich even spent lavish amounts of money on their
   a. guns
   b. pets
   c. movies
   d. city parks

4. During the Gilded Age, wealthy people often spent the spring in
   a. New York
   b. "Millionaire's Row"
   c. Europe
   d. the Vanderbilts' mansion

5. In the summer season, the wealthy women must have worried a great deal about their
   a. clothes
   b. husbands
   c. education
   d. children

VOCABULARY

Using your knowledge of the underlined word, circle the word or phrase that best completes each statement. *(50 points)*

6. Furniture and other objects that were <u>gilded</u> would probably have been
   a. expensive
   b. stolen
   c. traded
   d. free

7. The <u>elaborate</u> parties, mansions, and carriages were
   a. ignored
   b. secret
   c. decorative
   d. identical

8. This <u>lavish</u> lifestyle mainly served to
   a. teach children
   b. help others
   c. make enemies
   d. show off

9. The <u>rigid</u> behavior code of the wealthy required people to
   a. follow strict social rules
   b. follow certain religious beliefs
   c. participate in political activities
   d. show consideration for the less fortunate

10. Socializing with other people was <u>obligatory</u>, which meant that men and women
    a. could ignore their neighbors
    b. had to visit certain individuals
    c. could make easy excuses for missing a party
    d. could change or bend attendance rules

Selection Test

The Great Galveston Hurricane
from *Weatherwise*
by PATRICK HUGHES

COMPREHENSION QUESTIONS

Circle the letter of the best answer to each of the following items. *(50 points)*

1. Victims of the 1900 hurricane may have been killed by any of the following **except**
   a. swift water
   b. starvation
   c. fierce wind
   d. crumbling buildings

2. Adding to the city's danger in a hurricane was its
   a. closeness to Houston
   b. position five miles inland
   c. location on an island
   d. short distance from an earthquake

3. According to the selection, several victims showed concern for
   a. neighbors' pets
   b. children
   c. clothing that could be packed up
   d. musical instruments

4. One major health problem after the storm was
   a. a destroyed seawall
   b. numerous corpses
   c. ill sightseers
   d. air pollution

5. We may conclude from the article that
   a. Galveston wasn't prepared for the hurricane
   b. the people ignored urgent warnings
   c. houses were poorly built
   d. the United States government had refused to help

VOCABULARY

Using your knowledge of the underlined word, circle the word or phrase that best completes each statement. *(50 points)*

6. The debris in Galveston included
   a. damaged homes
   b. stranded survivors

7. Many of the victims were submerged, or
   a. forced under water
   b. floating on water

8. The city's benevolent institutions
   a. vaccinated people
   b. helped people

9. If a house is habitable it is
   a. clean
   b. livable

10. People who were maimed in the storm needed
    a. a hospital
    b. fire station.

11. Disintegrating buildings were
    a. falling apart
    b. in the suburbs

12. The estimated cost of rebuilding was
    a. low
    b. approximate

13. If a boat capsized, it
    a. turned upside down
    b. leaked

14. A protruding nail would be
    a. hammered
    b. sticking out

15. A barricade gave at least some
    a. protection
    b. warning

Name _____ Class _____ Date _____

Selection Test

COMPREHENSION QUESTIONS

Circle the letter of the best answer to each of the following items. *(50 points)*

1. The Maple Leaf Club was open during
  a. the Civil War
  b. an era of segregation
  c. an era of integration
  d. the 1970s

2. One instrument that was most likely to be needed to play ragtime is the
  a. piano   **c.** violin
  b. tuba   **d.** harp

3. Scott Joplin often went to The Maple Leaf Club because he
  a. had trouble sleeping
  b. was serious about his music

  c. liked to shoot pool
  d. he easily won card games

4. Joplin was convinced that some people did not like ragtime because
  a. its melodies were boring
  b. it was too much like church music
  c. rock and roll was more popular
  d. the lyrics contained unwholesome words

5. Scott Joplin was considered the king of ragtime because he was
  a. the son of a former slave
  b. friendly and polite
  c. dedicated and talented
  d. ashamed of his family

VOCABULARY

Using your knowledge of the underlined word, circle the word or phrase that best completes each statement. *(50 points)*

6. The integrated crowds who heard Joplin's music were
  a. highly educated
  b. of various races

7. A musician with lofty ambitions wants
  a. to be famous
  b. to be unknown

8. The popularity of Joplin's music was indisputable because
  a. he made money from tips
  b. people came to hear him

9. Someone who feels dominated feels
  a. unimportant
  b. powerful

10. Joplin treated his listeners amiably by
  a. arguing
  b. smiling

11. A few people can cause a commotion by
  a. waiting quietly
  b. talking loudly

12. When Joplin improvised music he
  a. made it up
  b. borrowed it

13. The Maple Leaf Club was not respectable because of
  a. the piano playing
  b. the drinking

14. Diligence requires
  a. determination
  b. laziness

15. Someone who thought ragtime music was not legitimate
  a. imitated it
  b. disapproved of it

Selection Test

from **The Railroad Unites America**
from *The Iron Horse:*
How Railroads Changed America
by RICHARD WORMSER

COMPREHENSION QUESTIONS

Circle the letter of the best answer to each of the following items. *(50 points)*

1. The time period of this selection is mostly
   a. before the Civil War
   b. during the Civil War
   c. after the Civil War
   d. during World War I

2. The transcontinental railroad was built
   a. from west to east only
   b. from the west and the east
   c. from north to south only
   d. only from the mountains through the deserts

3. Who had the easiest job building the railroad?
   a. General Dodge and the Union Pacific
   b. Collis Huntington and the Central Pacific
   c. President Lincoln and the U.S. Army
   d. soldiers and Indians

4. The American Indians most resented the railroad developers for their
   a. appetite for buffalo meat
   b. greed for land
   c. employment of immigrants
   d. steel manufacturing

5. We may infer from the selection that the author of the article
   a. doesn't find fault with either whites or American Indians
   b. is related to Colonel Custer
   c. sympathizes with the American Indians
   d. thinks the railroad cost the government too much money

VOCABULARY

Using your knowledge of the underlined words, circle the word or phrase that best completes each statement. *(50 points)*

6. When the American Indians plundered the trains, they mostly wanted
   a. train parts   c. to seize cargo on board
   b. to ask for peace   d. to exchange gifts

7. The railroad companies wanted the American Indians subdued so that the Indians would
   a. make war
   b. imitate European immigrants
   c. feed the buffalo
   d. surrender and stop fighting

8. The killing of countless American Indians has become a notorious part of American history because
   a. most people believe it was justified
   b. most people voted for President Lincoln

   c. most people still want to argue about the Civil War
   d. most people believe the American Indians were treated unfairly

9. To enjoy the massacre of many people a person would have to be very
   a. athletic   c. cruel
   b. charming   d. friendly

10. When the army began to wipe out peaceful American Indian villages, the Cheyenne started their retaliation by
   a. offering a peaceful solution
   b. joining the railroad effort
   c. striking back and killing railroad crew
   d. escorting settlers across the plains

Selection Test

A Gentleman's Agreement
from *Shadow Ball: The History of the Negro Leagues*
by GEOFFREY C. WARD AND KEN BURNS, WITH JIM O'CONNOR

COMPREHENSION QUESTIONS

Circle the letter of the best answer to each of the following items. *(50 points)*

1. Marcus Garvey was a famous black
   a. baseball player   **c.** musician
   b. coach   **d.** nationalist

2. Garvey encouraged African Americans to help themselves by writing,
   a. "No more spilled blood"
   b. "No more fears"
   c. "No more injustice"
   d. "No more of this nonsense"

3. Rube Foster's strategy of bunts, steals, hit-and-runs, and crafty pitching was called
   a. "fast ball"
   b. "hard ball"
   c. "black baseball"
   d. "smart baseball"

4. In contrast, white baseball managers focused on
   a. hitting home runs
   b. stalling tactics
   c. illegal ruses
   d. marketing

5. Foster's nervous breakdown was probably a result of
   a. family problems
   b. the strain of running a league
   c. ill health
   d. a traumatic car wreck

VOCABULARY

Using your knowledge of the underlined words, circle the letter of the word or phrase that best completes each statement. *(50 points)*

6. Confirmation of one's suspicions that one was not doing so well in a class would include
   a. a failing grade on a test
   b. a passing grade on a test
   c. an excellent grade on a test
   d. an announcement to begin one's test

7. An example of aggressive behavior is
   a. shaking hands when introduced
   b. frowning at strangers
   c. snatching a piece of paper from someone
   d. asking politely for a glass of water

8. Baffling a player during a game means
   a. confusing him or her
   b. acting on impulse and instinct at all times
   c. telling every player to do his or her best
   d. trying hard

9. A player who becomes enraged during a game might show this by
   a. smiling and waving to the crowd
   b. shaking a fist and yelling
   c. hitting a home run
   d. sitting quietly on the bench

10. If a team prevails, that means it
   a. wins the game
   b. loses the game
   c. collapses at times of stress
   d. is not very reliable

Name _____ Class _____ Date _____

Selection Test

from "You're Under Arrest"
from *Rosa Parks: My Story*
by ROSA PARKS WITH JIM HASKINS

COMPREHENSION QUESTIONS

Circle the letter of the best answer to each of the following items. *(50 points)*

1. How old was Rosa Parks when she decided not to give up her bus seat?
   a. twelve
   b. twenty-two
   c. forty-two
   d. seventy-two

2. When Rosa Parks refused to move, the bus driver
   a. threw her off the bus
   b. yelled at her until she moved
   c. hit her and called her names
   d. called the police

3. The first African American mayor of a major American city was
   a. James Blake
   b. Ruby Bridges
   c. Tom Bradley
   d. Jesse Jackson

4. In what decade did Rosa Parks refuse to move from her bus seat?
   a. 1940s
   b. 1950s
   c. 1980s
   d. 1990s

5. In which city did Rosa Parks's stand against segregation take place?
   a. Montgomery, Alabama
   b. Atlanta, Georgia
   c. Detroit, Michigan
   d. Tallahassee, Florida

VOCABULARY

Using your knowledge of the underlined word, circle the letter of the word or phrase that best completes each statement. *(50 points)*

6. The item that best fits the description of vacant is
   a. an abandoned building
   b. a basket full of ripe apples
   c. a bus with two or three passengers
   d. a vase with one flower in it

7. Complying with an order to be quiet would mean
   a. shouting at the top of one's lungs
   b. speaking at a reasonable volume
   c. not talking
   d. apologizing profusely

8. An example of segregation is
   a. attacking a person for his or her religious beliefs
   b. separate seating for blacks and whites
   c. separate bathrooms for men and women
   d. an age requirement for a driver's license

9. Someone experiencing a resurgence might be
   a. a singer who has always been well appreciated
   b. a popular politician falling suddenly into disfavor
   c. a baseball player having a streak of bad luck
   d. a once-popular actress regaining fame

10. Violations of civil rights would include
   a. discriminating against someone because of his or her race
   b. joining a march in support of the passage of an important civil-rights law
   c. giving a speech praising Martin Luther King, Jr.
   d. affording equal opportunity to all, regardless of race

Selection Test

The New Immigrants
from *Junior Scholastic*
by NAOMI MARCUS

COMPREHENSION QUESTIONS

Circle the letter of the best answer to each of the following items. *(50 points)*

1. Today's immigrants to the United States are mostly from
a. Asia and Latin America
b. Europe
c. Africa and Asia
d. Canada

2. All of the following are reasons why immigrants are maintaining closer ties to their native lands **except**
a. cheap long-distance phone rates
b. cheap airfares
c. satellite TV programming
d. less strict United States immigration policy

3. Foreign-born residents account for approximately what percentage of the U.S. population?
a. 10 percent   **c.** 30 percent
b. 20 percent   **d.** 40 percent

4. At the turn of the century, most immigrants were
a. Africans, Egyptians, and Israelis
b. Irish, Italians, and Eastern Europeans
c. Chinese, Japanese, and Korean
d. British

5. All of the following items are part of the profile of the new immigrants **except**
a. being fairly well educated
b. being more prosperous
c. adapting more easily to a new home
d. staying more connected to their homelands

VOCABULARY

Using your knowledge of the underlined word, circle the letter of the word or phrase that best completes each statement. *(50 points)*

6. Common <u>customs</u> particular to the United States include
a. baseball, driving on the right side of the street, and celebrating Thanksgiving
b. large, well-built highways
c. having to be at least 35 years of age in order to run for the office of president
d. murder being illegal

7. <u>Residents</u> of the United States are
a. the Stars and Stripes and the eagle
b. all the people living in the country
c. *E pluribus unum*
d. football games and fireworks displays

8. A person who fits a <u>profile</u>
a. is doing some light carpentry work

b. usually requires a file cabinet to do so
c. is extremely thin and wiry
d. matches the description of a person or group

9. A fair description of someone who <u>flees</u> a prison is someone who
a. returns
b. shoots a gun
c. escapes
d. searches for something hard to find

10. A <u>stable</u> stock market would mean one that is
a. sharply rising in value
b. up and down
c. steady
d. sharply declining in value

Name _____ Class _____ Date _____

Selection Test

A Girl Among the Whales
from *Storyworks*
by EVE NILSON

COMPREHENSION QUESTIONS

Circle the letter of the best answer to each of the following items. *(50 points)*

1. The author says she has had all of the following experiences **except**
   a. swimming to freezing waterfalls
   b. running through fields of wildflowers
   c. riding on the back of a dolphin
   d. being chased by a grizzly bear

2. The author says she has seen whales bigger than a
   a. desk
   b. refrigerator
   c. school bus
   d. commercial aircraft

3. When they are not off the coast of Alaska, humpback whales usually go to
   a. Hawaii or Mexico
   b. Antarctica
   c. China
   d. the Gulf of Mexico

4. To catch more fish, whales work together to make a net out of
   a. seaweed
   b. their fins
   c. barnacles
   d. bubbles

5. When startled, herring crowd together in order to
   a. be harder to swallow all at once
   b. appear as a single, bigger creature
   c. disguise themselves as a piece of debris
   d. deflect the whale's natural form of sonar

VOCABULARY

Using your knowledge of the underlined word, circle the letter of the word or phrase that best completes each statement. *(50 points)*

6. A marine biologist studies life
   a. on the moon
   b. on islands
   c. only on a microscopic scale
   d. in the ocean

7. An example of a cooperative strategy is
   a. a basketball team passing the ball to allow the open player the shot
   b. a farmer using fertilizer to enrich the soil
   c. a chess player planning three moves ahead
   d. a beaver cutting down a tree to use in a dam

8. If a person developed a new batting technique in baseball, he or she would have devised
   a. a new kind of baseball
   b. a rule batters must follow
   c. a method of hitting
   d. a new kind of bat

9. Condensed milk is milk that has been
   a. reduced in volume
   b. allowed to spoil
   c. mixed with bacteria for making cheese
   d. mixed with chocolate powder

10. A whale that has breached has
    a. given birth
    b. broken the surface of the water
    c. used sound to stun prey
    d. eaten too much food

Selection Test

Is Anyone Else Out There?
from *The Planet Hunters: The Search for Other Worlds*
by DENNIS BRINDELL FRADIN

COMPREHENSION QUESTIONS

Circle the letter of the best answer to each of the following items. *(50 points)*

1. FM radio waves travel endlessly through space
   a. at 50 miles per hour
   b. at 1,000 miles per minute
   c. at 18, 600 miles per hour
   d. at 186,000 miles per second

2. If in the year 1999 extraterrestrials thirty light-years away received our radio signals, they received our broadcasts from
   a. 1969
   b. 1990
   c. 1940
   d. 1929

3. Radio contact with extraterrestrials would
   a. make an interesting television show
   b. satisfy our hopes of finding company in the universe
   c. develop a new kind of music
   d. be followed by video contact

4. Around the year 2018, the United States plans to send astronauts to
   a. Mercury
   b. Mars
   c. Venus
   d. Pluto

5. What question does the author say humans have been asking since first gazing at the stars?
   a. "What does it all mean?"
   b. "Where did we come from?"
   c. "What's going to happen?"
   d. "Is anyone else out there?"

VOCABULARY

Using your knowledge of the underlined words, circle the letter of the word or phrase that best completes each statement. *(50 points)*

6. A person who has temporarily stopped working will probably
   a. never work again
   b. go back to work soon
   c. never try again
   d. go back to work after many years

7. A person who is skeptical about the possibilities of space travel
   a. enthusiastically believes in the concept
   b. somewhat supports the concept
   c. is doubtful about the possibilities
   d. thinks that space travel will never happen

8. An average, ordinary radio emits
   a. knobs and dials
   b. electricity
   c. sound
   d. water

9. Simultaneous events are events that happen
   a. as a cause and effect
   b. one after another, but unrelated
   c. at the same time
   d. with a long period of time in between

10. An example of intercepting something is
    a. crossing the street
    b. riding a horse
    c. catching a ball passed to another person
    d. running to catch the bus but failing to get there in time

Content-Area Reading Strategies

for the
Language Arts Classroom
by DR. JUDITH IRVIN
Florida State University

While teaching social studies in middle and high school, I worked primarily with students who struggled with reading and writing. In my desperate attempt to help them learn the content of history, geography, world cultures, economics, and so forth, I did what many good teachers did—I avoided the textbook. I engaged the students in inquiry, conducted simulations, showed videos, created maps and charts, and led lively discussions and debates. Oh, I trotted the textbook out occasionally to use the pictures, diagrams, and primary source material, but it was simply too difficult (or too much trouble) to ask students to read it.

When I did ask students to read, I used the only approach I knew—round-robin reading. This familiar classroom practice of having different students read paragraphs worked about as well as it did when I was in school. The students counted the paragraphs to see which one would be assigned to them and then agonized until their turns were over. No one really concentrated on what was being read. The strong readers were bored, and the struggling readers were embarrassed. I modified this approach by having students volunteer or call on the next reader. I even employed what is now called jump-in-reading, in which volunteers just start reading when another stops. These modifications created slightly more interest in the material, but they didn't stimulate any thought or motivation to learn. So, in desperation, I simply gave up using the textbooks.

How I Learned to Teach Reading

Shortly after I shelved my textbooks, our principal made the announcement, "Every teacher is a teacher of reading." I learned that I was supposed to set aside my beloved history and geography to teach "finding the main idea" and "locating information" through skills worksheets. In my class, this generated even less enthusiasm than round-robin reading.

I became resentful. I nodded dutifully at in-service sessions and talked about how important it was that students read and write better. Then I shut my door and went back to my way of teaching social studies because I was annoyed at being asked not to teach what was important to me and to my students.

After a few more years, I began my Ph.D. studies in social studies education at Indiana University. During this time, I began taking courses in reading education. To my amazement, I discovered that I had been using very effective learning strategies through the social studies methods I had learned and applied in my classroom. But I fell short of helping students apply those concepts when reading their textbooks.

I finished my doctorate in reading education and wrote a dissertation that incorporated both social studies theory and reading theory. In all fairness to my former principal, the field of reading education was redefined during the period between his mandate and my doctoral studies and has continued to evolve over the past two decades.

The Study of Reading

The research in reading falls into four categories:

- the text
- the context for learning
- the learner
- the learning strategies

These four factors can be conveniently separated for the purposes of discussion, but of course they are intricately linked and occur simultaneously. The figure below shows how these influencing factors interact with each other.

The Text: Narrative to Expository Good readers have expectations from text. When I curl up with a romance novel, I rarely bring a highlighter. Being residents of Florida, my husband and I read our homeowners' insurance policy very carefully after a hurricane. This is not the same way I read poetry or a menu. Good readers are flexible with a variety of text; poor readers read everything pretty much the same way.

Elementary students read primarily narrative text. Likewise, teachers teach children how to read a story by thinking about the setting or characters or by answering comprehension questions. Yet when elementary teachers embark on a social studies lesson, they generally jump straight to the content. They spend no time at all on how to read the textbook. When students enter middle school,

the demands for reading informational or expository text are much greater. Textbooks filled with new concepts replace stories. Charts and diagrams replace pictures. The vocabulary is more difficult and often essential in understanding the text.

Who in middle and high schools helps students read and write expository text? When I ask this question of a school faculty, the language arts teachers point to the social studies and science teachers because they are the ones with these types of textbooks. The social studies and science teachers point to language arts teachers because they "do" words. Even when students attend a reading class, what is usually taught is more narrative and on a lower reading level. What happens when students enter a social studies class and no one has helped them understand how to read the textbook?

Teachers often comment that students do not read anything outside of school. In reality, students read all kinds of text. They read e-mail, notes, magazines, TV listings, cereal boxes, video game instructions, T-shirts, movie posters, signs, song lyrics, and much more. We can connect to our students' real-world literacy by creating links from what they read outside of school to what we want them to read in school. We can connect song lyrics to poetry, movies to short stories, Internet

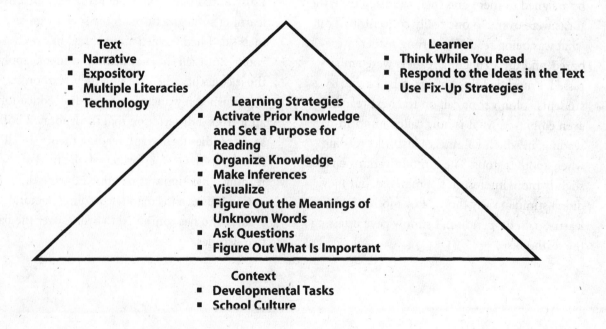

Text
- **Narrative**
- **Expository**
- **Multiple Literacies**
- **Technology**

Learner
- **Think While You Read**
- **Respond to the Ideas in the Text**
- **Use Fix-Up Strategies**

Learning Strategies
- **Activate Prior Knowledge and Set a Purpose for Reading**
- **Organize Knowledge**
- **Make Inferences**
- **Visualize**
- **Figure Out the Meanings of Unknown Words**
- **Ask Questions**
- **Figure Out What Is Important**

Context
- **Developmental Tasks**
- **School Culture**

sites about rock stars to biographies, video game instructions to expository text. Unless we recognize and provide links to the kinds of reading and writing that adolescents encounter in the "real world," they may never value what we are trying to teach them.

The Context for Learning Middle and high school students are immersed in life. The developmental tasks of becoming autonomous, forming a positive self-concept, learning social skills, progressing academically, and engaging in abstract thinking are all very important. To facilitate these developmental tasks, educators can create positive climates that reward effort as well as ability, provide a relevant curriculum, and motivate students to learn. We teachers have to ask ourselves, "What is worth knowing for adolescents in today's society?" and "How do we present this knowledge so that it makes sense to the lives and experiences of our students?"

The Learner Our students come to us knowing a lot of "stuff." This prior knowledge includes all that they have experienced, including their values, beliefs, and culture. You can think of this accumulated prior knowledge as a file cabinet. We all have multiple file folders, skinny or thick, on a variety of topics. For example, I have a big, thick file folder on soccer. My husband is a soccer coach; my daughter and son play soccer; and I played on a recreational team. On the other hand, I have a skinny file folder on football. I rarely attend a game and do not know much about the players.

Sometimes our job as teachers is to hand students a folder and have them label it and put things in it (building background information). Sometimes our job is to have students retrieve folders and read through them (activating prior knowledge). Sometimes our job is to help students organize their folders, placing labels on different parts so they can use this information in a new context (organizing knowledge). A good guiding principle is that students cannot learn anything new unless they are able to connect it to something they already know. To become strong readers, students must engage with the text in various ways.

- **Think While You Read** Many students see reading as something to get through, rather than something to absorb, integrate, synthesize, and extend. Their eyes glance over the words, but they may not learn or remember the information because they have not thought about it.

- **Respond to the Ideas in the Text** When students are engaged in reading, they respond to the ideas in some way. They ask themselves questions, organize the ideas in a map, and connect the ideas with what they already know.

- **Use Fix-Up Strategies** Strong readers keep track of whether things make sense to them and do something to "fix up" their comprehension if things do not make sense. They might use the glossary, re-read, read ahead, think about the topic, or ask someone.

- **Activate Prior Knowledge and Set a Purpose for Reading** Before reading, good readers activate what they know about a topic by looking at the table of contents, glossary, titles, captions, section headings, and/or graphics. They make connections from the text to their experience and prior knowledge. They may skim the structure of the text for main ideas and think about what they will be expected to do with reading.

- **Organize Knowledge** During and after reading, strong readers summarize the major ideas. They may skim the text and re-read portions to take notes or to create a concept map or an outline. This organization and reorganization of knowledge helps students understand, remember, and use the major concepts presented in the text.

- **Make Inferences** Strong readers make inferences throughout their reading. That is, they connect what is in their heads with what is on the page. If they see a building with an onion-shaped dome, they might infer that the setting is in Russia. Accurate inference making depends on the background knowledge of the reader.

- **Visualize** Proficient readers visualize the information presented in text. Nonproficient readers, on the other hand, do not seem to be able to create pictures in their minds. Having students sketch images or create concept maps, diagrams, charts, or other visual representations of the information helps them create these visual images.
- **Figure Out the Meanings of Unknown Words** As students read increasingly complex text, they encounter words they do not know. Previewing text for key vocabulary and using context and structural analysis can help students increase their understanding and their vocabularies.
- **Ask Questions** Before and during reading, strong readers ask themselves questions such as, "What do I know about this topic?" or "What is the meaning of a concept in bold print?" These questions indicate that students are thinking about the reading and connecting the ideas in the text to their prior knowledge.
- **Figure Out What Is Important** One of the most common question types on standardized tests is "finding the main idea." To comprehend text, readers must identify, remember, and summarize the major ideas presented in the text. Figuring out what is important in the text should be tied to the purpose for reading. Taking notes from text, constructing a concept map, or creating an outline all involve identifying what is important in the text.

You can talk to students about how effective and efficient learning takes place. If talking about effective reading behaviors becomes a natural part of classroom instruction, students can add these ideas to their repertoires and become stronger, more flexible, and more proficient readers.

The Learning Strategies Veteran teachers have heard the terms *skills* and *strategies* thrown around for many years. Skills must be automatically and consistently applied and require fairly low levels of thinking. Skills take practice. This fact became abundantly clear to me the first time I was in the car with my sixteen-year-old son, who had just gotten his driver's license. Making a left-hand turn in traffic takes a high level of driving skill and, initially, a lot of concentration. Checking both mirrors, gauging the distances of oncoming cars, and signaling the turn became automatic after practice. My son can now negotiate the same turn while carrying on a conversation and eating a candy bar.

While driving gets easier with practice, we all need a plan when navigating unfamiliar territory. We consult a map, ask for directions, and formulate a strategy for getting to our destination. A strategy is an overall plan requiring higher levels of reasoning. It is flexible in application and involves awareness and reflection.

Proficient reading takes both the execution of skills and a strategy for fulfilling the purpose for reading. With some practice, taking notes becomes a fairly automatic process of identifying important points and recording them in a way that can be used later. But it takes a strategy to put the pieces together to write a report. Before reading, strong readers use strategies to connect with what they know about the topic, while reading to maintain concentration and reflect on ideas in the text, and after reading to organize major points to fulfill the purpose for reading. The learning strategies in this book are designed to engage students in the behaviors of strong reading until these behaviors become part of the readers' repertoire.

Helping Struggling Readers Become Strong Readers

Struggling readers can do the same thing as strong readers, but they need more help, more support, and more scaffolding. For example, my husband purchased a boat that sits very high in the water, which is wonderful when you are in the boat looking down. After snorkeling one day, I learned the downside of a high-riding boat. When it came time to get back in the boat, the platform and the one step were too high. I wanted two more steps—the scaffolding I needed to start climbing into the boat. Struggling readers have a similar dilemma. They often have difficulty getting started, and then they easily give up.

To avoid this, introduce each strategy with fairly simple reading so that students learn the steps of the strategy and do not have to face the additional challenge of difficult text. As you select an appropriate strategy, consider the students' prior knowledge about the topic, the type of text, and the purpose for reading. You will find that some strategies lend themselves better to the study of world cultures, and others to the study of history or economics. You will also find that you prefer some strategies over others. My purpose is to provide you with options to use in any teaching and learning context. It is my fervent hope that you find that these strategies enhance your instruction by engaging students more actively in learning.

Good Luck and Best Wishes,
Dr. Judith Irvin

Read More About It

Irvin, J. L. *Reading and the Middle School Student: Strategies to Enhance Literacy* (2nd edition). Boston: Allyn and Bacon (1998).

Irvin, J. L., Buehl, D., and Klemp, R. *Reading and the High School Student: Strategies to Enhance Literacy*. Boston: Allyn and Bacon (2002).

Irvin, J. L., Lunstrum, J. P., Lynch-Brown, C., and Shepard, M. F. *Enhancing Social Studies Instruction through Reading and Writing Strategies*. Washington, D.C.: National Council for the Social Studies (1995).

STRATEGY 1: PREVIEWING TEXT

When facing a textbook reading assignment, most students just plow in and try to finish it as quickly as possible. They may leaf through the chapter or passage to see how long it is, taking note of how many pages they can skip because of pictures or graphs. Proficient readers, on the other hand, take a moment to consider the following things *before* they begin a textbook reading assignment:

*P*urpose of the reading
*I*mportant ideas
*C*onnection to prior knowledge

This strategy of previewing text is therefore known as PIC. You can use the PIC strategy to help your students develop good reading habits by encouraging them to spend just a few moments organizing their thinking and setting their goals before beginning a reading assignment. In addition, this process leads students to speculate about the main idea of the passage before they start reading. After reading, they may change what they thought the main idea was or confirm that their prediction was correct.

How Can the Strategy Help My Students?

The PIC strategy can get your students into the all-important habits of setting a purpose for their reading, identifying the most important ideas, and connecting with what they already know. Often when students read, they do not think about what is really important to remember. Previewing reading assignments helps students focus on the most important information and facilitates storing that information in long-term memory. If students take a few moments to go through the steps described below, they will better understand and remember the material they read.

Getting Started

Here are the steps to the PIC strategy:

Step 1: Purpose for Reading. Make sure students know what they will be doing with the information after reading. (That is, what is the assignment or purpose for reading? What will they do with the information?) Have them peruse the structure of the assignment, noting special features such as summaries or guiding questions. Ask students to use the table of contents and glossary of the book to locate information. To establish a purpose for reading, students can ask the following questions.

- What am I going to do with this information when I finish reading?
- How does this text fit in with the material before or after it?

Step 2: Important Ideas. Students should flip through the assignment, noting any headings that indicate the major points in the reading. They should try to understand how this passage fits within the larger chapter, unit, or book. Students should also be familiar with any key vocabulary in boldface type or italics. These words are probably the most important concepts in the text. To identify important ideas, students can ask the following questions.

- Is there anything in the table of contents, index, or glossary that can help me understand the "big ideas"?
- What are the key vocabulary terms I should understand?

Step 3: Connect to What You Know. Students need to think about what they know about the topic before they start reading. Encourage them to wonder about the topic, asking themselves, "What would I like to find out?" Finally, students should identify questions they want answered about the topic. They can organize their ideas with a chart like the KWQ Chart below.

Using the Strategy in Your Classroom

After students have read the text, they should go back to their KWQ charts to see if their questions were answered and to make sure they understand the key vocabulary. Feel free to vary the strategy as students become accustomed to previewing their assignments. You may wish to move from having students complete KWQ organizers to having them address just the purpose for reading, important information about the topic, and connecting-to-prior-knowledge questions in a quick discussion or pre-reading assignment. You can also add an after-reading component by asking students to discuss, in small groups or as a class, the questions they still want answered. (**See Strategy 7, Graphic Organizers 6 and 7, and KWL and KWLS Charts.**) They may have some questions that were not answered in the text. These questions can be the basis of further research or projects.

Extending the Strategy

Books use diagrams, charts, maps, and pictures to help the reader understand the content. As students become more familiar with previewing, you may wish to direct their attention to these graphic features, asking them in what ways these items will extend or support their learning.

The PIC strategy is simply a guide to help students preview the text before reading and focus on the most important points. It can be used in conjunction with other assignments or modified to serve as an aid for studying for a test or writing a report. For example, before students read you can ask them to sketch out a graphic organizer or a concept map (**See Strategies 3 and 4**) to fill in after they read. They can then use this organizer as a writing or study guide. (**See Graphic Organizer 3, Cluster Diagram.**)

Some Final Thoughts

The purpose for previewing text is to get students to recognize the text's main idea, which could be a theme, something important to students, or the first sentence in a paragraph. However, helping students identify the main idea of a text passage is often a difficult challenge. David Moore (1986)

▶ What I *Know* About the Topic	▶ What I *Wonder* About the Topic	▶ Questions I Would Like to Have Answered

suggested that you engage students in stating what the text is about in one or two words and then add two or three other words to go with it. This usually comes closer to the author's intended main idea.

When students first use the PIC strategy, the process will seem very time-consuming. But as they become more familiar with the format and steps, they will move through the strategy more quickly. Feel free to modify the strategy to suit the needs of your students.

Read More About It

Alvermann, D. E. "Graphic Organizers: Cueing Devices for Comprehending and Remembering Main Ideas." In *Teaching Main Idea Comprehension,* J. F. Baumann. Newark, DE: International Reading Association. 1986.

Avery, P. G., Baker, J., and Gross, S. H. "Mapping Learning at the Secondary Level." *The Clearing House* 70 (5) 1997: 279–85.

Heimlich, E., and Pittleman, S. D. *Semantic Mapping: Classroom Applications.* Newark, DE: International Reading Association. 1986.

Romance, N. R., and Vitale, M. R. "Concept Mapping as a Tool for Learning: Broadening the Framework for Student-Centered Instruction." *College Teaching* 47 (2) 1999: 74–79.

STRATEGY 2: UNDERSTANDING TEXT

When you come home at the end of the day and flip through the mail, you probably don't read each item the same way. You would read a letter from a friend differently than you would read a notice from a lawyer you do not know. The items *look* different, use different vocabularies, and have different structures. Strong readers know how to adjust their reading depending on the text and their purpose for reading.

A textbook contains different forms of text. Students must interpret pictures, diagrams, figures, and charts. They read narrative accounts, diaries, and documents that support the major concepts. Then, there is the text itself. Expository

or informational text is generally structured in one of the following five forms.

- cause and effect
- comparison and contrast
- description
- problem and solution
- sequence or chronological order

Particular content lends itself more or less to one structure or another. For example, while history is generally conveyed in a sequence or chronological order, geography may be best learned in a descriptive format. In addition, one or more forms may be used within a passage. The more that students can detect the structure of text, the better they can prepare themselves to think in a way that is consistent with that structure.

Signal or transition words usually indicate the structure of the text. Proficient readers intuitively notice the words that indicate the type of thinking required while reading. Signal words tell readers what is coming up. When you see *for example* or *for instance*, you know that examples will follow. On the next page is a chart with some of the most common signal or transition words.

An important reading strategy based on these words is called "Double S: *S*ignal Words That Indicate *S*tructure." This strategy is designed to help students recognize and use signal words to detect the structure of the text.

How Can the Strategy Help My Students?

Good readers are flexible thinkers. Signal or transition words such as *different from, the same as,* or *compared with* indicate that the authors are presenting information that will compare and contrast at least two ideas. This comparison-and-contrast structure is read differently from one in which ideas are presented in sequence or chronological order. Signal or transition words indicate what the structure of text might be. When students notice these words in the text, especially before reading, they tend to get ready to think in a certain way. Struggling readers need to have these words pointed out to them and to be instructed on the function of these words while reading or writing. In time, they should be able to use signal words and move to more complex forms of text.

When students are learning to write expository text and must demonstrate that skill on a task such as producing a sample for a standardized test, these signal or transition words can help them express their points more clearly. As students recognize and use transition words and different text structures, they will (1) comprehend text more effectively, (2) produce more coherent expository writing, and (3) think more clearly and flexibly.

Getting Started

Here are the steps in the Understanding Text strategy.

Step 1: Survey the Text. Have students flip through the text and list all the different types of items they will be reading, such as documents, charts, diagrams, maps, short stories, or expository text. Usually, the expository writing in textbooks explains or informs the reader. But primary source material, such as a diary, may be read differently. The primary source probably supports one or more of the major points presented in the text.

Step 2: Identify the Signal Words. Have students list transition words in the text or allow students to attach self-adhesive notes to the text page to help them locate the transition words.

Step 3: Identify the Structure of the Text. Using their list of transition words, students, individually or in small groups, should identify the main structure of the text: cause and effect, comparison and contrast, description, problem and solution, sequence or chronological order. They should ask themselves, "What kind of thinking will be necessary to understand the information in the text?" and "How would I best display the information after reading?"

Step 4: Predict the Main Idea of the Passage. Using what they know about the signal words and the structure of the text, students should write a sentence stating what they think the main idea of this passage will be.

SIGNAL WORDS				
Cause and Effect	**Comparison and Contrast**	**Description**	**Problem and Solution**	**Sequence or Chronological Order**
because	different from	for instance	the problem is	not long after
since	same as	for example	the question is	next
consequently	similar to	such as	a solution is	then
this led to … so	as opposed to	to illustrate	one answer is	initially
if … then	instead of	in addition		before
nevertheless	although	most importantly		after
accordingly	however	another		finally
because of	compared with	furthermore		preceding
as a result of	as well as	first, second …		following
in order to	either … or			on (date)
may be due to	but			over the years
for this reason	on the other hand			today
	unless			when

Step 5: Read the Text.

Step 6: Revisit the Main-Idea Prediction. After reading, students should go back to their prediction of the main idea of the passage. They should then display the information on a graphic organizer appropriate to the text structure. (**Graphic Organizer 2, Cause and Effect; Graphic Organizer 11, Comparison and Contrast; Graphic Organizer 3, Description; Graphic Organizer 9, Problem and Solution; or Graphic Organizer 10, Sequence or Chronological Order.**) Then students may write a summary or in some other way organize what they have read.

Using the Strategy in Your Classroom

We know that good readers use signal or transition words to help guide their understanding and their thinking. Struggling readers do not. So teachers can help struggling readers to recognize and use signal words through the Double S strategy. This does not mean asking students to memorize lists of words. Some teachers find it effective to write signal words on posters around the room or to give students a page to put in their notebooks. Students should also add their own signal words to such lists as they find them in the text. In time, they will use these words intuitively, and they will not need to go through the steps of identifying signal words before reading.

Discussing the structure of text is a little more difficult. The best way for students to "see" the structure is through graphic organizers (presented in Strategy 3). The more that students have these conversations about text, the more proficient they will become at recognizing and using text structure to guide their thinking.

For additional help in identifying and discussing text structures, refer to the Text Structure Reference Chart on pages 164–165. In addition to listing and defining the five main expository text structures discussed here, the chart lists the most common signal words associated with each text structure and provides a sampling of questions that students can use to help them recognize the structures and further analyze them.

Extending the Strategy

After students practice locating signal words and identifying text structure, you can link this strategy with Strategy 3: Using Graphic Organizers. The Double S strategy may also be linked to the PIC technique discussed in Strategy 1.

Traditionally, reading and writing have been taught separately. But practice with the Double S strategy also can help students write more effective expository pieces. Writing expository text is a major component of most state assessments.

Some Final Thoughts

Unfortunately, not all texts are written in a format that has an identifiable structure. Similarly, there may be no signal words in the text. The text may also change structure within the passage. These more complex structures demand increasingly sophisticated reading ability. However, the Double S strategy can get students started on the road to becoming independent learners.

Read More About It

Britton, B. K., Woodward, A., and Binkley, M., Eds. *Learning from Textbooks: Theory and Practice.* Hillsdale, NJ: Lawrence Erlbaum Associates. 1993.

Garner, R., and Alexander, P. A., Eds. *Beliefs About Text and Instruction with Text.* Hillsdale, NJ: Lawrence Erlbaum Associates. 1994.

Harvey, S. *Nonfiction Matters.* York, ME: Stenhouse Publishers. 1998.

McMackin, M. C. "Using Narrative Picture Books to Build Awareness of Expository Text Structure." *Reading Horizons* 39 (1) 1998: 7–20.

Quiocho, A. "The Quest to Comprehend Expository Text: Applied Classroom Research." *Journal of Adolescent and Adult Literacy* 40 (6) 1997: 450–54.

TEXT STRUCTURE REFERENCE CHART

Structure or Pattern	Signal Words		Questions for Patterns
Description, Simple Listing, Enumeration Information about a topic is presented through description, listing characteristics, features, and examples.	*to begin with* *characteristics are* *most important* *the following* *in many ways* *for example* *such as* *to illustrate* *furthermore*	*also* *in fact* *finally* *as well* *for instance* *while* *in addition* *another*	What is the main topic? What did the author say about (topic)? How did the author present these ideas? What ideas (or facts) are discussed? Can you think of other ideas or facts about . . . ?
Sequence or Chronological Information is presented in sequence, usually in numerical or chronological order.	*first, second, third* *next* *then* *finally* *after* *until* *before* *first/lst*	*on (date)* *at (time)* *not long after* *now* *as before* *when* *initially* *lastly* *preceding* *following*	What was the first important idea discussed? When did it occur? What is the sequence of events? Why did the author tell about this process in this order? What would be included on a time line of the events? What is the chronological order of the steps?
Comparison and Contrast Information is presented by showing likenesses (comparison) and differences (contrast).	*different from* *in contrast* *alike* *same as* *on the other hand* *however* *but* *as well as* *not only . . . but* *in a like manner* *difference between* *instead of* *compared with*	*either . . . or* *while* *although* *unless* *similar to* *yet* *nevertheless* *also* *likewise* *as opposed to* *after all* *and yet* *as well as*	Why do you think the author wrote about this topic by showing likenesses and differences? What is being compared here? How were they alike? How were they different? What do they have in common? Can you think of other ways these (topics) are alike or different?

▶ Structure or Pattern	▶ Signal Words		▶ Questions for Patterns
Cause and Effect Facts, events, or concepts (effects) come into being because of other facts, events, or concepts (causes).	*reasons why* *if . . . then* *as a result of* *therefore* *because (of)* *thus* *on account of* *due to* *may be due to* *effects of*	*since* *consequently* *this led to* *so that* *nevertheless* *accordingly* *for this reason* *then, so* *in order to*	Can you tell me the cause of _____? What was the effect of _____? How should causes and effects be arranged on a chart? Can you think of any other causes that might produce these effects? Are there any other effects that can result from this cause? Can you think of similar causes and effects?
Problem and Solution or Question and Answer Information is stated as a problem and one or more solutions are presented. A question is asked and one or more answers are presented.	*a problem is* *a dilemma is* *a puzzle is* *solved* *question . . .* *answer* *a solution* *the best estimate* *one may conclude*	*why* *when* *where* *how* *what* *who* *it could be that* *how many*	What were the problems discussed here? Are there solutions to this problem? What are they? What caused the problem? How was it solved? Can you think of any similar problems? How were they solved? How would you solve this problem?

STRATEGY 3: USING GRAPHIC ORGANIZERS

Graphic organizers are made up of lines, arrows, boxes, and circles that show the relationships between and among ideas. They are sometimes called webs, semantic maps, graphic representations, or clusters. These graphic organizers can help students organize their thinking and their knowledge. While textbooks contain many types of text, the largest portion of text is expository or informational. Expository text has five major structures:

- cause and effect
- comparison and contrast
- description
- problem and solution
- sequence or chronological order

In this strategy, four types of text structure will be presented. Description will be presented in Strategy 4 because this type of text is best displayed with a concept map. The four types of text structure with accompanying graphic organizers are shown below and on the following pages.

Cause and Effect: Cause-and-effect patterns show the relationship between results and the ideas or events that made the results occur. (**See Graphic Organizer 2, Cause-and-Effect Chart.**)

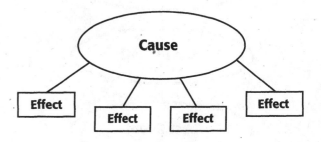

Problem and Solution: Problem-solution patterns identify at least one problem, offer one or more solutions to the problem, and explain or predict outcomes of the solutions. **(See Graphic Organizer 9, Problem and Solution Chart.)**

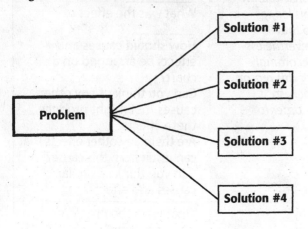

Comparison and Contrast: Comparison and contrast, or Venn, diagrams point out similarities and differences between two concepts or ideas. **(See Graphic Organizer 11, Venn Diagram.)**

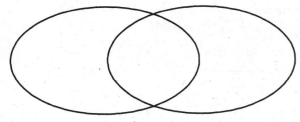

Sequence or Chronological Order: Sequence or chronological-order diagrams show events or ideas in the order in which they happened. **(See Graphic Organizer 10, Sequence or Chronological Order Chart.)**

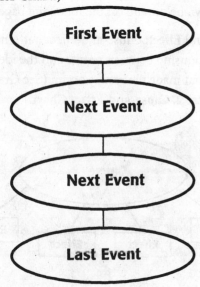

How Can the Strategy Help My Students?

The way that ideas are presented in a textbook dictates the type of thinking that is necessary to understand and remember those ideas. Graphic organizers help students visualize the connections between and among ideas. They also help students organize knowledge so they can use it later to study for a test or write a report. The act of organizing information engages students in learning and helps them make connections to what they already know. In addition, discussing which graphic organizer might best display the information helps students "see" and use the structure of text to understand and remember more effectively.

Getting Started

Any single piece of text can be displayed in more than one way, depending on the purpose for reading and the reader's prior knowledge of the topic. Below are the basic steps in one approach to using graphic organizers.

Step 1: Students preview the material to be read.

Step 2: Students hypothesize which of the four graphic organizers would be best to display the information and their understanding of the material. Their discussion should include the purpose for their reading, and they should note any signal or transition words that may indicate the type of thinking required for the reading and the best way to display the information. Be sure to tell students that the organizers can be modified to meet their needs. For example, the cause-and-effect graphic organizer has room for four effects, but the text may only state one or two.

Step 3: Students read the text silently, taking notes.

Step 4: Students work in cooperative groups to create a graphic representation of their understanding of the text.

Step 5: Students present the finished product to others in the class.

Using the Strategy in Your Classroom

Previewing the text is essential for students to get an idea of the text's "layout." It helps students get ready to think and organize their ideas in a particular way. If students have not had any previous experience using graphic organizers, you may wish to introduce them to the students a little at a time. Here are some tips for helping students become more proficient users of graphic organizers.

- Begin the explanation of graphic organizers with simple text that has an obvious structure.
- Present one graphic organizer at a time.
- Then, move into having students compare and contrast representations.
- Help students use signal or transition words to determine the structure of a text. These are words such as *for instance, similar to, different from,* and *because* that indicate how ideas are related in a text.
- Then, have students use two, then three, then four types of organizers.

As students become more accustomed to discussing and using graphic organizers, they will be able to adapt them to both their purpose for reading and the type of text they are reading. Eventually, students should be able to generate graphic organizers on their own and use them in their note taking.

Extending the Strategy

If students are using webbing in other classes, explain that using graphic organizers is much the same process as creating webs. This would also be a good time to talk to students about the differences in narrative and expository text. Occasionally, pieces of narrative text are inserted in textbooks to elaborate on a point. Students can be shown the different functions of each type of text—graphic organizers are the perfect vehicle for achieving this goal.

Graphic organizers can also be used as a stimulus for writing expository essays. Students learning to compose essays in cause-and-effect, comparison-and-contrast, problem-and-solution,

or sequence or chronological-order patterns should capture their ideas in a graphic organizer before they begin writing.

Previewing the text is essential in deciding which graphic organizer is most appropriate. Therefore, you may wish to connect this strategy with Strategies 1 and 2.

Some Final Thoughts

Unfortunately, not all texts are neatly packaged into the tidy structures I have presented so far. Sometimes text does not follow a definite structure, and sometimes it changes from one structure to another in the same chapter. When this happens, it is wise to discuss the author's purpose for the text and help students construct their own way of organizing the ideas presented.

Read More About It

Dye, G. A. "Graphic Organizers to the Rescue! Helping Students Link—and Remember—Information." *Teaching Exceptional Children* 32 (3) 2000, 72–76.

Irwin-DeVitis, L., and Pease, D. "Using Graphic Organizers for Learning and Assessment in Middle Level Classrooms." *Middle School Journal* 26 (5) 1995: 57–64.

Robinson, D. H. "Graphic Organizers as Aids to Text Learning." *Reading Research and Instruction* 37 (2) 1998: 85–105.

STRATEGY 4: CONSTRUCTING CONCEPT MAPS

As you saw in Strategy 3, graphic organizers can help students visualize and make sense of expository text. The type of graphic organizer we will focus on now is the concept map. A concept map, sometimes called a semantic map or a cluster diagram, allows students to zero in on the most important points of the text. The map is made up of lines, boxes, circles, and arrows. It can be as simple or as complex as students make it and as the text requires.

How Can the Strategy Help My Students?

Struggling readers often get bogged down in the first three paragraphs of an expository text because they are having difficulty with comprehension. Consequently, they miss the most important points in the passage and never really figure out what the text is about. The concept map is designed to help students focus on and organize the most noteworthy points in the text so they can use them later for a discussion, a writing assignment, or a test. When students preview a reading passage and then work through a reading assignment, they can arrange and rearrange important concepts as needed.

Getting Started

Previewing helps students see the structure of the passage. With a description-type structure, students may notice signal or transition words such as *for instance, for example, such as, in addition*, or *furthermore*. These signal words indicate that the text is describing or explaining important concepts. The following steps may be helpful in having students complete a concept map:

Step 1: Preview the Passage. Previewing can help students determine which kind of structure might best display the ideas in the text.

Step 2: Sketch a Concept Map. Looking at the boldfaced type, headings, and general structure of the text, students should sketch out a map to display the ideas in the passage.

Step 3: Read the Passage.

Step 4: Construct a Map. Using boxes, lines, arrows, bubbles, circles, or any other figure, students can display the ideas in the text in a concept map.

Using the Strategy in Your Classroom

When first introducing the concept map to students, you may wish to create most of the map yourself and have students complete it after they have used a prereading strategy and have read the text. The mapping strategy is most effective, however, if students create their own concept maps. They can embed definitions and examples within the maps to help remind them of the meaning of particular concepts. As students create their own maps, they should consider the content of headings, the signaling power of boldface type, and the organization of the text to help them choose the most important points.

Concept maps work best with text that explains one or more ideas and provides supporting examples. A concept map may be displayed hierarchically, as in the example below, or in a more free-form style, as in the example on page 169.

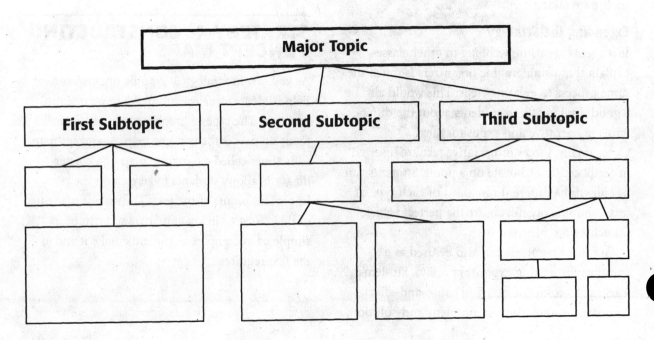

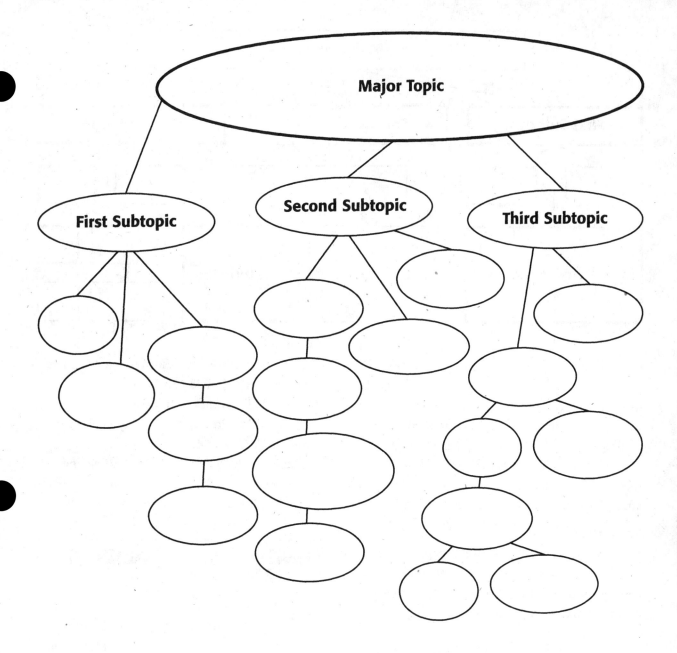

Any combination and organization of circles, bubbles, squares, triangles, lines, or arrows can be used to construct a concept map. Previewing helps students see the overall picture. Sketching gives students an idea of how the key concepts can best be displayed. Constructing the final map helps students understand how the concepts relate to one another. Some teachers suggest sketching the ideas via self-adhesive notes and then constructing the final concept map when students are happy with the display. If some students are more comfortable having a structure to work with, offer them cluster diagrams (**See Graphic Organizer 3**),

and ask them to fill in as many levels as they need and to add boxes if appropriate.

Extending the Strategy

Struggling readers may need more help to begin a task such as creating a concept map. A Cloze Concept Map may support such readers. After students complete a pre-reading strategy on the topic at hand, you can give them an almost-completed map. Some of the boxes should be left blank and have bold lines around them, as shown in the example on the following page.

If you think students may have difficulty even with this task, you may wish to provide a word

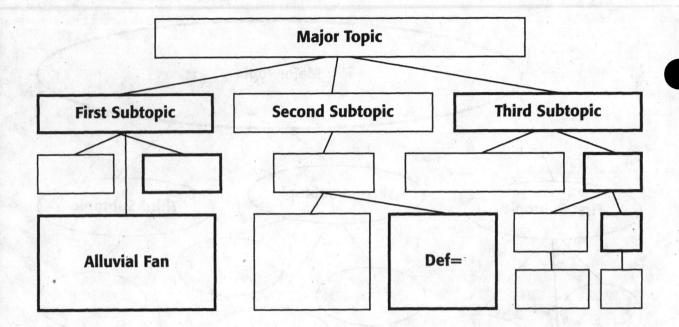

Major Topic

First Subtopic   **Second Subtopic**   **Third Subtopic**

Alluvial Fan   **Def=**

box with the deleted items listed. As students become more proficient at completing this Cloze Concept Map, more boxes can be left blank. As time goes on, once students have finished a pre-reading strategy, you can give them a blank concept map to fill out as they read. Eventually, they should be able to construct their own maps after previewing the text and making a sketch.

Some Final Thoughts

When first introducing a concept map, use a short and fairly simple text before moving on to a more complex and longer one. Although it is sometimes a challenge, it is best to limit concept maps to one page. That way, when students prepare to study for a test or use the information in writing, the text's most important ideas are displayed in a handy and easy-to-use format.

Read More About It

Chen, H. S., and Graves, M. F. "Previewing Challenging Reading Selections for ESL Students." *Journal of Adolescent and Adult Literacy* 41 (7) 1998: 570–71.

Cunningham, J. W., and Moore, D. W. "The Confused World of Main Idea." In *Teaching Main Idea Comprehension*, J. Baumann. Newark, DE: International Reading Association. 1986.

Dana, C. "Strategy Families for Disabled Readers." *Journal of Reading* 33 (5): 30–35.

Huffman, L. E. "What's in It for You? A Student-Directed Text Preview." *Journal of Adolescent and Adult Literacy* 40 (1): 56–57.

Salemblier, G. B. "SCAN and RUN: A Reading Comprehension Strategy That Works." *Journal of Adolescent and Adult Literacy* 42 (5): 386–94.

STRATEGY 5: VISUALIZING INFORMATION

Textbooks are full of charts, diagrams, pictures, illustrations, cartoons, and maps. These visual aids enhance the learning of the content. In their rush to complete an assignment, students often skip over the visual information that may actually improve their comprehension.

The Information Age has certainly bombarded students today with visual images. Some say that the beautiful picture books, the television, the Internet, CD–ROMs, and so forth may have taken away a student's need (and perhaps ability) to visualize. Others may argue that youth today think in visual images. Whatever the case, proficient readers visualize as they read—struggling readers generally do not.

How Can the Strategy Help My Students?

Visual information displayed in a textbook can be flipped over and ignored or studied and incorporated. What students *do* with the visual information is the important ingredient to comprehending text. Rakes, Rakes, and Smith (1995) suggested that a teacher can help students use information on increasingly interactive levels. The teacher can:

- Provide written or oral directions immediately before students "read" the visual information, such as "On this map, you will notice . . ."
- Direct students' attention through study questions to the important accompanying visuals, such as "This chart displays the most common transportation in America during the Industrial Revolution . . ."
- Encourage students to evaluate the graphics in the text and think about how the graphics and text relate to one another. You might ask, "Given the most important point of this passage, is this graphic representative of . . ."
- Ask students to create their own visuals depicting the information represented in the text. When students draw a sketch or picture of the information in the text, they have made a connection between what they know and what they are reading. Illustrations can be used to summarize text, and graphic organizers and concept maps (Strategies 3 and 4) can assist students in integrating new knowledge with existing knowledge.

The more that students are involved in creating visual images, the more engaged they will be with the ideas in the text. Depending on the purpose of the assigned reading, you may wish to direct students to visuals, have them evaluate the visual information presented, and/or have students create their own graphic representations of the ideas presented in the text.

Getting Started

Here are the basic steps to the Visualizing Information strategy:

Step 1: Preview the Text, Noting the Visual Information Presented. This information may be in the form of charts, diagrams, pictures, or illustrations.

Step 2: Ask How the Visual Information Relates to the Text or Why the Author(s) Included This Information. It is important that students create a link between the text and the visual. You may wish to have students use a transparency over the text to draw arrows between the text and the visual.

Step 3: Generate Questions Raised by the Visual Aid. Students should list two to three questions that arise from this visual aid.

Step 4: Read the Text.

Step 5: Go Back and Review Visual Aids in the Text. Students should evaluate whether the visual accurately displays the most important ideas in the text.

Using the Strategy in Your Classroom

This strategy can, of course, be modified to suit the needs of your students and their purpose for reading. Based on Rakes, Rakes, and Smith's levels of interaction presented above, you could:

- simply direct students to notice the visual element
- provide study questions based on the visual element
- have students evaluate how the visual element helps them better understand the text
- have students sketch their own understanding of the topic of the reading

In addition, questions can direct students' understanding of how the visual element fits with information presented before and after it.

Extending the Strategy

Some educators suggest that after reading, students be asked to draw the visual from memory. This works particularly well for diagrams explained in the text. The act of creating a graphic helps students process it better and connect to the information presented in the text. In addition, this activity can certainly be used to assess how well students understood the text.

Student-created graphics can be extended through group work by having students explain their graphic to other students. They benefit from hearing and seeing the various perspectives of other students. Without employing competition such as "whose graphic is the best?", students can be guided to give feedback on other students' graphics. Giving and soliciting feedback helps them process the ideas in the text more deeply and become better consumers of displays of visual information.

Some teachers have used a Visual Reading Guide (Stein, 1978) for many years. This study guide is simply constructed to direct students to preview the visual information in the text before they read, answering some preliminary questions before and after reading.

The graphic organizers and concept maps presented in Strategies 3 and 4 are additional ways of encouraging students to visualize and organize the ideas in the text. (See Graphic Organizer 2, Cause-and-Effect Chart; Graphic Organizer 9, Problem and Solution Chart; Graphic Organizer 11, Venn Diagram; and Graphic Organizer 3, Cluster Diagram.) Some computer software allows students to flip between graphic representations and an outline of the material.

Some Final Thoughts

Not all text has strategically placed visual infor-mation that is well explained and connected to the text in the caption. If this is the case, then having students evaluate and/or redraw graphics may be useful. Also, because of time constraints, a teacher can not give this type of attention to every visual aid in the text. But when the visual infor-mation does help students better understand the ideas in the text, this strategy can be most helpful. Most students—but especially struggling read-ers—can benefit from learning how to use the visual aids that often accompany texts.

Read More About It

Hyerle, D. *Visual Tools for Constructing Knowledge.* Alexandria, VA: Association for Supervision and Curriculum Development. 1996.

Rakes, G. C., Rakes, T. A., and Smith, L. J. "Using Visuals to Enhance Secondary Students' Reading Comprehension of Expository Text." *Journal of Adolescent and Adult Literacy* 39 (1) 1995: 46–54.

Scevak, J., and Moore, P. "The Strategies Students in Years 5, 7, and 9 Use for Processing Texts and Visual Aids." *The Australian Journal of Language and Literacy* 20 (4) 1997: 280–88.

Stein, H. "The Visual Reading Guide (VRG)." *Social Education* 42 (6) 1978: 534–35.

STRATEGY 6: BUILDING BACKGROUND INFORMATION

Have you ever tried to read a computer manual or some other highly technical book when you lacked the background knowledge really to understand it? It is frustrating to read something on a topic you know little about. Students encounter that feeling often when they attempt to read many textbooks. You can help students build the information they need to be successful before beginning a reading assignment.

One strategy for achieving this goal is the Predicting and Confirming Activity (PACA). Teachers find this strategy a good way to teach their content. The strategy helps build back-ground information before students read about something they know little about so they will have a context for understanding the ideas presented. (Graphic Organizer 8, PACA.)

How Can the Strategy Help My Students?

Students often have no personal connection with much of what we hope they learn in classrooms. They have a context for American history and geography, but often struggle with subjects such as world cultures. For students to learn anything new, they must connect it in some way to some-thing they already know. Good teachers help students make the connection between new information and what students already know.

Getting Started

Here are the steps for the Predicting and Confirming Activity. The Predicting and Confirming Activity uses student predictions to set a purpose for reading. Students make these predictions based on an initial set of information provided by the teacher. Given additional information, students can revise their predictions (or hypotheses) and pose them as questions to be answered during reading.

Step 1: Provide Some Initial Information and Pose a General Question. Provide students with a list of words containing the important concepts in the reading as well as ten to fifteen more familiar terms that students will know. Then, ask them questions about the reading. A word list and a question are usually enough to help students make predictions. But if they are not, you can couple the word list with a short overview of the topic.

Step 2: Write Predictions Based on the Initial Information. These predictions can be discussed and written on the chalkboard or written by individual students or groups of students.

Step 3: Provide New Information. This can be in the form of pictures, charts, diagrams, maps, or other visual information from the textbook, a video, or from reading a story.

Step 4: Review Predictions. Students may revise, confirm, or reject their original predictions. Then they turn the predictions into questions for reading. Based on the new information, students discuss—as a class or in small groups—which of their original predictions they want to keep and which they think no longer apply. They may also revise some predictions to be more accurate. They then turn these predictions into questions they want answered during reading.

Step 5: Read the Text.

Step 6: Revisit Predictions and Answer Questions. Students once again look at their predictions and answer the questions they generated earlier. At this point, students go back to their original predictions and see which ones may be revised or confirmed. They may also check to see if their questions were answered. From here, depending on the purpose of the reading, you may wish to ask students to write about their new learning, formulate study questions and answers, or use some graphic representation of their learning.

Using the Strategy in Your Classroom

The Predicting and Confirming Activity is simply a method for building background information before reading. When students read after completing this strategy, they will be able to connect what they are reading and what they now know about the topic. The predictions turned into questions help guide their reading as well.

When constructing the initial word list, it is important to include both words students will know and some they will encounter in the reading. While discussing these words in small groups in order to write their predictions, students may guess at the meanings of unknown words, or someone in the group may know the word.

If students do not know enough about the topic even to begin predicting, then you could start off with a reading or an overview of the topic or have students leaf through the textbook to get some ideas. You could also direct students to write a sentence using two or more words in the list to construct the prediction.

Extending the Strategy

After questions are formulated and predictions are made, you may wish to use a jigsaw design to complete the reading. Groups would be assigned to answer specific questions about the topic—each group forming an expert group. Then one student from each group would share his or her "expert" information with the base group to complete the synthesizing activity.

If students need additional help in processing new information, you could ask them to visualize. They could also organize their newfound knowledge into a graphic organizer or employ a sketch or diagram. Additionally, they could extend and organize their thoughts by writing a summary or report.

Some Final Thoughts

When using a Predicting and Confirming Activity, students risk forming misconceptions by making predictions based on limited information. Revisiting the predictions is an important part of this strategy, because it is your opportunity to correct these misconceptions and expand students' knowledge about the topic. For this reason, some teachers prefer to display the predictions on an overhead or on the chalkboard. A classroom environment in which students are free to guess and be wrong is an essential component to implementing this strategy.

Some pictures in books are rich with information and some are not. You may need to supplement the text with videos, pictures, or stories. The purpose is to build background information where none or little exists so that students can be more successful when they read their textbook. In the process, students may learn that making and confirming predictions is an essential part of effective reading.

Read More About It

Beyer, B. K. *Inquiry in the Social Studies Classroom*. Columbus, OH: Charles E. Merrill Publishing Company. 1971.

Harmon, J. M., Katims, D. S., and Whittington, D. "Helping Middle School Students Learn From Social Studies Texts." *Teaching Exceptional Children* 32 (1) 1999: 70–75.

Nessell, D. "Channeling Knowledge for Reading Expository Text." *Journal of Reading* 32 (3) 1988: 231–35.

Weir, C. "Using Embedded Questions to Jump-Start Metacognition in Middle School Remedial Readers." *Journal of Adolescent and Adult Literacy* 41 (6) 1998: 458–68.

STRATEGY 7: MAKING PREDICTIONS

Making predictions is one of the most important strategies students can use when approaching a new reading assignment. Hilda Taba (1967) was one of the first educators to suggest a method for encouraging even young children to think at higher levels. Her concept-formation model was later adapted as List-Group-Label, a strategy to activate what students know about a topic, build and expand on what they know, and organize that knowledge before they begin reading.

Building on Taba's original work, reading educators later added the "map" step. This strategy can also be used as a diagnostic instrument to find out what students know about a subject before they read and as an organizational tool to facilitate higher level thinking through making predictions. Because the strategy involves the categorization and labeling of words, List-Group-Label-Map also makes an excellent preceding strategy for a vocabulary development lesson.

How Can the Strategy Help My Students?

When students begin reading without activating what they know first, they often miss the connections that would help them store that information in longer-term memory. In addition, many students lack the ability to categorize and classify information. This process of grouping concepts helps students understand the relationships between ideas. Classifying and categorizing concepts before reading helps students connect to what they already know about a topic and better understand the concepts in the text. Creating a concept map before reading gives students the opportunity to "see" the ideas and their relationships while reading.

Getting Started

Here are the steps in the List-Group-Label-Map Strategy.

The List-Group-Label-Map strategy works best when students already know something about a topic. During the initial discussion, teachers may ascertain how much students already know about a topic and correct any misconceptions they may have.

Step 1: Make a Word List. Direct students to an initial piece of information and ask them to list as many words related to the topic as possible. Pictures are the best and easiest stimulus for this activity, although other visual information in the textbook can be used. These words may be associations they come up with from memory if the topic is very familiar. Many teachers also use videos to elicit words. If you conduct the discussion with the entire class, write the word lists in columns on the chalkboard or on an overhead transparency. If the discussion occurs within a small group, a student can record the words.

Step 2: Look for Word Associations. Students group items by indicating which words belong together. Only one student in a group should indicate which words go together. The teacher (or a student in a group) then marks the words with an *X* or *O* or some other symbol. If another student wants to add to the grouping, it is important that the first student be consulted because he or she may be thinking of a different category. Students can use words more than once.

Step 3: Label Word Groups. Then the student who came up with the original groupings goes back and labels each group. These labels represent concepts, and the words are then examples of these concepts.

Step 4: Make a Concept Map. Individually or in small groups, students use the words listed to create concept maps, following the process described in Strategy 4. (**See Graphic Organizer 3, Cluster Diagram.**)

Step 5: Read the Text. During reading, students may note whether the concept map they created was consistent with the ideas presented in the text.

Step 6: Revisit the Concept Map. After reading, students take another look at their concept map and add information from the reading. Encourage students to elaborate on their maps using the

ideas in the text. These expanded maps connect what they knew before reading with what they learned while reading.

Using the Strategy in Your Classroom

Any picture, video, or other information can be used to generate the word list. Pictures that give a lot of information work best and can be used to build the background information necessary to understand the text. Pictures also help students visualize what they read. To get students started, simply ask them what they see in the picture (or remember from the video). Since the next step is to classify and categorize words, encourage students to choose words that describe what they see rather than make interpretations from the picture.

When students group words, it is important that one person state his or her grouping. If more students get involved, the original labels for the groups may be confused or lost. Words can be categorized in endless ways.

Whenever students are engaged in making predictions, they may form misconceptions about the information presented in the text. You can correct these misconceptions while reviewing their concept maps or during the ensuing discussion.

Extending the Strategy

After you have completed the List-Group-Label-Map process, you may wish to try any or all of the following extension activities:

- *Possible Sentences.* Students connect two or more words from the list and write sentences inferring what the text will be about. These sentences can be formulated into a paragraph, and students can compare their predictions.
- *Writing Summaries.* Using the list and the concept map, students can write a summary of the information after reading. A visual display of the ideas and words in a list can help students who have difficulty writing summaries.

■ *Comparing and Contrasting*. One approach is to lead students to compare and contrast one piece of information with another and then lead them, through carefully designed questions, to make a generalization using both sets of information. **(See Graphic Organizer 11, Venn Diagram.)**

List-Group-Label-Map can be combined with other strategies such as Understanding Text (Strategy 2). Depending on the needs of your students, how familiar they are with the topic, your instructional objectives, and the purpose for the reading, many of the strategies presented in this book can be used to support one another.

Some Final Thoughts

The List-Group-Label-Map strategy can be used by itself to generate information and inferences about a text before reading it, or it can be used with other strategies to extend students' thinking and help them summarize and make predictions. The strategy is a vehicle for using the wonderful visual information generally displayed in text-books to connect readers with text.

Read More About It

Blevins, W. "Strategies for Struggling Readers: Making Predictions." *Instructor* 108 (2) 1990: 49.

Caverly, D. C., Mandeville, T. F., and Nicholson, S. A. "PLAN: A Study-Reading Strategy for Informational Text." *Journal of Adolescent and Adult Literacy* 39 (3) 1995: 190–99.

Foley, C. L. "Prediction: A Valuable Reading Strategy." *Reading Improvement* 30 (3) 1993: 166–70.

Nolan, T. E. "Self-Questioning and Prediction: Combining Metacognitive Strategies." *Journal of Reading* 35 (2) 1991: 132–38.

Stahl, S. A., and Kapinus, B. A. "Possible Sentences: Predicting Word Meanings to Teach Content-Area Vocabulary." *Reading Teacher* 5 (1) 1991: 36–43.

Taba, H. *Teacher's Handbook for Elementary Social Studies*. Reading, MA: Addison-Wesley. 1967.

STRATEGY 8: ACTIVATING AND USING PRIOR KNOWLEDGE

Strong readers know that asking questions and thinking about ideas while reading help them understand and remember text. Students who begin reading a text with no preparation and no thought about the topic often can complete an assignment but do not seem to remember much about what they read. One way to help students clear this hurdle is the KWL strategy, which was developed by Donna Ogle in 1986 and further refined by Carr and Ogle (1987). KWL stands for What I *K*now, What I *W*ant to Know, and What I *L*earned. The purpose of this strategy is to activate students' prior knowledge:

BEFORE reading by adding background information and helping students monitor their learning

DURING reading by thinking about what they want to know or the questions they want answered about the topic, and

AFTER reading by helping them organize what they know through listing the things they learned about the topic.

The KWL chart looks like this:

▶ What I *Know*	▶ What I *Want to Know*	▶ What I *Learned*

How Can the Strategy Help My Students?

Students do not tend to use their prior knowledge about a topic when they read unless it is "activated." The KWL helps students review what they know about a topic, set a purpose for reading based on what they want to know, and organize what they learned after reading.

For struggling students, extra support can be given by the teacher or other students by helping them study the charts, diagrams, maps, and pictures in the book to make some inferences or guesses about the topic. Nonproficient and second-language learners can gain background information by listening to the discussion of others.

Getting Started

Here are the steps in the KWL strategy. The KWL activity is most successful when students know something about the material but need to build on what they know to comprehend the text. Students can complete the KWL activity individually, in a group, or as part of a class discussion.

Step 1: Fill Out the First Two Columns of the KWL Chart. Students should write down everything they *know* for sure about the topic. Then they should write down everything they *want* to know about the topic in the middle column. There is no set of correct answers, but misconceptions or wrong information can be flagged for further discussion. What they want to know should be phrased as questions.

Step 2: Read, View, and/or Listen to Content about the Topic.

Step 3: Fill Out the Learned Column. Students should work in small groups to elaborate on their answers.

Step 4: Construct a Concept Map. This map represents an integration of what students knew before reading and what they learned.

Step 5: Write a Summary. Using the concept map, students can write a summary of what they learned about the subject. The summary helps students focus on the most important points in the reading.

Using the Strategy in Your Classroom

The KWL strategy works best with topics about which students have some prior knowledge. If they know very little about a topic, students will have trouble filling in the first two columns of the chart. The purpose of the strategy is to *activate* what students know about a topic and, through discussion and further learning, *build background information.* If students are unsure how to identify what they know, they can scan their reading and make questions from subheadings. If the topic is too broad and students know a lot about it, they may get bogged down making a list. Sometimes you will not know how much prior knowledge students have until the brainstorming begins. To solve this problem, you might have your students create a concept map first so they can organize their thoughts about the topic. Then have them summarize the key points in the What I Know column. (**See Graphic Organizer 6, KWL Chart.**)

Another possibility is that when you ask students what they want to know, they will respond "nothing." That's why I like to refer to the middle column as "what you *think* you know." These statements of what they think they know can then be turned into questions they want answered in the reading. (**See Graphic Organizer 7, KWLS Chart.**)

Extending the Strategy

Because KWL is such a popular strategy, teachers have devised numerous variations. One variation, known as WIKA, was developed by Richardson and Morgan (2000). WIKA stands for *What I Know Activity*. Some teachers find that the original format for KWL does not fit into the before-during-after framework, which is more clearly identified in the WIKA.

In this variation, the before-during-after instructional framework is clearly identified above the five columns.

WIKA

Before Reading		During Reading	After Reading	
What I Already Know	What I'd Like to Know	Interesting or Important Concepts from the Reading	What I Know Now	What I'd Still Like to Know

Other teachers have used these variations:

KWHL

What I *Know*	What I *Want* to Know	*How* I Will Find Out	What I *Learned*

Or:

KWLS

What I *Know*	What I *Want* to Know	What I *Learned*	What I *Still* Want to Know

Some Final Thoughts

Feel free to modify the KWL strategy for your topic and the special needs of your students. If your students need more help thinking of what they know about a topic, you can show them a video, bring some pictures to class, have them leaf through their textbook, or read them a story. The first time you use any strategy, pick an easy text and keep the directions clear and simple. As students become more proficient using the strategy, more difficult text and variations may be used.

Some teachers are frustrated using a KWL because it takes longer to get "through" content. Keep in mind, however, that students tend to retain the information longer when they use this strategy. True, it takes some time for students to understand the KWL steps, but the purpose is to get them in the habit of thinking of what they know about a topic before they start reading.

Read More About It

Bryan, J. "K-W-W-L: Questioning the Known." *The Reading Teacher* 51 (1) 1998: 618–20.

Cantrell, J. "K-W-L Learning Journals: A Way to Encourage Reflection." *Journal of Adolescent and Adolescent Literacy* 40 (5) 1997: 392–93.

Carr, E., and Ogle, D. "K-W-L Plus: A Strategy for Comprehension and Summarization." *Journal of Reading* 30 (7) 1987: 626–31.

Heller, M. "How Do You Know What You Know? Metacognitive Modeling in the Content Areas." *Journal of Reading* 29, 1986: 415–22.

Huffman, L. E. "Spotlighting Specifics by Combining Focus Questions with K-W-L." *Journal of Adolescent and Adolescent Literacy* 41 (6) 1998: 470–72.

Ogle, D. "K-W-L: A Teaching Model that Develops Active Reading of Expository Text." *The Reading Teacher* 39 (6) 1986: 564–70.

Richardson, J. S. and Morgan, R. F. *Reading to Learn in the Content Areas*. Belmont, CA: Wadsworth. 2000.

STRATEGY 9: ANTICIPATING INFORMATION

Anticipating what a text is going to be about helps readers connect the text with what they already know. Activating and using prior knowledge is an essential component of comprehending text. A strategy known as the Anticipation Guide was developed by Harold Herber in the early 1970s and has been used and modified over the years. The strategy is particularly well suited to teaching informational or expository content and helping students clarify their opinions and ideas about a topic.

How Can the Strategy Help My Students?

Middle- and high-school students love to debate, discuss, and voice their opinions. The Anticipation Guide uses this natural tendency to connect the ideas in a text with students' experience and knowledge. The Anticipation Guide helps students

- activate knowledge about a topic by voicing an opinion before they read
- focus their attention on the major points during their reading
- provide a structure for discussing the text after they read.

As students state their opinions about a text's topic, they become more engaged and invested in supporting their viewpoint. This discussion alerts them to the important ideas in the text. In addition, students have a structure for discussing these ideas, and teachers can ask additional questions or make comments that expand student thinking.

Getting Started

Here are the steps to the Anticipation Guide strategy.

Anticipation Guides work best with material that prompts students to form an opinion. For example, one teacher started a unit on comparative governments with this statement: "It is fair that some people make more money than others." The impending discussion on either side helped students understand socialist and democratic philosophies before reading about them. The steps of an Anticipation Guide are as follows:

Step 1: Identify the Major Concepts. Before students begin the activity, determine the main ideas of the reading selection, lecture, or film and write several statements that focus on the main points in the text and draw on students' backgrounds. Four to six statements are usually adequate to generate discussion. The statements can be presented in a chart like one below. **(See Graphic Organizer 1, Anticipation Guide.)**

Step 2: Identify Agree/Disagree Statements. Students point out statements with which they agree or disagree, then write *agree* or *disagree* in column A. Rather than analyzing too much or second guessing, students should merely respond to the statements. Students respond individually—either negatively or positively—to each statement and can then compare responses in small groups.

Step 3: Engage in a Prereading Discussion. You may wish to get a hand count of responses to the statements and ask students to justify their responses with reasons or evidence. Then engage students in full discussion of the pros and cons of each statement. You may wish for students to compare answers within a small group before moving to a large group discussion.

Step 4: Read the Text. Students should be directed to look for ideas either that support or contradict the statements they just discussed.

Step 5: Revisit the Statements. Students should look at the statements they chose earlier to see if they have changed their opinions and then write *agree* or *disagree* in column B. The purpose of this strategy is not to engage students in competition to see who is right or wrong, but rather to activate their opinions about issues that are related to the text and to expand their thinking.

Step 6: Engage in a Postreading Discussion. Looking again at the statements, students should compare their before-reading reactions to their after-reading reactions. Ask them to justify their new or continuing beliefs based on the reading.

Using the Strategy in Your Classroom

The challenge in designing an Anticipation Guide is creating statements, rather than questions that may signal students that there is a right or wrong answer. The statements also need to connect what students already know with the major ideas in the text. In a sense, the statements represent the "so what" of the reading; that is, how this selection relates to the lives of the students.

Duffelmeyer (1994) maintained that effective statements

- convey a sense of the major ideas that the student will encounter.
- activate and draw upon the students' prior experience.
- are general rather than specific.
- challenge students' beliefs.

After reading, students may wish to add to the statements or modify them in some way. The statements can be the basis for a writing assignment or an essay answer for a test.

Extending the Strategy

Writing assignments are a natural extension of the Anticipation Guide. Writing a persuasive essay

A	Statements	B
Before Reading Agree/Disagree		**After Reading** Agree/Disagree

is required on many standardized tests. Students could be encouraged to take one or two of the statements, document them with evidence found in the text, and construct a persuasive essay. You may wish to work with an English/language arts teacher on this assignment.

As students get more proficient at using an Anticipation Guide, you can include some distracter statements that have little to do with the content. Critical readers can detect irrelevant comments as not central to the main argument. For students who are not yet ready to read this critically, these statements can be discussed after the reading.

Some Final Thoughts

While exchanging information with their classmates, it is easy for students to form misconceptions. It is particularly important that you correct these misconceptions during the prereading and postreading discussion. Creating a classroom environment where students are free to make predictions and venture opinions is the key to stimulating discussions. But monitoring those discussions is also an important role of the teacher.

The Anticipation Guide is an excellent method for promoting active reading, directing students' attention to the major points in the text, and helping them to use evidence to modify erroneous beliefs. Using the natural propensity of adolescents to debate and argue engages them in the content by connecting the topic to their lives.

Read More About It

Conley, M. "Promoting Cross-Cultural Understanding Through Content-Area Reading Strategies." *Journal of Reading* 28 (7) 1985: 600–05.

Duffelmeyer, F. A. "Effective Anticipation Guide Statements for Learning from Expository Prose." *Journal of Reading* 37 (6) 1994: 452–57.

Erikson, B., Huber, M., Bea, T., Smith, C., and McKenzie, V. "Increasing Critical Reading in Junior High Classes." *Journal of Reading* 30 (5) 1987: 430–39.

Herber, H. L. *Teaching Reading in Content Areas.* Englewood Cliffs, NJ: Prentice-Hall. 1978.

Merkley, D. J. "Modified Anticipation Guide." *Reading Teacher* 50 (4) 1996–97: 365–68.

STRATEGY 10: TAKING EFFECTIVE NOTES

Identifying the most important ideas in a text and capturing them in the form of notes for study or writing a report can be a formidable task for many students. Any of the prereading strategies suggested in this book can help students focus on the most important points before they read. The INSERT Method (Interactive Notation System for Effective Reading and Thinking) was developed by Vaughn and Estes (1986) to assist students in clarifying their understanding of the text and making decisions while they read. This strategy can help students concentrate on important information and can provide the structure to organize those ideas after reading.

How Can the Strategy Help My Students?

Most students, especially those who struggle with reading assignments, do not understand that comprehending text involves *responding* to it in some way. In fact, some struggling readers do not realize that *thinking* is necessary while reading. Strong readers integrate the information in the text with what they already know. They constantly make decisions or have a running conversation with themselves such as the following:

- This point is important, but this one is a detail.
- This seems like an example used to help me understand the text.
- I already knew that.
- I didn't know that.
- This is in boldfaced type—must be a major concept.
- I don't understand this explanation.
- This map must be here for a reason— probably to illustrate the important ideas.

The INSERT Method prompts students to have these types of conversations while they read. It also provides a structure for students to organize effective notes after they read.

Getting Started

Vaughn and Estes suggested that the INSERT Method helps students think more and better while they read. I adapted this method into the steps below to extend this strategy and help students capture the most important ideas into effective notes.

Step 1: Introduce Students to Symbols in INSERT. An endless set of symbols can be used to help students focus on the text. Which ones you choose depends on the purpose for reading and type of text. Some examples are listed below.

- ✔   Knew this already
- ***   Important information
- ++   Supporting detail
- Ex   Example of important concept
- ??   Don't understand this

Step 2: Read the Text and Respond Using Symbols. Students are not normally allowed to write in textbooks. But the INSERT Method requires that students respond in writing to the ideas in the text. Some teachers fold a sheet of paper lengthwise into three sections, place the INSERT symbols at the top with a line to indicate the page number, and instruct students to place this sheet alongside the book for notetaking. Other teachers have students record their responses with a felt-tip marker on blank transparency sheets. Still others prefer to have students mark passages in the text using self-adhesive notes with colors corresponding to symbols or with preprinted symbols.

Step 3: Use Symbols to Organize Notes from the Reading. This is a good time to have students compare notes. Students can meet in small groups to share what they thought were the most important points, the details, and/or the examples presented in the text. The discussion helps students understand how to find the main idea in passages and organize information. They can then organize these main ideas in the form of notes. Depending on the purpose for reading, the notes could be arranged in different ways. The information could be placed in a concept map or used as part of a larger essay.

Using the Strategy in Your Classroom

The INSERT Method engages students in the major points of the text and helps them organize their thinking. Feel free to change the symbols depending on your purpose for having students read a selection. For example, if students are reading a position statement of some sort, you may wish to use the following symbols:

- A   Agree with this statement
- D   Disagree with this statement
- I   Interesting statement

Categorizing the ideas in the text engages students in thinking and making decisions about the text. In time, students will make these distinctions on their own as they comprehend text.

Extending the Strategy

Taking notes from text is an important skill that must be used to write a report or make a presentation. The Cornell, or divided-page, note-taking system is a popular system used in many middle and high schools. In this system the important points are listed on the left side of the paper, and the details are listed on the right. The page might look like the example on the top of page 183. (**See Graphic Organizer 5, Key Points and Details Chart.**) This information can also be translated into a concept map (see Strategy 4) or a graphic organizer (see Strategy 3) to help students see the relationships between ideas.

Some Final Thoughts

The INSERT Method is a simple yet powerful strategy for helping students respond to reading informational or expository textbooks. This strategy is most effective when used with a prereading strategy that activates what students

▶ Key Points	▶ Details

know about a topic before reading or a postreading strategy such as creating a concept map or graphic organizer. The purpose of this strategy is to help students think about and respond to text.

Read More About It

Czarnecki, E., Rosko, D., and Fine, E. "How to Call Up Notetaking Skills." *Teaching Exceptional Children* 30 (6) 1998: 14–19.

Randall, S. N. "Information Charts: A Strategy for Organizing Student Research." *Journal of Adolescent and Adult Literacy* 39 (7) 1996: 536–42.

Rankin, V. "The Thought That Counts: Six Skills That Help Kids Turn Notes into Knowledge." *School Library Journal* 45 (8) 1999: 24–26.

Tomlinson, L. M. "A Coding System for Notemaking in Literature: Preparation for Journal Writing, Class Participation, and Essay Tests." *Journal of Adolescent and Adult Literacy* 40 (6) 1997: 468–76.

Vaughn, J. L., and Estes, T. H. *Reading and Reasoning Beyond the Primary Grades.* Needham Heights, MA: Allyn and Bacon. 1986.

Weisharr, M. K., and Boyle, J. R. "Notetaking Strategies for Students with Disabilities." *The Clearing House* 72 (6) 1999: 392–95.

STRATEGY 11: DEVELOPING VOCABULARY KNOWLEDGE

All readers encounter words they do not know; strong readers have strategies for determining what to do about those words. Proficient readers use any or all of the following strategies when they encounter an unknown word:

- Skip it and read on.

- Reread.
- Think about what they are reading.
- Sound out the word to see if they have heard it before.
- Look at the headings and subheadings of the text.
- Guess at whether the word is a noun or an adjective.
- Associate the parts of the word (prefixes, root words, suffixes) with more familiar words.

In my opinion, teaching students strategies to use when they encounter an unknown word is more useful than teaching them a host of vocabulary words in isolation. If they don't use these words in writing or see them in reading, students tend to forget them after the weekly vocabulary test.

The Contextual Redefinition strategy helps students learn to use context and structural analysis to determine the meanings of unknown words. An important element in this strategy is teacher modeling of the process of determining the meanings of words. This can be done by sharing the associations that come to mind when using structural analysis.

How Can the Strategy Help My Students?

Structural analysis (or morphemic analysis) involves determining the meaning of an unknown word by associating the word's prefixes, root words, or suffixes with meaningful parts of other words. When applied to informational or expository texts, structural analysis can be paired with contextual analysis to create a powerful strategy for determining the meanings of unknown words.

Context present at the sentence level is not always helpful. The larger context of the paragraph or the entire passage should be used.

Questions such as "What is this passage about?" or "What type of word would go there?" help students make good predictions about the approximate meaning of a word. Depending on the word or its function, an approximate meaning is often enough to comprehend the text.

Another helpful question is "How important is this word to understanding the passage?" Strong readers make good decisions about when to simply guess at a word's meaning and when to stop and determine the meaning. Consider the following sentence: "Her mauve skirts fluttered as she fell over the precipice." A proficient reader might guess that *mauve* is a color and move on without determining the exact color. However, the same reader might stop to determine the meaning of *precipice* since it explains what the woman fell over.

Getting Started

Contextual Redefinition is a good strategy for introducing the key vocabulary in an informational or expository selection. The strategy helps students learn and engage deeply with the important concepts of the reading selection, and helps them practice the behaviors and thinking that proficient readers use to figure out unknown words.

Step 1: Identify Unfamiliar Words. Before students begin reading, select the word or words likely to be unfamiliar to them. Words that contain meaningful morphemes for analysis work best, so select words with familiar prefixes, suffixes, and root words that students can associate with other words. Having students guess the meanings of particular morphemes is far better than just telling them the meanings. By guessing, students become actively involved in the reading.

Step 2: Guess Word Meanings. Present the word in isolation and ask students to make guesses about its meaning. The only clues they have at this point are their associations with the prefixes, root words, and suffixes. Some of these guesses will be wrong or even funny. Remember that the

process of using structural analysis is important, not proving someone's guess right or wrong.

Step 3: Refine Guesses. Using the unfamiliar word, write (or borrow from the text) a series of sentences, including more contextual cues in each one. Have students refine their guesses about what the word means as you present each sentence.

Step 4: Verify Meanings. Have students verify the word's meaning in a dictionary or glossary. If students have no idea what a word means, a dictionary or glossary may not be helpful because many words have more than one meaning. Therefore, a dictionary or glossary should be the last place they go, not the first. The purpose of these references is to verify an already good guess about the word's meaning. (**See Graphic Organizer 4, Contextual Redefinition Chart.**)

Using the Strategy in Your Classroom

Most people use a variety of strategies simultaneously to comprehend text. Structural and contextual analysis are two of the most helpful. Another helpful strategy is to examine the syntax of the sentence or the way that the word functions in the sentence. While presenting the sentences with increasingly rich context, make sure to help students see how each sentence gives them the very important clue of syntax.

When using structural analysis to help students associate new words with known words, you should point out that these conventions do not always apply. For example, *-er* at the end of a word usually means "someone who does something," so a painter is one who paints. But is a mother one who moths? Is a father one who faths?

The powerful component of the Contextual Redefinition is the teacher modeling. Struggling readers in particular need to experience successful models of reading behavior and thinking.

Extending the Strategy

Wordbusting, also known as CSSD, is a parallel strategy to Contextual Redefinition. The steps to Wordbusting are as follows:

- *Context.* Use clues from the surrounding words and sentences.
- *Structure.* Look for familiar roots, prefixes, or suffixes.
- *Sound.* Say the word aloud. It may sound like a word you know.
- *Dictionary.* Look up the word.

Some Final Thoughts

Educators are desperate to teach vocabulary because students can use these words to write, speak, and think more clearly. Vocabulary is also a common component of standardized tests. Well-meaning teachers often assign lists of words with instructions to use them in sentences or copy their definitions. When presented in relative isolation from any meaningful content, these words are only slightly learned and rapidly forgotten.

Contextual Redefinition enables students to determine the meanings of unknown words during reading. In addition to learning strategies, students need to practice these strategies by reading narrative and expository text that contains unfamiliar words.

Read More About It

Cunningham, J. W., Cunningham, P. M., and Arthur, S. V. *Middle and Secondary School Reading.* New York: Longman. 1981.

Gifford, A. P. "Broadening Concepts Through Vocabulary Development." *Reading Improvement* 37 (1) 2000: 2 –12.

Ittzes, K. Lexical "Guessing in Isolation and Context." *Journal of Reading* 34 (5) 1991: 360–66.

Simpson, P. L. "Three Step Reading Vocabulary Strategy for Today's Content Area Reading Classroom." *Reading Improvement* 33 (2) 1996: 76–80.

Watts, S., and Truscott, D. M. "Using Contextual Analysis to Help Students Become Independent Word Learners." *The NERA Journal* 32 (3) 1996: 13–20.

NOTES

GRAPHIC ORGANIZER *for Content-Area Reading Strategies* 1

ANTICIPATION GUIDE

A **Before Reading** Agree / Disagree	Statements	B **After Reading** Agree / Disagree

GRAPHIC ORGANIZER *for Content-Area Reading Strategies*

2

CAUSE-AND-EFFECT CHART

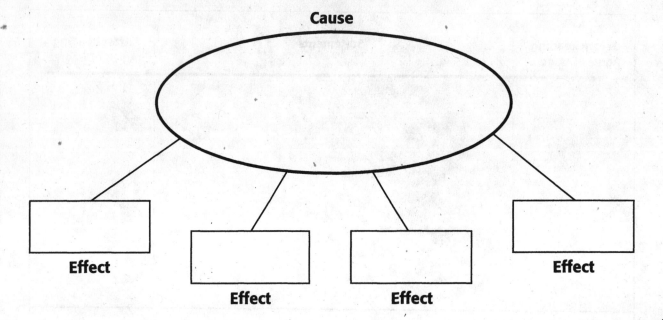

Cause

Effect

Effect

Effect

Effect

GRAPHIC ORGANIZER *for Content-Area Reading Strategies* ③

CLUSTER DIAGRAM

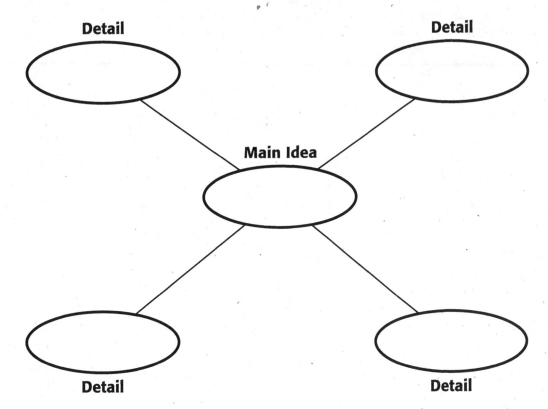

Detail

Detail

Main Idea

Detail

Detail

GRAPHIC ORGANIZER *for Content-Area Reading Strategies*

4

CONTEXTUAL REDEFINITION CHART

▶ Identify Unfamiliar Words	▶ Guess Word Meanings	▶ Refine Guesses	▶ Verify Meanings

GRAPHIC ORGANIZER *for Content-Area Reading Strategies* (5)

KEY POINTS AND DETAILS CHART

▶ Key Points	▶ Details

KWL CHART

What I *Know*	What I *Want to Know*	What I *Learned*

Name ______________________ Class ______________ Date __________

GRAPHIC ORGANIZER *for Content-Area Reading Strategies* 7

KWLS CHART

What I *Know*	What I *Want* to Know	What I *Learned*	What I *Still* Want to Know

GRAPHIC ORGANIZER *for Content-Area Reading Strategies*

PREDICTING AND CONFIRMING ACTIVITY (PACA)

▶ General Information	▶ Prediction	▶ Confirmation

Name _____ Class _____ Date _____

PROBLEM-AND-SOLUTION CHART

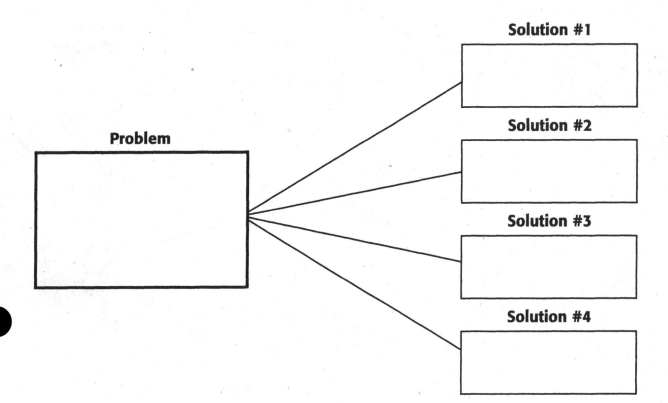

GRAPHIC ORGANIZER *for Content-Area Reading Strategies* **10**

SEQUENCE OR CHRONOLOGICAL ORDER CHART

First Event

Next Event

Next Event

Last Event

GRAPHIC ORGANIZER *for Content-Area Reading Strategies* **11**

VENN DIAGRAM

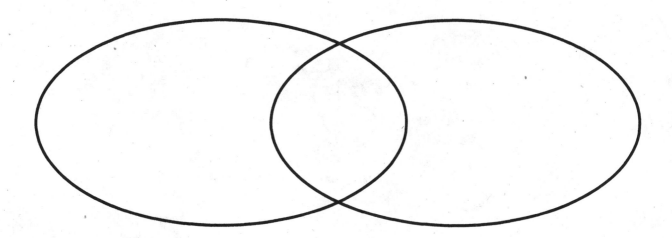